THE
magic
AND
craft
OF
media
writing

carl sessions stepp

NTC Publishing Group

Library of Congress Cataloging-in-Publication Data

Stepp, Carl Sessions.
    The magic and craft of media writing / Carl Sessions Stepp.
       p.   cm.
    Includes index.
    ISBN 0-8442-2053-1
    ISBN 0-658-00874-9 (trade)
    1. Journalism—Authorship.   I. Title.
PN4775.S69   2000
808′.06607—dc21
                                             99-056108
                                               CIP

Acknowledgments
Pages 47–48: © 1992, *The Washington Post*. Reprinted with permission.
Page 53: © 1996, *The Washington Post*. Reprinted with permission.
Pages 133–34: © 1992, *Los Angeles Times*. Reprinted with permission.

Cover design by Jennifer Locke

TO MY CHILDREN,
ASHLI, AMBER, AND JEFF

Contents

Chapter 9   Writing for Drama 133

Chapter 10   Polishing Your Work 155

Preface

I was mowing my backyard when the breakthrough idea for this book pierced my daydreams. By the time I put away the lawn mower, I was deep into a brainstorm, atumble with thoughts, careening toward coherence. As I showered, the first few phrases were coming to me. As I exited the shower, wrapped in a towel, I began scrawling them on wet paper. You are reading them now.

It was magic—a classic burst of inspiration, the kind of transcendent moment that has blessed artists from Mozart to Toni Morrison to regular mortals like me. But it was more than magic. It was a payoff for years of hard work.

I had been noodling on this idea for five years. I had created an outline and filled manila folders with clippings, ideas, and shreds of sentences. I had drafted several chapters. The raw materials had been marinating inside me for an age. The magic moment—what my author friend Patricia Cornwell calls the "through-the-looking-glass experience"—had been prepared for by long years of craftwork. A sudden shot of magic was my reward.

What was this revelation? My breakthrough idea was that every great piece of writing needs a breakthrough idea. I suppose that sounds mundane enough, but at the time it forcefully brought together many loose strands of my thinking. I believe that writing involves endless rounds of hard work, which I call craft. But I also believe in the magic of writing: those inklings of inspiration that seize us unexpectedly and lift our work into the next stratum of excellence. What magic most often confers, I realized that day in my backyard, is the special breakthrough concept that gives an article its uniqueness, its appeal. Every piece of writing needs a breakthrough idea to make it special, and that is the starting point for the book you are holding.

This book proposes a system for success that combines craft and magic into a twin-engine approach for conceiving, reporting, organizing, and writing articles for the mass media. I call it the WRITE approach, an acronym representing Work, Release, Inspiration, Technique, and Energy. As I explain in the first few chapters, this approach capitalizes on the combined powers of the hard-working artisan and the inspired artist within every writer.

From the domain of craft, it is possible to derive a step-by-step guide to becoming a better writer. I can almost guarantee it will succeed. Hard work on the fundamentals of writing virtually always pays off.

Beyond craft, it is possible to enhance our access to magic by living, thinking, and working in ways that flex our imagination and provoke visits from the muses.

Together, craft and magic unite into a synergistic method for progressing toward writing excellence.

Unfortunately, writers both young and old sometimes regard craft and magic as polarized choices rather than an inseparable team. They tend to see themselves as artisans or artists, craftworkers or magicians, one or the other. In truth, I believe, artisanship and artistry are two dependent components of good writing. One without the other is incomplete. Show-stopping writing is like splendid jazz, both meticulously scored and extravagantly improvised. Or like gourmet stew, begun with a prosaic recipe but crowned with a chef's grand epicurean flourish.

To approach writing only as a craft or only as a magical art is, almost literally, to use only half the brain. Craft derives from the left brain hemisphere—the logical, orderly, serial side. Magic emanates from the right hemisphere—the visual, musical, intuitive realm.

This book rests in a simple premise: To become a great writer, you must cultivate both craft and magic. It offers specific advice for advancing in both domains.

Throughout the book I cite advice and examples from the dozens of outstanding writing books already on the market. Many talk about writing as a craft or process. Many talk about writing as magic or art. However, few combine both craft and magic into an approach specifically aimed at journalistic writing. To help fill that need is my goal.

Acknowledgments

Much of what you read here germinated elsewhere, in classes with my students, articles in journalism magazines, and workshops with professional writers and editors. I could never begin to name everyone who has inspired and helped in the development of my thinking, but I feel compelled to mention at least a few names.

First, I should especially acknowledge *American Journalism Review* magazine, where I originally explored many of these ideas, and its outstanding editors, Bill Monroe and Rem Reider. My dean, Reese Cleghorn, and my University of Maryland colleagues, especially Nan Robertson, were unflaggingly helpful and supporting. Friends and colleagues graciously cheered me on. My editor at NTC/Contemporary, Marisa L. L'Heureux, was a skilled and understanding collaborator who encouraged me from day one. I also want to thank every writer, editor, and publication whose work and words I cite. All were unfailingly generous. We are all part of an ongoing writers' conversation.

Finally, I thank my wife, Laura, and my children, Ashli, Amber, and Jeff. From them, I know what magic truly is.

Part 1

The Craft and Magic of Writing

Chapter 1

Writing in
an Age
of Change

Let's begin with the joy of writing. What joy of writing, you may ask? Doesn't everyone understand that writing wreaks pain and anguish? Isn't the tormented author a stock character? Can't every pretender quote sportswriter Red Smith's observation that "There's nothing to writing; all you do is sit down at a typewriter and open a vein"?[1]

Here is a secret from the inside: Writing is fun. To be free to write is one of life's grandest gifts; to be paid for writing is a treasure. Writers work hard and face frustration, they whine and they brood, they occasionally even suffer. But few would trade places with their landlord or their accountant. Writing is a calling, and those who follow it feel the privilege of the chosen.

Writers enjoy artistic power and independence that others can only envy. They cruise blissfully through the marketplace of ideas. They dare to create, to trawl for fresh truths, to savor the tastes and sounds of word and thought. Writers know the thrill of composing a faultless phrase, the satisfaction of encountering their byline, the fulfillment of unveiling their work before admiring audiences.

How many other professionals can enjoy the gratification of laboring over a precious article and then seeing it within weeks, days, or hours, emblazoned in cover-story print or home-page glory before thousands of eyes? To this day, I tenderly recall the tingle of my first byline some 35 years ago, a reaffirming and revitalizing spark that I wanted to repeat again and again and again.

Sometimes writing even seems easy. Some days writers, like athletes and musicians, glide into a mysterious zone of creativity and productivity, and

---

[1]   Jon Winokur, ed., *Writers on Writing* (Philadelphia: Running Press, 1987) 78.

glorious prose pours onto their pages. Words flow as if from a cistern deep inside the soul. Stories unfold spontaneously in seamless entirety.

This is the joy of writing. Few feelings are more exhilarating, and to a writer who has struggled they bestow sublime redemption: a payoff more than worth the suffering.

Yet do not discount the struggle. Writing is a complicated enterprise, at times exasperating. It demands a trunkful of discipline and not a little luck. It is hard on the impatient. It looks so easy; it turns out to be so hard. This book is intended to help. This chapter offers an overview of today's writing environment and introduces an approach—simultaneous attention to both craft and art—designed to help writers improve at every level.

THE MINGLING OF ART AND CRAFT

To write is to inhabit paradoxical realms. First comes the humdrum but vital world of craft, consumed with attention to technique and method. This is a realm of outlines and outtakes, of false starts and fifth drafts. It concerns itself tediously with every detail from commas to cohesion.

Then comes the mystical, magical world of art, apart from yet intimately linked to the routines of craft. Here, writers draw on the mysterious creative chambers of the subconscious, sometimes confounded by a barrenness of imagination, occasionally blessed by unheralded visits from the muse.

This book treats both domains. Its premise is that writers improve the most by heeding lessons from both the realm of craft and the realm of magic. In parallel, these forces offer an ideal approach that inspires the best possible writing—whether news or features, investigations or profiles, conventional or innovative.

The book offers a system and something of an antisystem: an explication of the rigors of craft and an entreaty to the gods of magic. It is a combined approach that banks on hard work and great artistic leaps. The objective is to adapt for media writers a creative spiral that for centuries has characterized the work of phenomenal artists: *hard work, followed by a period of detachment, followed by a shock of inspiration, followed by more hard work.*

This spiral can be abbreviated into an acronym called the WRITE approach: Work, Release, Inspiration, Technique, Energy. Respect and apply the approach, and you can catch a natural wave that will redouble your creative powers:

- **W**ork: It begins with step-by-step attention to every detail of the writing process, from idea to research to focus to writing to revision.
- **R**elease: Intermittently as you think, research, and prepare to write, you must release yourself from the material, back off for a bit, let your mind

play with the possibilities, and prime yourself for the discovery of the breakthrough idea.

- Inspiration: Magic strikes. Combined, the discipline of hard work and the serendipity of subconscious contemplation set off a kind of chain reaction of creativity. Good ideas hit you "out of the blue."
- Technique: Back to the hard work. The material and ideas must be forged into good writing, an operation that requires additional meticulous attention to craft which, in turn, will re-bless you with more rounds of magic.
- Energy: Writers need stamina. The spiral goes on indefinitely.

This book concerns itself mainly with writing for the mass media, especially newspapers, magazines, newsletters, and their online counterparts. It is aimed toward writers producing both news and features for the media. But nearly all writers face similar problems, whether they produce news or advertising, novels or corporate memos; whether they work online or on paper or on the air. Every writer, novice or master, can gain from better understanding the processes and principles of writing and from applying all elements of the WRITE approach.

Writing is without a doubt very hard work. The craft is the conscious part, demanding diligence and discipline. The magic is the intuitive part. As you apply yourself to the craft, your brain independently engages itself, assaying and sorting and splicing the impulses you send it and occasionally projecting them back to your consciousness in surprising and delighting reconfigurations. Nearly every writer has, at one time or another, leaped from bed in the middle of the night, pulled the car quickly to the side of the road, or hopped dripping from the shower in order to record a fleeting revelation.

Teachers and editors are often asked, "Can you really teach someone to write?" The question usually comes in a skeptical tone, implying that writing talent is an immutable inborn gift. The answer is simply this: anyone can learn to write *better*. Certainly, some people begin with more talent than others; a few are even prodigies. But most writers benefit measurably from serious attention to the fundamentals of their craft. Good teaching and editing help raise even the best work to new levels of quality.

Much of this book concentrates on the practices and procedures of good writing. Applying oneself to these fundamentals will improve the writing of beginners and professionals alike. For this reason, this book chooses to stress the joy and magic as well. Together, we should celebrate writing.

For some of you, writing may be, at least at first, just a job or a class requirement. The further you pursue it, however, the more you will find that writing is not merely a process: it is a way of life. What you write today is more than the product of a few hours or days of current research. It is the culmination of a lifetime of reading, writing, observation, and contemplation.

Today's reporting is the latest stage in your never-ending, generative growth as a writer. The words and ideas that emerge today, triggered though they are by the demand to produce an article now, may well have had a gestation of a lifetime, lying fallow in the literary subconscious until called forth, after proper cultivation, for today's occasion.

It is important to stress, of course, that the magic of writing is not as random and casual as it may at first seem. Like any other kind of magic, it thrives on preparation and application. The magic of writing and the craft of writing derive power from each other. Harnessed, they create a symbiotic energy of transcendent value. The harder writers work at craft, the more receptive they become to magical interventions.

Aspiring writers need both technical expertise and magic tricks. Their work demands that they nurture both the methodical, analytical sides of their brains (associated with the left hemisphere of the brain and often called "left-brain" traits) and the magical, unbridled parts (associated with the right side and often called "right-brain" thinking). This is no book about brain chemistry. But viewing craft as part of left-brain process and magic as right-brain inspiration can provide powerful symbolic insight into how writers can and should work best. In setting out here, then, the goal will be twofold: to better master the rules and to unleash the muse.

THE WRITER'S IDEALS

When we talk of good writing, what do we mean? Though we write for many different reasons—to inform, to entertain, to provoke, to inspire, to persuade, to sell—some standards apply universally.

Some ideals are technical in nature: copy should be accurate, precise, and clear, for instance. Others are creative: copy also needs drama, surprise, and specialness. Today's and tomorrow's changing media environment will serve simply to underline the never-ending importance of each of these values.

Accuracy is paramount. Nothing outranks the writer's responsibility to the truth. In pursuing truth, which of course can be elusive and disputable, writers should do everything humanly possible to document every assertion, use the most authoritative sources and evidence, and double-check and corroborate all material. Sloppy reporting, lazy note-taking, careless assumptions, and unreliable sources can undermine a writer's effectiveness and credibility. This point is fundamental and uncompromisable.

Precision is related to accuracy but implies additional attention to selection and arrangement of information. Facts and assertions that are technically accurate can still be rendered in misleading ways. There is an old story about a two-person race: the loser brags about finishing second and scoffs at the opponent for coming in next-to-last. Both statements are accurate, but of course they are deceptive. In seeking precision, good writers devote themselves scrupulously to such matters as nuance, balance, proportionality, and context.

Clarity is necessary because even the best information loses all impact if the reader cannot understand it. A writer begins with a thought and tries to transport that thought as faithfully as possible into the mind of the reader. Unambiguous words help, as do simple and direct sentences. Almost all writers have at times produced writing they know to be too confusing. But few if any writers could ever be criticized for writing too clearly.

Drama arouses and entices the reader. Writing fails if it does not move the reader's emotional needle. Good writing uses such techniques as characterization, setting, pacing, foreshadowing, and description to capture the audience's interest. It touches some emotion, whether it be anger, humor, pity, curiosity, or simply intellectual inquisitiveness.

Humanity should be a quality, if not of the writing itself, then of the transaction between writer and reader. Good writing is alive and organic, a conversation between a human writer and a human reader. Words-on-screen may appear to be inanimate objects, but what they convey and represent is fully alive. Writers enter into a dynamic commerce with their sources, their subjects, and their readers, and they should approach the transaction with respect and solicitude.

Surprise helps keep readers interested and makes them feel rewarded for their efforts. Barney Kilgore, a founding genius behind the *Wall Street Journal,* is often quoted as saying that "the easiest thing in the world is to stop reading." Good writers try to spread surprises throughout their copy. These payoffs delight readers and raise the prospect that they will stick with the copy.

Specialness addresses the question that all busy readers ask: why should I read this now? Good writing must establish, in the first sentence or two, why the reader should pay attention immediately. What makes this article special right now? What distinguishes it from every other article a reader may have read on this topic? What makes it must reading immediately as opposed to yesterday or tomorrow or an hour from now? To be worth writing, an article needs some unique and immediate selling point for the reader. This is the *breakthrough idea,* the result of an artistic leap. It is where magic most often tops off the hard work of craft.

THE WRITER'S CHANGING ROLE

Writing ideals may be permanent, but the writer's world changes by the nanosecond. Print's centuries-old domination succumbed to broadcast; while still in its infancy broadcast was overtaken by computerization; and the room-sized computers of just a short while ago speedily yielded to hand-held instruments promising to unite everyone in cyberspace. As the ongoing technological fair enchants us all—and as print falters, especially in its hold on young people—many despair for the very survival of the print medium. What awaits those who think of themselves, traditionally, as writers in journalism?

Many plant themselves happily among the optimists. They see in today's changing media environment a wonderful opportunity for journalists to seize the public mantle as never before, by becoming society's information experts and master storytellers. Here's why.

First, history stands with them. Old media don't die; they adapt. Radio didn't kill newspapers; television didn't kill radio; cable didn't kill networks; Nintendo didn't kill cable; and online news hasn't killed offline news. History's lesson is that the world of media and of information is ever-expanding and that those who persist and adapt can always thrive.

Second, society needs good writing more than ever. One of the ironies of our age is that the more information we have, the more confusing it seems. Every community can support—in fact, will require—central, common, printed sources of reliable and relevant information. If newspapers didn't exist, someone would be busy inventing them right now. If magazines disappeared, new species would instantly spring to life. If all broadcasting went dark, town criers would return to the streets.

Third, the allure of technology misleads us. What we experience today is an emerging information age in which the many new means of *delivering* information, while fascinating to contemplate and important in their effects, will remain subordinate to content. The key to success in the information age is fully as much in *gathering and managing information* as in the instruments for delivering it.

Clearly we stand on the brink of astounding innovations in information delivery, and few can predict what the next few years and decades will hold. Information tablets? Electronic notebooks? Home multimedia complexes? Avatars in hyperland? We can only imagine what new forms will gain ascendance for information delivery. And history tells us that whatever we imagine will undoubtedly be quaintly off-kilter. We are always underestimating and misjudging where technology will end up.

But we can have every confidence in this prediction: regardless of the forms of delivery, the demand for information will never decrease. We have embarked on an information age where the premium on reliable information rises higher and higher by the day.

The bottom line is strikingly simple: those who can find, gather, organize, and present information will remain in demand. Change will swirl around them and they will race to keep up with the times. But the primal human hunger for news and information shows no signs of diminishing, and every complicating change ripens the market for competent writers and editors.

With this optimism goes a warning, nevertheless: complacency will be fatal. The old ways of journalism, left smugly untouched, will not suffice. Writers must learn to operate in a dramatically changing environment. But this is not a threat. It is an opening.

THE MEDIA'S CHANGING ROLE

To help picture the media's evolving role, consider an analogy from the petroleum industry. For 150 years, the media, primarily newspapers, have sold the equivalent of mid-grade regular gasoline, a mainstream product for the typical consumer, and they have transported this product through the conventional pipeline of mass home delivery.

Now, imagine that petroleum companies strike it rich, finding the mother lode of oil resources beyond their wildest dreams. That is what has happened to mass media. As the information age gains momentum, a near-infinite volume of sources and data is suddenly cascading through the pipelines. Moreover, the distribution system itself, the means of delivering the information, is experiencing revolutionary upgrading, as the rusty old pipelines give way to high-tech connections that channel information with speed and precision and with individualized convenience.

What we face, then, are three transformational changes in the nature of journalism:

1. Increases in the volume of available information on a scale unimaginable even 10 or 15 years ago
2. Opportunities to deliver that information with expanding variety and efficiency
3. Interactive capabilities that bring consumers into the information flow from its very beginning

The question now is how these developments will affect writers. Several possibilities come to mind.

The Information Explosion

Writers must immediately cope with processing more information than ever before. Computers and databases now put at our fingertips virtually every piece of information in every library, documents collection, and database in the world. Just a short time ago, a typical news story might require conducting a handful of personal interviews and, perhaps, dropping by the courthouse to check a document or two. Now, the same assignment may require a series of electronic interviews over e-mail, a check of computerized databases to find everything that's been written about the topic *anywhere* during the past year, a visit to an electronic bulletin board where the topic is under discussion, and a search that produces *all*, not just a few, relevant documents in the local government computer library.

The change in order of magnitude is astonishing. Where once newspapers might examine 50 or 60 local tax assessments looking for patterns of unfairness, now every single assessment—tens of thousands—is cheaply accessible, and patterns can be almost instantly documented by computer spreadsheet. Where once, when a controversial new company moved into the community, a writer might haphazardly telephone reporters in the company's old location to inquire about its record, now the reporter can locate virtually every mention of that company in every newspaper, professional journal, government document, and court case for the past five years.

Information Supermarkets

With all this information available, we will increasingly see what might be called the vertical integration of the information marketplace. Media companies will become increasingly involved all along the information supply chain, from the "crude" stage (supplying raw information via fax, phone, cable, and computer) to refined premium (combing thousands of sources to produce reports of specialized value to audience segments willing to pay top dollar for them).

Consequently, as a writer you may have less rigid ties to one medium. Spending all your time reporting for one or two editions of a single newspaper will seem increasingly inefficient. Instead, you will likely gather information for use in a multitude of ways—for example, in a telephone databank, an ongoing computerized update, a commercially vended database, a book-length special report, an online information site, as well as in the next day's newspaper. News companies will become gigantic information warehouses and supermarkets providing material in a variety of forms to a variety of audiences.

A New Dependence on Writers and Editors

Consumers are likely to feel overwhelmed by the intimidating volume of all this information. What they will most need is help in managing it. Tomorrow's writers will enjoy three key roles:

- information specialists
- explanation specialists
- master storytellers

As information specialists, writers must not only master the traditional reporting skills of observing, interviewing, and following paper trails. They must become more complete information scientists who can expertly search the information universe, locate and retrieve relevant material, and sort, arrange, and assemble it—all under deadline. They will find many new challenges: how to coax an anonymous e-mail source onto the record, how to create a homemade database to evaluate all local drunken-driving incidents, what computer library carries the most comprehensive data on agriculture or toxic waste or treatments for the latest scourge.

As explanation specialists, they may face the greatest challenge of all: to synthesize and assimilate all this information, presenting it accurately, clearly, understandably, coherently, and—still—interestingly. One of the most valuable, and powerful, contributors in the information age will be the writer who can make sense of the proliferating and bewildering flow of information.

Amid all the change and turmoil, audiences will turn anew to master storytellers, as they always have. Harvesting byte-sized blips of data and retailing smart, quick analyses will have their places. But so will the ancient art of storytelling. From before the written word, societies have depended on storytellers to draw together the hopes, dreams, visions, fears and values of a culture. There is a reason we refer to the news as "stories." The yarn, the parable, the symbolic vignette all bring us truths just as powerful, and even more enduring, than data. Stories are the running narratives by which we make sense of our lives, and nonfiction stories will remain near the summit of journalistic service.

Does this sound like a world where writers will be in less demand? Anything but! Writers can welcome the coming changes just as pioneers and adventurers throughout history have seen opportunity in exciting times. In an information age, information professionals have little to fear and much to gain.

"Information professionals." Perhaps these words conjure the chilling image of soulless journo-robots spitting out data bits via computer chip. It is an unappealing image to most aspiring writers, who are filled with a passion for telling stories and expressing truths.

They should relax. There is little danger that data-shoveling will crowd out style and narrative. While some journalists will find a productive niche in delivering raw data directly to consumers, they will occupy just one corner in the information bazaar. As the ill-fated experiments with videotext attest, there is limited demand for such no-frills, telegraphic prose.

A good bet is that the preponderance of journalism will remain as highly personalized transactions between writers and audiences. In fact, in the frantic rush that characterizes the information age, the quality and style of writing stand to be more important than ever in capturing the attention of busy readers.

Precision, clarity and grace will remain the hallmarks of writing excellence. And the storytellers, with their power to engage and illuminate through irresistible narrative, will hold a commanding place in the competitive drive to produce explanation and meaning.

Writers will endure. You can take that to the automated teller machine.

THE MAINSTAYS OF WRITING

Changes come and go, but in the ageless and endless writing ritual, certain qualities abide. As we embark on a celebration and contemplation of writing, let's consider two other fundamental parts of the writing equation: the writer and the setting.

The Writer

Writers are human beings. To do their best work, they need gentle care and feeding. Throughout this book, which stresses both the craft and magic of writing, it is important not to lose sight of the organic, personalized nature of the process. Writing is produced by people, not machines, and people have idiosyncratic styles and temperaments that feed directly into their work. Good writers know this about themselves, and good editors recognize and capitalize on it. All this will remain true in an increasingly electronic era.

It takes a strong ego to write. Writing is among the most arrogant of acts, akin to leaping on a soapbox and expecting everyone to drop everything and pay attention to you. It requires a considerable amount of brazenness and self-esteem.

Yet few writers are fully secure. Most fret over every assignment. The most acclaimed writers still worry constantly about failure. And every writer knows that moment of gut-churning dread that surges up every time you turn over a new manuscript to an editor. It is a fear of rejection that never relents. Each time you leap onto the soapbox, there is the chance the audience will patronize you or spurn you or laugh at you. Or, worst of all, ignore you.

Even so, journalists do not have the luxury to be pampered prima donnas. They must muster their courage and get on with the work. But good writers should be introspective and self-aware. They should recognize their need for support, stimulation and inspiration. And they must appreciate that magic, like lightning, is most likely to strike when the conditions are best aligned for good conduction.

The Setting

Writing is a product of time and place. Good writers almost always benefit from time, and they do their best work in settings that let them relax and exercise their particular work habits.

While good writing can happen quickly, it usually requires investing considerable time in the prewriting stages. In general, it is fair to say that the overall process needs plenty of time. As *New Yorker* editor William Shawn once said, "It takes as long as it takes."[2] For most writers and most stories, nothing would bring more immediate improvement than spending more time on each step of the reporting and writing process. This, too, is a constant even in changing times.

But time, of course, is a leading problem for journalists, especially those on deadline. The rise of electronic information delivery, with its expectations of immediacy, has already intensified the tyranny of deadlines. More and more, writing is hurried, and that haste carries a lamentable price tag. Some of the most frustrated writers are those forced, in the sacred name of deadline, to take shortcuts at every stage.

As journalists, we must be realistic and accept that, at times, the deadline demands copy. But perhaps we have come to acquiesce too placidly to this coercive newsroom routine. In this age of constant concern over declining readership and viewership, publishers and editors would do well to heed some simple advice: *good writing requires more time than it may seem, and until media managers provide ample creative time, their writing, and therefore their readership, will suffer.*

Given a world of deadlines, how should writers respond? One sound piece of advice: pick your shots. Learn to meet deadlines but also find ways, whenever possible, to buy time to undertake special assignments. Not every writer of every story in every medium can take all the time needed. No one would advocate paralyzing the process by which timely news is engineered. Every media writer, as a fundamental professional skill, should know how to produce accurate, reliable copy on deadline.

But at the same time, all who love writing should heed some obvious lessons. Good editors should make sure that each writer, at least occasionally, is given time to produce top-notch work, and they should insist that, on key projects, extra time be allocated.

Perhaps an even bigger failure of newsrooms, at least in regard to writing, is that they create some of the worst possible conditions under which to write. Writing is like any other kind of performing: the performer needs to be relaxed and comfortable. And writing is a highly personal, even intimate, act, one that is risky to attempt in public.

---

[2] John McPhee, "Remembering Mr. Shawn," the *New Yorker,* 28 December 1992, 137.

So how do newsrooms work? By violating almost every commonsense tenet about how to achieve a comfortable, relaxed writing place. They typically herd writers into large, boisterous, rowdy central pens. They prop them up in uncomfortable chairs in front of poorly arranged computer setups. Under crushing deadlines, with editors screaming in their ears, phones ringing and people sidling by to chat, writers are then expected to settle in and do their best work.

Does this make sense to you? Of course not. You cannot emphasize enough the importance of *getting ready to write* and of *writing while relaxed.* As with baseball or piano playing or bricklaying, attention to some simple fundamentals will bring instant rewards.

1. Writing quality is intimately related to time invested.
2. Productivity is directly related to working conditions.

In both cases, some wise investment can pay priceless dividends for writers and those who employ them.

SUMMARY

Writers can progress with confidence and enthusiasm into the new age of communications. They are needed and always will be. But their world will grow ever more competitive and their work ever more complicated.

Producing good writing is much harder than it looks, and it is getting harder. Tomorrow's professionals will have to process more information, faster, in more ways than ever before. They will need every traditional writing and editing skill, plus sophisticated computer mastery, plus the ability to impart unprecedented depth and perspective, all under deadline-a-minute pressures.

The survival of writing is not in question, but the success of individual writers is never guaranteed. Some will excel; some will fail. This book is designed to help writers lift themselves into the class of winners, to not only survive but thrive. By connecting the linear, left-brain craft aspects of writing with the underappreciated, less linear, right-brain imaginative powers, writers can profit from a unified, redoubled approach to conceiving, researching, organizing, and presenting their material.

The following points represent a manifesto that informs this book and that will inspire those who take it seriously:

1. Great writing is a product of both craft and magic.
2. Most writers by nature rely more heavily on one or the other. This self-confining polarity ("I'm either left-brained or right-brained") should yield

to a deliberate bilateralism ("I'm going to get better at both"). For maximum improvement, writers should exercise and strengthen both their analytical powers and their creative chambers. We can call this *creative balance.* The WRITE approach can help you unify and apply both forces.

3. Moving simultaneously on parallel tracks is not as easy as it may sound. Linear methodicalness can make a writer's less linear side edgy; creative messiness can offend the left side's sense of orderliness. This tension can be turned into a positive force, but it takes discipline and desire.

Hold this image in mind: think of craft and magic not as opposite extremes on a line. Instead, think of them as base points on a triangle. Above them, at the apex, fully dependent on support from the both sides of the base, is the ideal that is literally and figuratively the highest point. That is where we find great writing.

Practicing Craft and Magic

The earliest chapters of this book center on how you think about writing. Later chapters will delve with increasing specifics into techniques and methods. But all chapters assume that you are actively writing from the very beginning. As you work, then, try to apply the insights about craft and magic, building on them as you proceed through the book.

1. Start with the WRITE approach. Select a writing project (whether it is your idea or an assignment from someone else) and invoke the creative spiral: work hard, back off, probe for inspiration, return to technique, maintain the energy to continue the spiral.

2. Remember that craft comes first. Work steadfastly toward the ideals discussed in this chapter: accuracy, precision, and clarity.

3. Let magic enter in. Stretch toward the breakthrough idea and strive for drama, humanity, surprise, and specialness.

4. Whenever you are tempted to reject or resist an idea about writing, try to open your mind. "Both-and" thinking almost always trumps an "either-or" attitude. Human beings are quite capable of juggling conflicting views and benefiting from the resulting creative tension. We will call this the *power paradox.*

5. Use this book in your double role as artist and artisan. Work with it—the tips, the techniques, the linear models that lead to step-by-step improvement. But also play with it—read it aloud, puzzle over the magical impulses. Use it as a starting point to brainstorm for your own words and images and inspirations.

Chapter 2

Writing
as
Craft

Writing isn't just writing.

Writing is more than writing, more than the literal act of scribbling words onto paper or typing them onto a screen. Writing is a process consisting of many stages, and each stage affects the outcome. When you report, you are, in a way, writing. When you organize your notes, you are writing. Even when you sit quietly over coffee, contemplating your next article, you are writing. Writing is an act of mind at least as much as an act of pen or keyboard.

Viewed in this way, writing can be seen as a craft, a series of steps carried out systematically. Like most other crafts, it demands technical expertise and artistic skill, and, like most other craftspeople, writers can improve their work through discipline, diligence, and attention to the fundamentals. No one becomes a great writer by craft alone, but everyone can become a better writer by improving at craft. This chapter sets out to dissect the writing process, identify its component steps, and explore how writers can, through craft, steadily raise the level of their work.

To create and publish their material, writers must complete a series of steps. Some occur before the actual writing and some follow it. Neglecting any step can compromise the final product just as much as a failure during the actual writing phase. Neglecting the early stages, for example, is the most common cause of frustration or writer's block. Neglecting the later stages is the most common reason that work falls short of the writer's aspirations.

All writers, of course, operate as individuals, with their own idiosyncratic work styles. Do not misunderstand this chapter as suggesting that every writer must confirm to rigid models and formulas. That is not the point at all. Every craftsperson has a signature style, and so it is with writers. Much of writing is mystical and magical, defying efforts to analyze and deconstruct it, and few should ever presume to dictate writing style to others. At the same time, however, we can all recognize that craft begins with mastery of the basics. Thus, it is easy to see the virtue of better understanding the writing process and applying those lessons to our personal ways of working.

Most writers strive constantly to improve at the craft. To do so requires hard work and discipline. Like any complex activity, whether it is hitting a tennis ball, playing a concerto, or conducting a biochemistry experiment, writing requires a command of the fundamentals that comes from careful attention to detail and technique, from drill, practice, and repeated experience. As in any field, there are a few prodigies who make writing seem deceptively easy. But even they are usually working much harder than we imagine. As the novelist Thomas Mann once richly observed, "A writer is a person for whom writing is more difficult than it is for other people."

Anyone can write, just as anyone can hack at a golf ball or splash paint on a canvas. But artistry and mastery require, for most of us, more than raw talent.[1]

Good journalism usually begins with a big idea and ends with a complex, completed masterwork. In between comes a process that plays out step by step, word by word. A key principle for writers seeking improvement is to understand how to break down this huge challenge—to produce a major work—into a series of smaller steps, each of which can be defined and confronted systematically.

This is the linear aspect of writing. It is craft. It is hard work. It is attention to detail. And devotion to craft almost always repays the effort. Any writer, from greenest amateur to decorated laureate, can become better by systematically improving at each step of the writing process.

A MODEL FOR WRITING

What is the writing process? Many scholars, teachers, editors, and others have outlined various versions, using slightly differing terms and orderings, and you can read about them in detail in the literature of composition. Most versions describe the process similarly, as a series of steps something like the following:

- **Launching.** The starting point. Settling on the idea and assignment; determining the purpose; considering the audience.
- **Reporting.** The research phase. Including interviewing, the use of documents and databases, and sometimes personal observation.
- **Focusing.** The conceptual key. Sorting and organizing the material, articulating a theme, choosing an approach, developing an outline or road map to carry it out.

---

[1] Donald Murray, *Writing for Your Readers,* 2d ed. (Old Saybrook, CT: Globe Pequot, 1992) 226.

- **Limbering.** The warm-up. Getting oneself relaxed and ready to write, in a place and frame of mind conducive to your best work.
- **Writing.** The act itself.
- **Rewriting.** The second wind, the reinvigorated surge. Establishing enough critical distance from your copy to make helpful revisions, which can range from top-to-bottom reworking to polishing one sentence again and again.
- **Copyediting.** The final polish. Working with one or more editors to finally prepare the copy for publication.

The coming chapters will examine these stages in detail. Here, they can be briefly described in the order in which they usually occur, along with some objectives a writer has at each stage.

Launching

Writing begins with an idea. It can be the writer's own proposal or an assignment from an editor. It can be vague or concrete, wispy or fully formed. It can start as an inspiration, a tip, a deduction, a question, a hunch, or a surefire certainty.

This is a fairly obvious point. To write, you must have a subject. But the launch is a vital stage, and writers sometimes shortchange it in their hurry to get on with the action of reporting and writing. So it is always worth investing a few minutes at this embryonic stage to ensure that a strong foundation is in place for your entire writing project.

In some respects, launching a story resembles launching a rocket. You need to know where you are aiming, and you need to appreciate the impact of small, early calibrations. If you launch a spaceship toward Mars and the initial heading is off by a fraction of a degree, you will miss Mars by millions of miles. But a quick early correction gets you back on course with little harm. The farther the flight goes without correction, the more costly, time-consuming, and risky the whole business becomes. The same pattern pertains to writing. Early adjustments save time, energy, and agony.

Here, the principle of creative balance applies. At the launch, the writer needs to move on several tracks. You need private thinking time, something various writers have called daydreaming or noodling, to let the idea float and incubate in your own mind. You need public talking time, preferably with a trustworthy editor, to listen to the idea, try to frame it in words, and test others' reactions to it. And you need writing time, to toy with the idea on paper or on screen, to begin to corral your freethinking into a coherent theme or storyline.

Nothing is more helpful at this point that a good collaborator. Your collaborator can be a teacher, a colleague, a coach, or a friend, but the job is really that of an editor. Typically, the editor represents the boundaries of the real world and generally controls such important practical matters as how much latitude you have to develop the assignment and how much time and space you will have. More importantly, the editor should represent an intellectual ally, a smart and friendly teammate specifically deputized to help you produce better work.

Sometimes, writers and editors see each other as adversaries and, from the beginning, build unnecessary, destructive tension into their relationship. This behavior is not only counterproductive, it is downright foolish. It is far better to form a partnership with your editor from step one, to harness the editor's power to your own. After all, you both have the same goal: producing high-quality work. You both have direct personal and professional stakes in the outcome. You both earnestly want the project to succeed.

Instead of an adversary, think of the editor as something supremely more positive: an extra brain on loan, an intellectual reinforcement whose ideas, energy and inspiration all are made available to serve the writer's needs. Why squander such a resource?

With the help of an editor, you want to accomplish several important objectives during the launch stage.

- You want to consider *audience* and *purpose,* asking the two questions central to any writing project: who is my intended reader, and why am I writing this? Mass media audiences are by definition large and diverse, but their range is enormous, from the massive viewership of a network news program to the heterogeneous subscribers of a hometown newspaper to the far more specialized patrons of online information sites. The more you know about your audience, its characteristics, and its expectations, the better you can shape your reporting and writing for maximum effectiveness. Your purpose in writing will vary, from informing to entertaining to provoking. Is your main goal to convey new and important information, to explain the complicated, to tell a good tale? Settling on a clear purpose gives direction to your reporting, organizing, writing, and presentation.

- You want to clarify the assignment as much as you can. Sometimes complete clarity is impossible; an editor may, for example, instruct you to look into a situation for a while before settling on a specific story idea. And you should not be overly rigid; you seldom want to lock down an idea before you have researched and thought about it. Still, you need to settle on a preliminary theme that is as specific as possible. It is like identifying your destination when you set off on a cross-country drive. You may not know exactly where you will stop along the way, but you need to know where you are headed.

- You want to ensure that you, your editor, and any other relevant colleagues (photographers, artists, designers, producers, other writers contributing to the project) have the same idea in mind and coordinate among yourselves to stay in harmony.

- You need a surge of energy and inspiration, a hearty exhortation from your editor that, along with a deep breath, propels you into the game.

Reporting

If you remember only one thing from this book, make it this: *the single biggest step toward better writing is better reporting.* The quality of your writing is a direct function of the quality of your material. The better you research and report, the better your articles turn out. A mediocre writer working with extraordinary information will almost always produce more interesting stories than an extraordinary writer working with mediocre information. Material matters most.

Reporting, therefore, is a crucial stage in the writing process. It is hardly an exaggeration to say that your success at this stage reliably predicts the ultimate quality of your article. The material you get through reporting creates a sort of upper limit of potential. Your work will never get any better than the material allows.

Luckily for us all, reporting can be systematically improved through concentration on technique. Many journalists tend to consider themselves as better at either reporting or writing. Those who regard themselves as "writers" in the artsy sense sometimes dismiss or underestimate the necessity for painstaking reporting. This is, of course, a mistake, and as craftspeople they should exercise their reporting muscles every chance they get.

The principal objective at the reporting stage is simple enough to describe. You want to employ personal observation, interviews, documents research, and online reporting to compile as much relevant information as time permits. And, time always being an oppressor, you want to collect your information as efficiently and systematically as possible.

Here, an outside-in principle applies. The best reporters are resourceful and imaginative, casting a wide net as they begin their quest. They circle around the borders of a story, reconnoitering the territory, chatting informally with gossips and secondary sources, soliciting ideas and advice from anyone and everyone, vacuuming up any tips and materials that might conceivably help.

Gradually, depending on available time, they stalk the center of the story, closing in from the outer rings to the interior, where the key, primary sources reside. Many reporters talk of *overreporting*, of gathering three or four times as much material as they will use, in order to be able to choose the very best from an ample supply. Others use terms like *mastering* the material or *immersion reporting*. The goal is to reach the greatest possible depth of understanding.

On a parallel track, reporters have one more vital objective during this phase. While compiling their information, they should also spend time *thinking as a writer*. This means devoting a portion of their brain to toying with leads, sketching preliminary outlines, and evaluating whether their reporting is producing the kind of facts, insights, quotes, anecdotes, and details that will feed into a dynamic, understandable article.

Too often, writers find themselves with a working personal understanding of their subject, but without the specific ingredients necessary for compelling writing. Recognizing such problems early, rather than later, allows for timely calibration.

Focusing

If stronger reporting is the number one route to better writing, then more thoughtful organizing is number two.

Yet this is a stage too many writers skimp on or even skip. In a hurry to convert the precious raw material from their reporting into finished goods, they rush to the terminal, ponder momentarily over the lead, and soon begin clicking furiously at the keyboard. Too often, the result is not an orderly article so much as a random collection of miscellaneous interesting items.

Disorganization is the archenemy of good writing. The best writers anticipate that danger and account for it in their craftwork. Top writers almost invariably turn out to be individuals who expend special effort on organization.

But these writers tend to be exceptional. The most common methods of so-called organization are these two: thinking about the story while driving from the reporting scene back to the newsroom, and reading quickly through notes while sitting at the desk just before writing. These are both fairly useful brain stimulators, but they are seldom sufficient substitutes for the punctilious craftwork of true organization: choosing a focus and a storyline and making an outline.

We know the effects of disorganized writing, those rambling, gassy, blurry pieces that befuddled readers abandon after a few paragraphs. Few faults make it easier for readers to lift their eyes off the page than a piece with no clear angle or storyline.

Perhaps the problem lies in the writer's eagerness to proceed. Perhaps the yoke of deadline is to blame. But a few minutes devoted to focusing can turn an unformed, vague abstraction into a well-planned narrative with a compelling point and an approach calculated to grab and hold reader attention.

Good organizers use many techniques. They sort and sift their notes using various systems, make lists and outlines, ask themselves questions that help cut to the storyline, draft summary statements, list key words, and take many other steps. We will return to these techniques in greater detail later, but for now, just keep in mind your crucial objectives for this stage.

- You want to systematically reduce your mass of notes and research materials to smaller and smaller "piles," usually through a several-step filtering process. For example, you might first inventory your material and sort it by rough topic; then make a one- or two-page list of all your potential points and topics; next, consolidate the topic list down to the five or six most important points, ranked in the order you want to write about them; and, finally, derive from all this material a clear, interesting central *theme* that can be expressed in a sentence or two.
- You also want to settle on a *storyline,* a way of writing about this theme that unifies all your material and provides both journalistic and literary structure, coherence, and drama.
- You want an *outline* or *road map*—and this should be written, not simply mulled over in your head—that shows clear beginning and ending points, along with three or four key stages in between.
- You want to feel a mastery of your material and a confidence in your approach. When you feel on top of your material, you are just about ready to write.

Limbering

Writing is an intimate act that journalists regularly must perform in public. It is best suited to solitude and serenity, but journalists typically do it in crowded, noisy news halls. It is a physical and mental exercise, but journalists often begin without any warm-up at all.

The lesson should be obvious. Run without first stretching your muscles, and you risk hurting yourself. Write without first limbering your mind, and you risk hurting your copy.

Like athletes, musicians, and performers of all kinds, writers work best when they feel relaxed and loose. Unfortunately, the news business seems a gigantic conspiracy to make it as hard as possible for writers to relax. If you wanted to create the worst possible writing environment, you could not do much better than the typical newsroom, where journalists write under atrocious conditions, with phones ringing and people milling around, editors scowling from across the room or, worse, peering over their shoulders, and huge wall clocks ticking down the minutes to the unbending deadline.

These conditions help explain why so much journalistic writing seems cramped and bloodless. Stifled in any effort to be creative, journalists reduce their writing to formulaic templates that can be churned out assembly-line style. It is a coping mechanism that lets writers meet the minimal standard under tough conditions.

But things do not have to be that way. Even inside a newsroom, journalists can construct safe, creative writing zones, both physical and intellectual. Among your objectives at this stage are the following:

- **Build a comfortable *place* to write.** You may have only a six-by-six cubicle, but make it cozy. You need a snug chair oriented suitably (for example, do you prefer to face other people, a blank wall, a window?), easy access to your tools (such as notes, reference materials, favorite pencils, and coffee mugs), and any appropriate fortifications to mark your space.
- **Determine the best *time* to write.** In a newsroom, you seldom fully control your time, but most of us are more productive at certain times than others. If morning is your most efficient time, for example, try to write as often as possible then.
- **Allow yourself a few *writing rituals*.** Maybe you need to stretch or pace for a few minutes before you write. Many people nibble food or sip drinks, visit the restroom, arrange their writing tools in a special way. You do not want these preparations to be a distraction or a convenient way to postpone writing, and you never have limitless time in a newsroom. But for most writers a few moments of limbering can make the rest of the writing move much faster.

Writing

Writing, of course, is writing. It is the necessary and unavoidable climax to the entire process. Its secret, as author and teacher Natalie Goldberg has succinctly pointed out, is to "keep your hand moving."[2]

We all recognize that writing is not easy. But by now it should be clear that serious attention to process, step-by-step along the way, makes the actual act of writing consolingly easier.

To write well requires readying oneself. A writer applying the process model will spend a lot of time in activities that do not involve writing a word intended for publication. Yet consider the advantages, at the moment of writing, that accrue to writers who have succeeded at each preliminary step. They will have a compelling idea, a wealth of information to support it, a specific approach and storyline in mind, and a relaxed and comfortable setting in which to write. They are like investors who lock in interest rates early. No matter what happens next, they will benefit from wise planning. Sooner or later, though, they will have to write.

Two predominant patterns seem to characterize writers' work. Some writers move deliberately from start to finish, crafting one sentence at a time, reluctant to move forward until they are satisfied with the current section. Other writers work rapidly, filling screens with words as fast as they will come, then returning later to revise and polish.

Perhaps the biggest change in writing during the past generation has been the steady migration from the first camp into the second. More and more writ-

---

[2]   Natalie Goldberg, *Writing Down the Bones* (Boston: Shambhala, 1986) 8.

ers now write fast drafts, then refine them. The reason, it seems obvious, is the spread of writing via computer.

Writing in longhand or by typewriter was, and still is, painstaking. Revision is physically difficult and therefore psychologically discouraging. Traditionally, writers have responded by moving slowly, in hopes of reducing the amount of revision necessary.

Today, by contrast, computers let us write quickly and safely, since revision is effortless. Words on a screen seem less permanent, less expensively produced. Changing them is easy, both physically and spiritually.

This advance does carry a cost. Writing by hand and even by typewriter was marvelously tactile: you felt closer to the words, commingled with them intellectually and even physically. By contrast, words on a computer screen seem fluttery. Clinically encased behind a Plexiglas shield, they are off-limits to the rough-and-tumble of human contact, like premature babies in an incubator.

Ultimately, though, most of us prefer the new system. It liberates the writer to work recursively, writing and revising, circling back to troublesome passages, accelerating to take advantage of those moments of fleeting inspiration, and then braking when the inevitable curves and blind spots loom. Writing fast forces words up from the subconscious in a way that lets the message come forth uninhibitedly. And the form matters little. Whether the writing emerges fully ordered or as stream-of-consciousness jumble, it can easily be revised, shaped, and buffed. We can reap the blessings of fast writing when we need to and those of slow writing when we are ready.

Goals at the writing stage are clear-cut:

- You want a complete draft, with a well-conceived focus and shape.
- You want a lead that crystallizes the main idea in clear, compelling prose.
- You want an orderly, logical progression that presents the best of your information in an interesting, accessible way.
- You want copy that is within striking distance of meeting the specifications for length, style, and format.

Rewriting

Ernest Hemingway once told an interviewer he rewrote the ending to *A Farewell to Arms* 39 times. "What was it that had stumped you?" the interviewer asked.

"Getting the words right," Hemingway replied.[3]

Few writers believe that first drafts constitute their best creative work, but many journalists persist in publishing—and actually charging money for!—what amount to rough drafts.

---

[3]   *Writers at Work,* 2d series (New York: Viking, 1963) 222.

Under pressure of deadline, human nature seems to incline a writer to continue the forward motion of writing rather than undertake the more tedious chores of revision. Given an hour, a typical writer will write furiously for 55 minutes and give the copy a five-minute once-over for obvious and fatal errors. Invariably, however, far more substantial work will emerge if the writer follows 40 minutes of writing with 20 minutes of revising and polishing.

Revision serves the same purpose as adding the finishing touches to new furniture, homes, or cars. It burnishes rough work toward higher and higher levels of quality. Painters retouch spots they missed the first time. Carpenters correct misaligned angles and fittings. And good writers amend words and ideas to enhance accuracy, clarity, and drama. As John Kenneth Galbraith once observed, "There are days when the result is so bad that no fewer than five revisions are required. In contrast, when I'm greatly inspired, only four revisions are needed."[4]

Consumers recognize sloppy work by its inattention to detail, and they distinguish first-quality handiwork from seconds by the fineness of the quality control applied to it. Writing is no different.

Logically, the case for revision looks airtight. But writers need discipline and determination to overcome their natural resistance to allocating time for it. Their reward is that the more they revise, the more they improve—a cycle that, once activated, produces ongoing positive reinforcement.

For many writers, a good starting point is to practice *selective revision*, the art of reworking key parts rather than an entire piece. The very idea of rewriting can terrify a writer, carrying implications of starting over at a point when most writers have invested mammoth time and energy and can hardly bear the prospect of going through all those labors again. Selective revision is less forbidding. Instead of undertaking a full-scale, top-to-bottom reengineering, the writer surgically reworks parts of the piece that can most benefit from attention, for example, the lead or the ending or perhaps the exact configuration of the most important anecdote or scene. Even brief attention to the critical points can noticeably upgrade most articles. Devoting more time to revision usually continues the payoff.

Here, then, are the objectives for the rewriting stage:

- To critically review your information, themes. and writing compared to your goals and ideals
- To adjust the overall shape, outline, and presentation for accuracy, clarity, drama, and maximum impact
- To streamline syntax, sharpen focus, and power up language
- To locate and correct the careless errors, omissions, and clutter that accompany most first drafts

---

[4] James Charlton, ed., *The Writer's Quotation Book* (Wainscott, NY: Pushcart, 1985) 43.

- To fine-tune work to a professional level of excellence in content and structure

Copyediting

Revisions completed, you submit your copy to the editor and celebrate. Your work is done. Or is it?

Not so fast. The handoff to the editor marks a critical point in the process, and the writer has every incentive to stay closely involved.

Writing is a private act but publishing is public and corporate. What has been a writer's mostly individual work now must yield to the communal domain, a world of buzzing editors, designers, managers, and production technicians, who can overwhelm and even shove aside the writer whose creation is under consideration.

This handoff is unavoidable, but the writer and editor control whether it proves traumatic or therapeutic. Handled poorly, the transaction is almost like someone's snatching an infant away from its parents. If it is handled considerately, the work flows seamlessly into the production system under the watchful eyes of both writer and editor.

Editing should be a collaborative process, and the writer should play a direct and substantive role. Otherwise, the risks soar of added errors, capricious changes, or other indignities to copy. Working as a team, writers and editors produce better copy, learn together, and backstop each other.

What, then, is the proper role for the writer during the editing stage?

Ideally, the editor will have been involved all during the process. Editor-writer teamwork reduces friction and heads off problems, dramatically improving both copy and morale. Writers should recognize the importance of feeding editors' needs—for adequate quantity and quality of copy, for reasonable attention to deadlines, for respect and inclusion from beginning to end of the overall enterprise. Good writers know that part of their job is making the editor look good.

Therefore, the writer should consciously strive to produce copy that needs minimal editing and that contains no major surprises for the editor. Leaving typos, misspellings, or style errors undermines editors' confidence in a writer. And it tempts them to fire up the chain saw. Likewise, springing totally unexpected articles on an editor—something fundamentally different from what was discussed at the idea stage, for instance—is an invitation to a duel.

Next, the writer should be present during editing. Side-by-side editing is best, the editor working through the copy, the writer handy to answer questions and respond to changes on the spot. If side-by-side editing is not practical, then the writer should be available by phone or online or otherwise and should see any substantial changes before the copy gets published.

Good editors recognize that editing involves negotiation, and most welcome the writer's presence and contribution. Most of us have been burned, at one time or at many times, by a poor writer-editor relationship, and we instinctively recognize how poisonous it can be. So consider it important, on both sides, to show courtesy and restraint. Writers, for instance, should defend and explain their work but should also respect editors' judgment and avoid excessive argument. Editors, for their part, should appreciate writers' professional efforts, avoid condescension, and forgo the role of bully.

Never forget, if you are the writer, that the editor gets to be the editor. Ultimately, editors are in charge. Solomonic or sophomoric, their decisions stick. But a participatory writing and editing system proceeds more as a partnership and less as a hierarchy. It reduces quarreling and one-upmanship, casts everyone involved as equal professionals, and generates synergy rather than division. Best of all, it makes the copy better.

SUMMARY

Writing is a craft. Good writers advance methodically through a series of steps, each with important goals and standards: launching, reporting, focusing, limbering, writing, rewriting, copyediting. Attention to each stage affects the succeeding stage. Neglect any step, and quality suffers. But consummate each step, and the force of your writing multiplies with compounded intensity.

Craft demands practice and discipline, and those artisan's virtues promptly repay any investment of time and energy. The iron law of craft is that better technique turns out better work. Still, craft alone is insufficient. Writing is craft, but more than craft. Writing is also part magic. Discipline brings technical mastery, but inspiration elevates craft into art. The next chapter explores the magic of the writer's art.

Practicing Craft and Magic

1. Begin your next assignment by creating a checklist or flowchart of the steps in the writing process. Monitor the time you devote to each step. Is it sufficient? Is your time distributed in the most profitable way? Are you neglecting certain steps? Develop a plan to correct any imbalances you find.

2. Pay special attention to two steps that many novice writers speed past: focusing and revising. Produce a *written* plan or outline for the assignment. Once you have written, revise the lead at least twice. Identify what you consider the weakest writing in your article and spend some time rewriting it.

3. Address yourself daily to this overall goal: improving bit by bit at each stage of the writing process. If you are naturally linear, make lists and follow them. If you lean to artistic dominance, then exercise your left-brain hemisphere as if it were a flaccid muscle; post a copy of the writing stages at your desk, visualize each of them as you work, and compensate for any stage you may be shortchanging.

Chapter 3

Writing
as
Magic

Inspiration jolts every writer from time to time. You are cruising along a free-way or soaking in the shower, edging into sleep or savoring a stroll, and an idea flashes into your head, out of the blue.

But where is this blue from which inspiration leaps? What secrets abide there? What puts you in touch with them?

Welcome to the magic of writing, the mysticism that intertwines with the methodical. As we have seen, writing is certainly a craft, but it is far more. It is also a magician's art, influenced as much by abstruse rites and incantations as by order and process. It is a world whose magical interventions can trans-port writers into a dreamland where words and ideas form themselves, seem-ingly spontaneously, into the shapes and patterns of literature.

This chapter considers the nature and sources of inspiration, the writer's magic balm. It will discuss how writers' work styles can foster inspiration and will suggest some exercises for summoning those golden flickers of revelation that all writers covet.

Dedication to craft produces solid work and leads to constant improve-ment, but craft alone seldom generates the exceptional. It is magic that pro-vides the breakthrough idea, the grand artistic leap into excellence.

Yet magic is bedeviling and fanciful. At times, the muses whisper their rev-elations, and we write so effortlessly that it seems we will never run dry. Why are we so soon drained? At times, stories seem to emerge whole, with sudden authority and completeness. Why do so many barren hours, days, and weeks then ensue?

Why do the fickle muses tease us?

Perhaps the problem is that we fail to see that writing is holistic. Writing is a lifestyle, as well as an activity. It is a way of living, as well as a way of working. It requires treating craft and magic as companions, not enemies, and recognizing the synergistic, reinforcing potential of bringing our nonlinear artistry into synchronization with linear processing.

The great secret of writing is to bring craft and magic into unison rather than opposition, into creative fusion rather than immobilizing tension.

Too often, we resist. The craftsperson scorns the artiste as effete and touchy-feely. The artist eschews process as unworthy and demeaning. In newsrooms, for example, you often encounter two camps, the craftspeople and the artists, at work in the same place but squared off and antagonistic. Instead of learning from one another, they compete to impose one worldview atop the newsroom political hierarchy. They name-call (the "drones" versus the "prima donnas"), they snicker at each other's methods, they retreat into the rut of righteousness.

But the true secret to improving as a writer is to maximize the effort from both craft and magical powers: to discover your stronger side and capitalize on natural ability but, even more importantly, to recognize your weaker side and exercise it into full partnership.

It may be, then, that the problem is not that the muse is avoiding us—we are avoiding the muse. For the magic of writing, like almost all other forms of magic, involves some illusion. The shaman, the wizard, and the aesthete are more often than not artisans, too; and the magic that appears so preternatural and elusive springs from careful planning and precise execution.

Later, this chapter will suggest some specific ways to incorporate magical inspiration into your work. But first it is important to spend some time reflecting on how the imaginative powers apply to writers in general and on how those influences can be used by media writers on deadline.

In *Solitude: A Return to the Self,* Anthony Storr describes craft and magic as two worlds between which artists continuously shuttle:

> There are good biological reasons for accepting the fact that man is so constituted that he possesses an inner world of the imagination which is different from, though connected to, the world of external reality. It is the discrepancy between the two worlds which motivates creative imagination. People who realize their creative potential are constantly bridging the gap between inner and outer.[1]

This chapter delves further into the "inner world," the place writers must go in their search for the propitious zap of inspiration.

---

[1] Anthony Storr, *Solitude: A Return to the Self* (New York: Free Press, 1988) 69.

THE MAGICIAN INSIDE

In their typical imagery, writers often speak of inspiration arriving "out of the blue." It seems to come from somewhere outside, beyond and—somewhat forbiddingly—above themselves.

In reality, the opposite is more likely to be true. Inspiration comes not from above but from within. We may draw comfort from assigning our artistic fate to uncontrollable Olympian muses. To await the muse, after all, absolves us from responsibility and rationalizes delay and false starts. But the real muse is internal. We do not await it; it waits for us. It will tantalize us with stirrings and glimpses, vivid but fleeting reminders of its presence and latent power, like the fading images of a dream or the internalized melody of an old love song. We sense its nearness and shiver at its vast potentiality.

But how do you conjure its real presence? You act. You repudiate passiveness. You wire your work habits to connect to those internal currents that will summon inspiration.

Inspiration may be mystical, and it may be mysterious, but it is not accidental. It may seem magical, but it is ultimately explainable. The muses are not capricious; they come to those who work hard enough to deserve a visit.

Their arrival, however serendipitous it may seem, is a function of preparation, a reaction to forces you can set in motion. It is like a computer transmission whose appearance on screen, however amazing, is actually the controlled combination of dots and impulses. It is like a loaf of morning-fresh bread whose delicious and nourishing wholeness is perfectly expectable from the ingredients you measured into the machine the night before.

The magic of writing, in other words, is within your power to invoke, if not entirely to understand. Create favorable conditions, and the inner muse is more likely to spring forth.

The goal, then, is not to pine away aimlessly until some arbitrary muse deigns to bless you. You are not detached from your creative energies, and you are not in competition with them. You are connected to them, and the goal is to power up the connection. You want to ally yourself with the mystical powers within, to understand and nurture them, and to deliberately promote a work style where inspiration is most likely to thrive.

Magic, like craft, demands effort. There is no foolproof system. The computer image can blur, the homemade bread can gum up, and the creative juices can sour. But the likelihood of success multiplies with understanding and effort.

Novelist John Gardner believed that magic was responsive to the writer's perseverance in seeking it. The "soul of art," Gardner wrote, lay in those "queer moments" that precipitate the "altered state" of inspiration:

And young writers sufficiently worried about achieving this state to know when they've done it and feel dissatisfied when they haven't are already on their way to calling it up at will. . . . The more often one finds the magic key, whatever it is, the more easily the soul's groping fingers come to land on it. In magic, as in other things, success brings success.[2]

THE CREATIVE SPIRAL

If you study the lives and habits of successful artists, a recurrent pattern appears. In Chapter 1, I called it the *creative spiral:*

- hard work
- detachment
- inspiration
- hard work

Inspiration supplies the turning point, the magic moment that yields the artistic fruit. Repeatedly, you find creative people of all stripes—scientists and technicians, as well as writers and musicians—laboring toward what mathematician Henri Poincaré called "this appearance of sudden illumination, a manifest sign of long, unconscious prior work."[3]

As you read this section, pay attention to how various authors describe the methods and mindsets that drive their creative energies. From the thoughts of these artists, try to extrapolate those insights you can begin to apply in a more down-to-earth setting. Your goal is to understand the creative spiral and to find ways to tap into its powers for everyday assignments.

To reach the inspiration stage, both the work and the detachment seem indispensable prerequisites. Poincaré explains it this way:

[T]his unconscious work . . . is possible, and of a certainty it is only fruitful, if it is on the one hand preceded and on the other hand followed by a period of conscious work. These sudden inspirations . . . never happen except after some days of voluntary effort [which has] set agoing the unconscious machine and without them it would not have moved and would have produced nothing.

For writers, the pattern typically involves throwing themselves headlong into a story, then at some point backing off into a quieter period of reflection

---

[2] John Gardner, "Do You Have What It Takes to Become a Novelist?" *Esquire,* April 1983, 80.
[3] Henri Poincaré, "Mathematical Creation," in *Creativity,* ed. P. E. Vernon (Middlesex, Eng.: Penguin, 1972) 83.

that, to use Poincaré's marvelous phrase, can "set agoing the unconscious machine." In their book *Higher Creativity*, Willis Harman and Howard Rheingold describe how "incubation" leads to "illumination":

> At a certain stage in every creation, preparation ceases, and the ingredients have to be left to "cook" in order to allow the subconscious to operate on the problem. . . . As a result . . . a mysterious process produces the solution to our problem in a flash, from out of nowhere, in the form of a religious illumination, a literary image, a scientific understanding, the theme of a concerto, a business innovation, and so forth. . . . There is no doubt that this is an observation repeatedly confirmed by independent and reliable sources, a clue to the *state* in which deep insights occur.[4]

Harman and Rheingold also offer what they call "a more contemporary metaphor," comparing the human mind to a computer:

> As with a computer, part of the operation is automatic, taking place somewhere out of sight of the "screen" of our surface awareness. And as with the computer, this processor can be reprogrammed and debugged to help serve us better, allowing us to solve different and more difficult problems. . . .[5]

The composer Tchaikovsky once wrote to a friend about what he called "this magic process":

> Generally speaking, the germ of a future composition comes suddenly and unexpectedly. If the soil is ready . . . it takes root with extraordinary force and rapidity. . . . It would be vain to try to put into words that immeasurable sense of bliss which comes over me. . . . I forget everything and behave like a madman.[6]

Mark Twain described waiting weeks for a "call" that sent him into feverish writing spurts. He sometimes leaped from bed and wrote for hours. Writing *The Innocents Abroad*, he reported averaging 3,000 words a day for 60 days; working on *Roughing It*, he produced 30 to 65 pages per day. "I find myself so thoroughly interested in my work now," he said, "that I can't bear to lose a single moment of the inspiration."[7]

Arthur Miller commented that he produced the first act of *Death of a Salesman* in a similar state of creative fervor:

---

[4]   Willis Harman and Howard Rheingold, *Higher Creativity* (Los Angeles: Jeremy P. Tarcher, 1984) 26–27.

[5]   Harman and Rheingold, *Higher Creativity*, 9.

[6]   Peter Ilich Tchaikovsky, "Letters," in *Creativity*, ed. P. E. Vernon (Middlesex, Eng.: Penguin, 1972) 57.

[7]   Edward Wagenknecht, *Mark Twain: The Man and His Work* (New Haven: Yale University Press, 1935) 78.

> I started in the morning, went through the day, then had dinner, and then I went back there and worked till—I don't know—one or two o'clock in the morning. It sort of unveiled itself. I was the stenographer. [8]

Director Elia Kazan said of Miller: "He didn't write *Death of a Salesman;* he *released* it. It was there inside him, stored up waiting to be turned loose."

The creative spiral couples craft and magic in a self-sustaining cycle. Artists have long recognized this fact, and their insights have relevance for media writers as well; in perhaps more modest ways, you can use the craft-magic connection to bring more imagination into commonplace copy. We are referring to the writers' version of this cycle as the WRITE approach: Work, Release, Inspiration, Technique, Energy. The acronym may seem contrived, but it can provide an easily remembered guide to the important elements of good writing.

Whatever terminology or imagery you prefer, the vital point is that writers not discount the magic part as remote, capricious, or beyond influence. Magic is intimately tied to craft, it is responsive to stimulation, and it is just predictable enough that every writer should strive to comprehend its secrets.

CONJURING THE INNER MAGIC

If you, like many writers and most editors, are decisively linear, this talk of magic and mysticism may seem strained. But please bear with it. Remember this key point about learning: you have far more room to improve as a writer by nurturing your weaker side than by resting on your strengths and ignoring the growth potential elsewhere.

Most writers probably welcome the sparks of inspiration we have been discussing. But how many systematically apply themselves to coaxing up those sparks from the inner consciousness? It may seem oxymoronic to talk about systems and muses in the same sentence, but the oxymoron illustrates a central theme. Linking method and magic produces abundantly greater success than separating them.

A writer's lifestyle and work habits can directly raise the odds of arousing the inner magic. Although inspiration, like lightning, at first may seem whimsical and unpredictable, both are most likely to strike when the conditions are right. If you want to attract lightning, for example, you might fly a metal kite in a thunderstorm. If you want to invoke the muse, you need to pinpoint what prompts its presence.

In short, you want to make yourself into a walking receptacle calibrated to intercept messages from the muse. Or, in everyday language, you need to get yourself in the best possible position to catch any good ideas that go flying by.

---

[8] John Lahr, "Making Willy Loman," *The New Yorker,* 25 January 1999, 42.

WRITING AS A WAY OF LIFE

A writer was standing in the hallway when a colleague happened by. "You look confused," she greeted him. "What are you doing?"

"Writing," he said.

She walked away bewildered.

At the instant, of course, the writer was standing in public, staring off into space, and ignoring the comings and goings around him. It probably seemed rude, and it certainly did not look like writing. But he was writing, at least in the broad sense. He was trying to catch the muse.

Writing is a lifestyle and a mindset. When writers are not directly writing, they are preparing to write or recovering from writing, constantly on the alert for the muse.

If someone were to tell you that the room you are now sitting in was full of strange faces and voices, would you believe it? Look around. Do you see them and hear them?

No? Then turn on television. Magic happens. What one second before had been invisible waves and currents now form themselves into coherent, recognizable images and sounds. Were they present before you switched on the television? Of course. You simply had to tune the receiver properly.

Sad to say, writers cannot set their inspiration-receiving equipment with the same pinpoint accuracy as a television. No one can predict the absolute coordinates of where and when inspiration will strike. But you should know that it is a real force. You sense its presence. And you can do your best to tune it in.

In this effort, you should proceed both directly and indirectly. You stimulate the muse directly when you actively, consciously deliberate on your writing, siphoning ideas and approaches to the surface by, for example, thinking, talking, and writing about them. You can additionally take advantage of the brain's mysterious, subconscious creative power. Once you whet its interest directly, the mind will continue working on an idea even while you are doing other things, such as exercising and even playing. What we call inspiration is often an eruption from some subliminal region that has been diligently at work while the brain's conscious sectors were occupied elsewhere.

THE MUSE BY DIRECT ADDRESS

Here are some direct ways to conjure the muse.

Thinking

The writer thinking is employed in a frontal thrust toward the goal. Fans of detective novels come to recognize what is about to happen when Nero Wolfe closes his eyes and begins to purse his lips in and out, or when Hercule Poirot settles back to apply his "little gray cells." Insights and connections are imminent.

Thinking about a project does a writer good, at every stage. Thoughtfulness benefits the idea, the research, the focus, the writing, the revisions. But it is striking how seldom many of us clear our calendars for prolonged, applied sessions of thought. Perhaps it seems like wasted time, or makes us nervous. Perhaps we lack the discipline. Writers, after all, tend to be manic creatures. Perhaps we simply prefer action to contemplation. Perhaps thinking in public looks dangerously like malingering, offering an invitation for harried superiors to delegate us more work.

If you recognize yourself in these stalling rationalizations, then act to surmount them. Schedule a convenient time and place for thinking. If solitude is important, seclude yourself; if nosy superiors think you're goofing off, find a hideaway. If sitting up makes you nervous, then do your thinking horizontally, on a sofa or in a recliner; if lying down puts you to sleep, then think upright. If you need quiet, cut off the TV; if music soothes, play Mozart. If a change of scenery helps, take a walk or go for a drive.

The point is to apply yourself to thinking as if it were any other necessary chore. Program it into your schedule, select a propitious setting, treat yourself and your thinking seriously, and clear away as many distractions as possible.

Concentrated thought may be the writer's most underused rite.

Talking

Have you ever cradled a pile of playing cards after a game and found yourself holding a misaligned deck, with cards angling out in all directions? Then you begin to shake and bounce and massage the cards, and almost automatically they reconstitute themselves into the familiar cubelike pack.

Talking can have a similar effect on the ideas floating around in your imagination. It somehow seems to jiggle things into place, or at least in the right directions. Speech is by nature selective, an act of editing and priority setting that forces you to make quality judgments about what to reveal and in what way. Often, as you speak, you hear yourself expressing ideas, insights, and connections you never knew you had. Utter certain key words, and other phrases and concepts attach to them, almost as through magnetic force, forming groups and shapes of progressive orderliness.

An editor once coached a writer in the process of creating an intimate memoir. She was examining an important relationship in her life, but its meaning seemed elusive, hovering somewhere just out of sight, like a star in the sky that you can glimpse sideways but cannot detect when you look straight in its direction. The writer talked and fumbled and hesitated, and suddenly, in mid-sentence, she stopped. "I see it," she said. "I've got it."

Talking works best with a friendly listener, but do not overlook the value of speaking aloud to yourself. One writer tells of regularly chattering away during a 25-mile drive to work each day, creating leads in the air, trying out storylines, often pulling into a parking space to scribble a phrase or two in the ever-present pocket notebook. Talking is therapeutic and focusing, whether it is an individual act or part of a conversation.

But having a listener adds something irreplaceable. Listeners react, or sometimes do not. Talk about your material, and you can see in a listener's eyes what is interesting and what is boring. Ask for response, and the listener often articulates links and phrases you had overlooked, or expresses them in ways that provide new insights.

Talking, preferably with a sympathetic listener, is one of our most rewarding idea-processing tools. Whenever possible, talk out a story before trying to write it.

Prewriting

Words may seem like evanescent dots on a screen, but they have an undeniable tactile quality. Writers need to handle them, to knead them like dough or caress them like a violinist stroking the instrument before a concert. Before they read books, many people cannot resist playing with them, running their hands over the covers, opening the books at random to a few pages, literally getting a feel for the volumes and their contents. Writers often feel a similar physical connection to their words. They need to pet them and establish a bond, an easy familiarity with their companions-in-art.

Let's call this prewriting. Unlike composing or drafting, prewriting is preliminary and stimulative. It does not aim to produce ordered, polished copy or even coherence. Prewriting piques the imagination, alerts the mind's word sensors that the game is afoot. It is a call to action, a wake-up melody for the muse.

What exactly does prewriting consist of? *Written wordplay and wordwork of almost any kind.* Doodling and freewriting are common forms of wordplay, casual and undirected activities like a pitcher playfully tossing a baseball before settling into the serious warm-up regimen. Wordwork is more disciplined. It often involves experimenting with your material in different and unexpected formats; for example, try out headlines, memos to the editor, news digest lines, telegrams, ads, letters home.

As a creative, magic-inducing activity, prewriting can be eccentric or conventional, but mostly it is personal. Writers often like to do it fast. A few days or hours before beginning an assignment, for instance, try prewriting for half an hour or so, briskly typing stream-of-conscious style. Type as fast as possible, free-associating words, phrases, occasional complete thoughts in a great mishmashy tumble. Later, when making the transition from wordplay to word-work, you can connect some of the fragments, toy with headline concepts, and imagine magazine cover blurbs.

Sometimes prewriting yields instant rewards (for example, a lead or key phrase that winds up in the finished copy). But it is even more valuable for the delayed payoffs it almost invariably delivers. Prewriting seems to flip a mental creativity switch, setting into motion a subconscious idea machine. The machinery cranks on and begins spitting out ideas in a silent generative spasm, and over the next few days, periodically and apparently at random, many of the ideas will congeal themselves and float into conscious view. It is a process like waiting for ripe fruit to drop from a vine, wondrous in both its predictability and its spontaneity.

In an essay called "Toward a Theory of Creativity," therapist Carl Rogers linked creativity to "the ability to play spontaneously with ideas, colors, shapes, relationships" in wild, improbable ways:

> It is from this spontaneous toying and exploration that there arises the hunch, the creative seeing of life in a new and significant way. It is as though out of the wasteful spawning of thousands of possibilities there emerges one or two evolutionary forms with the qualities which give them a more perma-nent value.[9]

Pardon the mixed metaphors, but it is stimulating, as a brainstorming exer-cise, to summon as many visions as you can of this unfettered creative sub-consciousness in action: life springing from seedlings, solar flares radiating into the galaxy, bounty caught in a well-cast net, sparks pulsing from motor cylinders. In the mind, as you prewrite, image those quadrennial political convention extravaganzas, where someone empties a great bucket in the rafters and thousands of balloons fill the arena. Prewriting somehow fertilizes and catalyzes all these grand processes, to the writer's spectacular reward.

THE MUSE ADDRESSED SIDEWAYS

You can also probe indirectly for the muse.

Walking

Or running, swimming, or climbing the stair machine. Motion stirs the imag-ination. Exercise activates brain cells as well as muscle fibre. The writer-in-

---

[9]   Carl R. Rogers, *On Becoming a Person* (Boston: Houghton Mifflin, 1961) 355.

motion is abnormally alert and receptive, a mobile lightning rod for insight and inspiration. On certain rare and precious occasions, movement helps transport the writer into a state of hyper-awareness, where every synapse seems alive and conductive, and passing glimmers of inspiration are sucked into the center like winds in a vortex.

This is how we indirectly address the muse, by side glance and cocked ear. As a creative exercise, try to picture what is taking place inside the mind during these special moments of heightened consciousness.

Perhaps you will envision a busy airport, except that it is ideas, not jet planes, prowling the runways with all that pent-up energy bursting to erupt into takeoff. Or imagine a cooking range, with every burner fired up, a kettle boiling on one, a frying pan sizzling somewhere else, and, in the oven, a roasting casserole gradually gathering flavor from its own accumulating juices.

At least metaphorically, the mind is a multicylindered machine, throbbing with action and infinite in potential. What is nice is that the brain is capable of handling many tasks at once. Even when we are not paying direct and careful attention, all sorts of activities hum along simultaneously. While the brain's conscious regions are employed in walking or exercising or conversing, its other sections continue to simmer, sifting and digesting and processing the projects on file there.

It is easy to imagine our muses companionably accompanying us as we walk, jog, and run, occasionally, when conditions seem right, offering a nudge or a cheer. Or an idea, right out of the blue.

Playing

An acquaintance once described becoming stuck in a narrow crawlspace while working under a house. He found himself wedged tight, with no one around to help, and his first panicky instinct was to twist and wriggle, which only penned him worse. The more he thought about it, the tenser he became. Finally, he willed himself to relax and think of other things, and he was soon able to slither to safety.

Sometimes, for writers as well, the problem is that they are too tight and need to relax. Creative instincts are keenest when you are fresh and rested, but writers often drive themselves to the point of artistic overload, then press onward so stubbornly that their overworked imaginations rebel. Playing can be an effective antidote for the tension that keeps your inspiration bottled up. Activities such as gardening, tennis, or movie going can distract the mind just enough to loosen the blockages that keep ideas from surfacing.

Sleeping, of course, is a highly touted method of creative rejuvenation, and countless writers have offered testimonials about awakening in the middle of the night, semiconscious but aroused by the ember of a great idea that has somehow reached its flash point. Nor are writers the only people inspired in this way. Eugene Robinson, a longtime star professional football player, once told how he benefited from watching tapes of his opponents and then drifting to sleep thinking about how to beat them. "I like to lie in bed and let it marinate," Robinson said. "I watch for a while, then fall asleep and dream about making plays."[10]

Meditating is a more advanced, disciplined form of relaxation, but simply resting in an easy chair, listening to soothing music, can be a potent stimulant as well.

The message seems to be that artful distraction, in the form of almost any means of getting away from direct contact with our ideas, gives them time to ferment and coagulate into new shapes, tastes, and forms.

As mentioned earlier, to see a dim, far-off star, you sometimes have to avoid looking directly at it; focus your attention to one side or the other, and the star often swims into sight. Ideas are like these stars. You cannot stare them into existence. But sometimes, all you have to do is look away, and they will find you.

Laying in Tools

In the elaborate daily notebooks kept by the distinguished writer and teacher Donald Murray, you will find snatches of poems, leads-in-progress, and idle thoughts that filled his head. And, delightfully, every few pages you will run across photos and ads for an eclectic assortment of writer's tools: beautiful antique desks, comfortable chairs, personalized pens. It seems that Murray, like so many other writers, drew inspiration from these mundane appliances of his art.

An affinity for their tools is something that both craftspeople and artists have in common. There are plumbers whose attachment to certain wrenches matches any toddler's love for a teddy bear; baseball pitchers who wear the same sweat-stained cap for season after season; copyeditors who can function only with the prescribed set of No. 2 fat pencils at their side—even after they have converted to electronic editing.

Mike Phillips, a newspaper editor in Bremerton, Washington, once told me about learning an unexpected lesson about journalism when he began studying with a master wood-carver. The craftsman spent painstaking time making his own tools before he ever started carving. For Phillips, "being in control of my own tools" became more than a tenet of his hobby. It served as a metaphor for empowering both editors and writers.

---

[10] Austin Murphy, "Falcon Crest," *Sports Illustrated,* 18 January 1999, 40.

EXERCISES FOR MAGICIANS

Writers tend to align themselves with the traditions of craft more than with mysticism. They are more comfortable with talk of method than of magic.

History helps account for this tendency. Many people come to writing through reading, and for generations both reading and writing have been largely linear enterprises. You start at the beginning and read through, in a direct line, until the end. You write a first paragraph followed by a second paragraph and a third and so on. These sequential processes tend to attract people who are left-brain dominant and to echo in their work habits.

Other people, especially journalists, gravitate toward writing because of their interest in reporting. They commonly refer to themselves as reporters first, writers second. This path, too, tends to lure the left-brainers, because reporting demands the organized, step-by-step, logical procedures associated with the left hemisphere.

Of course, you find many exceptions. Every newsroom has at least a handful of right-brain-dominant writers, often tabbed by colleagues as "the creative types." You can often identify them by their artistic manner of dress or the whimsical decorations around their work spaces—or by the familiar lament that they feel stifled and unappreciated inside the news factories.

Changing times are rapidly reworking the left-brain, right-brain mix. As is discussed elsewhere in this book, linearity is no longer the dominant mode of experiencing the media. For centuries, we learned more from reading than from any other means except personal experience and word of mouth. Now, we learn far more from what we see in the media than from what we read. Television and online publishing are inexorably rewiring our internal information-processing systems. Instead of a beginning-to-end approach, we jump and skip, skim and surf. Information comes to us in bursts, from more than one direction. Online publishing allows a multidimensionality that lets us "gopher" and "tunnel" and "hyperlink" and "web" in personalized, nonsequential patterns that correspond far more to roundabout right-brain navigation than to left-brain straight-aheadness.

These changes, it seems clear, will attract more and more nonlinear writers into journalism. The lure will remain for the linear ones too, but the mix is likely to split more evenly.

In view of all these developments, then, writers will have to concentrate on developing their artistic aptitudes. Those who are naturally artisans *need* to improve their artistic powers, and all writers now find themselves in an environment where both craft and magic are indispensable to excellence.

Maybe there is some Darwinian law of selection that has, over centuries, honed the writer's left brain as the foremost survival tool for a linear world.

Now, to adapt to change, we should lose no time in revivifying the right brain. Luckily, there are many drills and exercises for the nonlinear side, and they can help us all.

Exercise 1: Stage Creative Moments

In her excellent book, *Writing on Both Sides of the Brain*, the writing teacher Henriette Anne Klauser makes numerous practical suggestions for stimulating right-brain response. Perhaps the best exercise is to identify the circumstances under which you seem most productive, and try to reconstitute them when you need inspiration. Specifically, pay attention to the times, the places, and the conditions where inspiration strikes you, and return to them when you need a lift. Klauser writes:

> Once you recognize the value of the words that come to you unsought from the right hemisphere . . . you will see that I am not being flip to suggest deliberately staging such moments. If your creative well has dried up, go for a walk, take a shower, drive around the block—allow yourself some reflective time. And bring a pad and a pen with you.[11]

Exercise 2: Perform a Mindstretch

Lay out, on paper or on screen or even in your mind, any or all key elements of your project: the idea or theme, the outline, the lead, the best quotes, anecdotes, and descriptions. Then try to stretch each one toward something better. Concentrate your brain and imagination on improving each element. Ask what would make it better, what is missing, what is overlooked. Ask yourself directly: is there a better story here, and if so what would it be? The more you stretch, the harder you think, the more likely you are to be inspired with some new and sparkling connection or combination.

Exercise 3: Draw a "Mind Spill"

This exercise comes from another outstanding teacher, Carole Rich, in her book *Writing and Reporting News.* Here is how she explains it:

> Get all the research together. Draw a circle in the center of a large piece of paper. Put the main topic in the center circle. Then draw circles, filling each circle with an idea. Take a colored pencil or highlighter, and mark the key components related to the main idea. Draw a line to connect one related idea

---

[11] Henriette Anne Klauser, *Writing on Both Sides of the Brain* (San Francisco: HarperSanFrancisco, 1987) 40.

to another so that all like information is grouped together. Then number the points, preferably in the order you will write them.[12]

Exercise 4: Create a Web

Similar to a "mind spill," a web is simply a free-associated collection of ideas related to your topic. One creative approach is to draw a web online, using a graphics program instead of word processing; label or color code the sections, or put main ideas in square boxes and secondary ideas in diamond-shaped boxes. The idea is to visually manipulate the information until you begin to sense connections and links. You can create a similar effect by imaging a tree trunk instead of a web and treating main ideas as branches and subordinate ideas as twigs sprouting from them. Gabriele Rico, in *Writing the Natural Way,* calls this process "clustering," advising writers to "simply let go and begin to flow with any current of connections that come into your head."[13]

Exercise 5: Brainstorm with Photos

Several journalistic writing coaches, including Adell Crowe at *USA Today* and Bruce DeSilva of the Associated Press, employ a version of this exercise. It works best with a group, but an individual can use it as well.

Begin with a photo. Study it for a few seconds. Give some thought to camera angle, lighting, and other compositional elements. Then write down as many details as you can, inspired by the photo, that could help in writing about the photo's subject. Rank the details, from most essential to trivial.

Exercises like this can sharpen both your powers of observation and your appreciation for information derived from various senses.

Exercise 6: Listen

You write with your hands, your eyes, your brain. But do not overlook your ears. Writing is musical, rhythmic, tonal. Listening both *to* and *for* good writing can help bring on an inspired thought. Listen to people's conversations, and write down interesting words and phrases. Let the sounds of daily life—music, television dialogue, sermons, lectures—stimulate your thinking about effective word usage. Listen to your own thoughts, and learn to recognize and capture creative moments before they vanish. Biographer Edmund Morris puts it this way: "to this day, when words won't come, I listen for them rather

---

[12] Carole Rich, *Writing and Reporting News,* 2d edition (Belmont, CA: Wadsworth, 1997) 264.

[13] Gabriele Lusser Rico, *Writing the Natural Way* (Los Angeles: Jeremy P. Tarcher, 1983) 35.

than look for them. Sooner or later one that sounds right will whisper itself onto the page."[14]

Exercise 7: Visualize Success

Finally, here is an exercise recommended by countless teachers, coaches, and advisers. Imagine the best possible outcome for your writing project and stride steadily toward it. Install this *success scenario* in your head, jot it down in your notebook, type it at the top of your document. Dangle it in front of your subconscious in every way possible, in the full expectation that it will be absorbed.

SUMMARY

Writing builds on but ultimately transcends craft. It is a magical art, rife with secret ceremonies and Delphic practices, with petitions and prostrations, invention and illusion. Writing casts its aspirants into a mysterious land of imagination, whose rules and ideals hover at the brink of our understanding—elusive, but sometimes exaltedly borne into our hands.

These are magical moments, but they are not entirely accidental. Through writerly habits, you can nourish your creative side and induce the coveted instants of inspiration. Through an optimal alignment of hard work and dedication, you can achieve the fusion of craft and magic that produces writing excellence.

To reach inspiration, you attend to your magical impulses both directly and indirectly, using every available means to focus the prodigious powers of the human brain. Active thinking, talking, and prewriting are generative processes that directly engage your mind. Exercising, relaxing, and carefully choosing tools and surroundings are indirect avenues; they occupy upper consciousness with constructive activity while, elsewhere, the mind continues to mull over the projects assigned to it.

The most fundamental key to improvement, at every stage, is to harness in unison—not opposition—the dual forces of craft and magic.

Practicing Craft and Magic

1. On your next assignment, deliberately select one direct method of addressing the muse (thinking, talking, or prewriting) and one indirect

---

[14] Edmund Morris, "Writing Life," *Washington Post Book World,* 27 September 1998, 11.

method (preferably walking or playing). Make a note to yourself of any payoff that seems to result.

2. As you apply the WRITE approach and the creative spiral in your assignment, put special emphasis on the "release" and "inspiration" segments. Even if you have only a few minutes or hours, take a break between the reporting and writing stages and let your brain work independently toward inspiration. Deliberately find the most comfortable place you know to do your writing. Be conscious of the effect such factors may have on your creativity, and program them into your future work.

3. Before you write, try any one of the above exercises for magicians. In subsequent assignments, keep experimenting. You may receive a quick reward, and at the least you will be exercising your creative faculties.

Chapter 4

The Three
Qualities
of Great Writing

A gifted newspaper writer, whose elegant articles had made him a newsroom star, once took time off to write a book. After a few weeks, he bumped into a friend who inquired about his progress. The writer hung his head. "I've written and rewritten and rewritten the first 100 pages," he said, "until I'm sure they are the very best that I can do.

"And," he added morosely, "they're not good enough."

Writers read. They read and read. They read so much that they can distinguish good writing from bad as quickly as most people can taste the difference between sweet and curdled milk. They know what good writing is. They see it in the mind's eye. And they agonize endlessly because their own work fails to match this ideal.

The passion for writing better is a trait nearly all writers share. Their insecurity is a great equalizer. From first graders to Nobel laureates, writers struggle inescapably with their next sentence. Wherever they rank on the scale of excellence, they want to move up. The "ones" long to become "twos." The "nines" hope to make themselves "tens."

Adjectives like *competent, adequate,* and *satisfactory* are archenemies of their enlarged aspirations. The good story is not good enough. The writing life is an unending quest for the great story.

What makes a great story? It is hazardous to be doctrinaire. Different readers and different writers have different reactions to different stories. As surely as one reader loves a certain piece, someone else cannot abide it; articles one editor rejects, others embrace. This makes dogma difficult. Excellence is, at least to some degree, inexpressible.

But not entirely. While tastes differ, it still should be possible to analyze and isolate some common characteristics of meritorious work. Writers need, at least, a sound working definition of the superior. To grandly aspire to write a "great story" poses too broad a challenge. If you can begin to put into words your ideas about excellence, if you can break down the huge overall goal into more manageable increments, then you will have a fair target at which to aim the discipline of craft and the devotion of magic.

So let's stipulate that exceptional stories generally share the following three virtues:

1. **Storyline**—a great idea
2. **Surprise**—great material
3. **Stylishness**—great words

Storyline, surprise, and stylishness. Notice how these qualities range from general to specific, from the relatively abstract arena of ideas to the tiniest of component parts, the words. A great story requires attention to the big things and the little things, to design and detail. That is why both craft and inspiration must be the writer's confederates.

Storyline, or a great idea, should be the starting point. You might call it the "high concept." An earlier chapter referred to it as the *breakthrough idea*, the magically induced theme and development that make your article different from any other piece ever written. A wonderful story begins with a wonderful idea, something that captures the essence of some universal mood or feeling, that attaches itself to one of the large natural themes to which readers can relate. A strong storyline needs to be concise, arousing, and expressible in a sentence or two. The storyline unifies and compresses all the writing's constituent ingredients into a concentrated force field, irresistible to the reader's imagination. Storyline helps a story mean something to the reader.

Surprise comes from great material, from information and impressions that drive home the storyline with vivid immediacy. It is no exaggeration to say, again, that the single quickest way to improve writing is to improve reporting. The better the material, the better the copy. If the content is dramatic, unexpected, and eye-catching, the reader will quickly engage. If readers fail to experience a compelling jolt of surprise from paragraph to paragraph, they will exercise their simplest option: they will look up from the story and stop reading.

Stylishness flows from the language. Great stories invariably include great words, words that sparkle and tickle and rankle and boggle, words that arouse and stir and awaken and stimulate. Powerful words pump energy into copy; flat words deflate it. Words bestow the musical undertones, the rich, dulcet melodies of artistic elegance.

SEEING THE STORY

An observant bird hunter who had practiced his hobby for nearly 50 years once described how he was trained to hunt. You stand very still, he said, and you focus on the distant sky. You scan your eyes slowly along the horizon, intently alert for the slightest movement. A flock, he explained, will appear first as a flutter, a ripple in your line of sight. Spot it early, and by the time it floats into full view you will be focused and ready.

His account could serve as an apt metaphor for how writers identify oncoming stories. They often begin with the flimsiest of notions, with almost a sixth sense that a good idea lurks just beyond their range of view. As they gather material and reflect on what they are learning—the equivalent, perhaps, of the hunter's staring into the horizon—they intuitively feel the idea coming closer and closer, until, at some magical threshold point, it suddenly materializes directly before them, presented in clear view and often in full form.

This is a powerful creative tool, in part because it makes use of the mind's mysterious ability to make connections for us and in part because it reinforces confidence in our intuitive powers. And, like a muscle, it can be strengthened with exercise.

This section will examine some examples of well-chosen ideas and storylines, and discuss ways to help writers fix their gaze on the best possible ideas early in the process.

Consider this small masterpiece, for example:

> They save this act for the very last, after the audience has already seen a man ride a tiger and three brothers dive from the flying trapeze, after the Bulgarian mother has balanced her daughter atop a pole on her forehead, after the elephants have danced in a chorus line. They save it for that moment when every thrill a three-ring traveling circus has to offer seems spent.
>
> Then the lights dim and the drums roll and the back flap of the canvas tent opens. Elvin Bale's incredible human cannonball act is about to begin.
>
> He designed this act nearly 20 years ago, when he was known as the greatest daredevil in all the world, so famous he had his own luxury car on Ringling's circus train, so thrilling he could bring a sellout crowd at Madison Square Garden to its feet, so fearless that Evel Knievel once shook his hand and told him he was crazy.
>
> The one, the only, the amazing Elvin Bale! A human bullet, shooting through space at 60 miles per hour, and this was the safest act in his repertoire, demanding little more than guts and a sturdy body.
>
> Now the cannon rumbles into the tent, its 30-foot barrel mounted atop a shiny red truck. The Human Cannonball looks tiny straddling the gray barrel as it slowly takes aim. He straps on a helmet and salutes the hushed crowd.
>
> "A final farewell!" the ringmaster intones.

The Human Cannonball disappears inside the gun. A beautiful blond assistant stands ready to fire it. The ringmaster urges the crowd to join the countdown. Five, four, three, two, one. The explosion rocks the bleachers and makes small children cry in terror.

Quietly, from the shadows below, Elvin Bale watches this grand finale.

His arms, still muscled and strong, grip his crutches in the sawdust, but his palms sweat and his eyes narrow and he can feel a phantom pain in his useless legs as the man he used to be flies past.

(Tamara Jones, *Washington Post*)[1]

This introduction meets the great writing test. It has surprise; we are shocked to discover that Elvin Bale is not the cannonball but the crippled observer. It has marvelous styling, deploying words and details with a drumroll tempo. And it has a brilliantly presented storyline: "he can feel a phantom pain in his useless legs as the man he used to be flies past."

Jones masterfully accomplishes one of the foremost feats of excellent writing: *moving from the physical to the metaphysical* in a way that links the particulars of one real-life story to the larger dramas of the universal human experience.

Her material is physical: a circus act, a cannon, a performer, a man on crutches in the sawdust. But the storyline, what this piece is really about, is metaphysical: how Bale feels, now incapacitated, watching "the man he used to be" fly past. In one superb phrase, Jones crystallizes the emotional guts of the story, connecting it to an eternal theme, the agony of lost glory.

Jones was asked how she managed to see this story. "I was hanging out at the circus with him," she replied. "Just seeing him standing there. . . . It came to me watching him."

Jones saw the Elvin Bale storyline almost literally, by observing him closely during her reporting. In other cases, she said, she comes to a storyline by thinking and then talking through her material. "I tend to do a lot of writing in my head before I ever sit down to write," she explained. "And I talk to people all the time. I'll whine and bellyache all through the process. I'll go to editors all the time and demand that they tell me what my story is."

By the time she settles in to write, Jones likes to have a theme statement on paper, along with a list of material that supports it. Then she often will write quickly, "from my mind," as she put it, rather than from her notes.[2]

Sometimes writers move from the physical to the metaphysical through a nimble play on words. Ken Fuson produced a fascinating *Baltimore Sun* series by following a troupe of high schoolers through a school production of *West Side Story*. The series was Shakespearean in its assortment of

---

[1] Tamara Jones, "Cannon Fodder," *Washington Post,* 15 September 1996, F1.

[2] Tamara Jones, interview by the author, 4 November 1997.

subthemes—love, jealousy, ambition, rivalry—evoking winces of recognition from readers thrown back to the emotional tumult of adolescence. Yet the overall storyline was captured impeccably in the simple title of the series: "A Stage in Their Lives."

Not every assignment has the built-in narrative tension of a circus tragedy or a high school melodrama. Gary Blonston of Knight-Ridder Newspapers took routine statistical data, figures on the aging of Baby Boomers, and carved a catchy, dead-on storyline out of a generation's trademark defiance:

> WASHINGTON—First, they didn't want to fight in Vietnam. Then they didn't want to get married when their parents said they should, have kids and a house, stick with the same employer, stick with the same spouse.
>
> They didn't want to pay cash, or save money, or pay taxes, or vote, or do much of anything else just because someone said they were supposed to.
>
> But now the dedicated individualists of the baby boom generation are encountering a fact of life they can't reject, sidestep or delay:
>
> Passing time.
>
> Those 76 million people aren't kids any more. They're becoming middle-aged.
>
> The youngest of them will turn 30 [this year]. The oldest already smell 50 on the wind. You can almost hear them chanting once again: "Hell, no, we won't go."
>
> But they will. . . .
>
> (Gary Blonston, KRT News Service)[3]

Blonston uses another effective tactic for locating storyline and finding the metaphysical in the physical: *connecting strands of raw information to a larger theme that unifies them.* By moving up one level of abstraction, Blonston turns a mishmash of data into a cohesive conceptual whole.

Here are three other examples of strong storyline construction:

- **Direct statement:** *Portland Oregonian* reporters Brian T. Meehan and Chastity Pratt spent months on the road with Jermaine O'Neal, at the time the youngest player in the National Basketball Association. In the first sentence of a lengthy three-part series, they offered their storyline:

  > In the lonely Los Angeles Memorial Sports Arena, the youngest player to lace up sneakers in the world's greatest basketball league swoops down the lane. . . .
  >
  > (Brian T. Meehan, Chastity Pratt, *Portland Oregonian*)[4]

---

[3] Gary Blonston, "Boom," KRT News Service, 21 December 1993.

[4] Brian T. Meehan and Chastity Pratt, "Hey, Kid," *Portland Oregonian,* 20 April 1997, A1.

- **Common links:** After tornadoes rampaged through the Carolinas, killing 61 people in a single day, *Charlotte Observer* reporters Frye Gaillard and Jim Walser produced a special report tracing the destruction chronologically from the first death to the last. But their storyline transcended simple chronology by focusing on a surprising redemptive thankfulness they encountered among survivors:

> It was a day made in heaven and hell. A 450-mile corridor of the Carolinas—once pastoral and serene—had been ravaged by unspeakable destruction and death, a fury the mind can barely grasp.
>
> The winds of Wednesday, March 28, are imprinted forever in the history of Carolinas disasters. At least 61 people were killed, more than 1,000 were injured, and property damage totaled at least $109 million. But in the minds and hearts of the thousands who survived, devastation brought with it a kiss of God's deliverance.
>
> (Frye Gaillard, Jim Walser, *Charlotte Observer*)[5]

- **Meaning in the mundane:** University of Maryland student writer Scott Silverstein found an original frame for his profile of an outstanding athlete. He illustrated his storyline, an athlete's competitiveness, by organizing his material around a day's worth of eating:

> Brian Dougherty's hungry, and it's not that unusual.
>
> He's munching on a sausage, egg and American cheese bagel at the Bagel Place on Route 1. . . . He eats here often before practice. . . .
>
> He likes to eat, he likes to watch SportsCenter, he likes to play Sega, he likes to win. It's a hunger he can satisfy only on Memorial Day, only in the NCAA Championship game, only by winning everything. . . .
>
> It's a hunger Dougherty's had since he started to walk, since he could hold a ball in his hands. . . .
>
> (Scott Silverstein, *The Diamondback*)[6]

TEN WAYS TO FIND A STORYLINE

Sometimes, storylines just walk up and say hello, as obvious as the sunrise. Most times, they do not come that easily.

For one thing, they seldom appear in your notebook. You can take a pad full of notes, collect a mountain of documents, and produce a full-fledged outline, and still not have a storyline. That is because the storyline usually is not one discrete point but something that connects many points; it is no single

---

[5] Frye Gaillard and Jim Walser, "Night of Fury, Time of Grace," *Charlotte Observer*, 1 April 1984, 1.

[6] Scott Silverstein, "Doc's Hungry," *The Diamondback*, 3 May 1996, 7.

thing a source told you, but something larger that unites many things many sources told you. Your notes are like a column of numbers; the storyline is the total. It is not enough to tell the reader that this piece is about the numbers 3 and 7 and 19 and 11. The bottom line, 40, is the most important figure, but it appears nowhere in the list. Your job is to supply it.

Writers, therefore, have to work to develop a storyline. They must immerse themselves in the material, inspecting and assaying and arranging and rearranging and pondering, stoking the imagination until flash point is reached.

Let me emphasize: *you are not ready to write until you have found your storyline, your breakthrough idea.*

Here are ten ways to help in the search for storyline:

1. **Find an editor with vision.** Great editors will listen to you describe your material, gaze at a point somewhere just past the horizon, and see the great story skulking behind the good story you are proposing. Writers commonly get too close to their material to see the larger patterns. Without that intimate attachment, editors are free to discard the clutter and to zero in on the core storyline.

2. **Apply the "eyes test."** Corner any reasonably friendly and intelligent person—an editor, a spouse, a colleague, a person next to you on the train—and talk about your story. Never let courtesy or phony compliments mislead you. The true reaction can be seen in their eyes: glazing over or sparkling? You want to make their eyes light up with interest. You want to make them exclaim, "Wow!" Until you see the eyes sparkle, you do not have a successful concept.

3. **Ask yourself what people will remember about your story a month from now.** Think about the books and articles you have read over the past few weeks. Other than breaking news stories, which ones can you remember? What made them memorable? Can you find a similar quality in the story you are about to present?

4. **Look for a symbol, a phrase, or an action that best exemplifies the truth you are trying to tell.** If your goal is to move from the physical to the metaphysical, then comb your material for something concrete to build on, a strand that can carry all the way through your article.

5. **Complete this sentence aloud: "This story is about . . ."** Force yourself to fill out the sentence over and over, aloud, until you are convinced you have made the most of your idea.

6. **Write a one-paragraph digest line that will sell your idea to the most skeptical editor you know.** Imagine that you have to break through the resistance of a jaundiced editor, and craft a summary statement that shows why your story will be compelling. In truth, readers are far tougher than editors.

7. **Get to WIRMI.** Talk about your material as much as you wish, but eventually get to a sentence that begins What I Really Mean Is . . . .[7]
8. **Find the turning points.** Great drama, and therefore great storylines, surrounds life's most serious turning points. Locate them, and you often find the key. Think of examples quoted earlier in this chapter: Elvin Bale's doomed cannonball flight; Carolinians mercifully saved from the wrath of killer tornadoes; a teenager presented a multimillion-dollar pro basketball contract. To repeat a common insight into writing, these are the moments after which life is never the same.
9. **Write the subhead.** The best headlines and book titles often begin with a three- or four-word play on words, a summary that grabs the reader. But then comes a secondary headline, often in sentence form, that crystallizes the overall idea for general consumption. Here is an example, from an article by Clint O'Connor in the *Cleveland Plain Dealer:*

    Headline: "A mother's demon, a daughter's rescue."
    Subhead: "How 5 words describing an alcoholic she never knew saved Kathi Hotchkiss from suicide."[8]

    The headline catches your attention. But the subhead lays out the storyline. Try writing your subhead in advance, and you are often forced to compress your material into a construction that can serve as your storyline.
10. **Visualize.** Just relax and look for the storyline, letting your artistic side roam free. Sit comfortably, close your eyes or stare into space, lightly sift your material, and try to see, in words or images, the most compelling way into your story.

SURPRISING THE READER

Suppose we could invent a device—let's call it a Writing Impact Meter—that could attach to every reader. It would work something like a voltmeter and would register its findings on a device resembling the heart monitors in emergency rooms. The monitor would create a chart for each reader, with jagged lines shooting up and down depending on how stimulated, or bored, the reader was at a given moment.

As I write, I sometimes picture readers hooked up to such devices, and I love to imagine the needles jerking wildly up and down, spasming almost out of control, as the overpowering energy of my writing drives readers into parox-

---

[7] I do not know who coined the phrase "WIRMI," but I first ran across it in Ronald T. Kellogg, *The Psychology of Writing* (New York: Oxford University Press, 1994) 121.
[8] Clint O'Connor, "A Mother's Demon, a Daughter's Rescue," *Cleveland Plain Dealer,* 12 December 1993, 1A.

ysms of rapture. Never, naturally, do I envisage the opposite—the monotonous blip-blip-blip from a reader whose pulse is barely stirred by the somnolence of my ragged prose.

For better or worse, the voltage of writing cannot be measured with scientific precision. But you can imagine what is going on, even if you cannot measure it. You know what arouses readers: surprise. Stimulation occurs when a reader encounters content that is unexpected and interesting. Even without a Writing Impact Meter, you know the result. Readers snap alert and read on hungrily. You also know what bores readers: content that is bland and mushy. And you know the consequence of feeding mush to readers. They quit reading.

The reader stops reading. The monitor levels out. Alarms sound. Doctors and nurses rush in. Resuscitators are activated. Heroic measures are applied. Quotes are streamlined, anecdotes are punched up, verbs are electrocharged. And readership is saved.

Your job as a writer, of course, is preventive. You cannot let low-energy copy anesthetize readers in the first place. You do not have monitors and resuscitators, and you have only one chance: you must pack enough voltage into your copy to keep the needle bouncing.

This calls for surprise, the second element of the great-story triad. Surprise gets readers' attention and keeps them going. A good writer begins with an engaging storyline, then scatters surprises, like candy treats, throughout the copy, rewarding and encouraging the loyal reader's progress.

Here is an example that delivers one eye-opener after another:

> Wednesday is Shop Rite day. The car may not be good for much—it's an '84 Tempo, only runs in second gear—but it always gets them to the grocery store, even though it won't go over 25 mph. Their budget for the trip is always the same, $30 apiece, and the shopping list is always the same. . . .
>
> Routine is important for them. On the morning before the trip, Fred, whose actual name is Eve, shaves her head bald. Charles Webb, who was once Eve/Fred's husband, doesn't mind this at all. Fred does it every day. Theirs is a solid relationship: They haven't spent a day apart in 30 years, even though they got divorced 10 years ago. . . .
>
> Charles and Fred Webb work in a nudist camp. They live in a small cottage in the woods behind a tall fence. They are not practicing nudists anymore, though; they are the caretakers, splitting a paycheck of $119 a week.
>
> They have no other income, although they are working to change that. Fred is an artist. Charles, a writer. He hasn't published a word in 14 years, but he's working on something, and it's possible he could strike it rich all over again.
>
> Not that they want to be rich all over again. Then they might have to give all the money away again.
>
> (Richard Leiby, *Washington Post*)[9]

---

[9]   Richard Leiby, "The Dropout," *Washington Post,* 20 December 1992, F1.

Leiby nimbly sprinkles nuggets all along the path here, raising curiosity and expectations sentence by sentence. The tone is understated, but the accumulating portrait of two exceptionally unusual people is irresistible. You are a dozen paragraphs into this story before you realize it.

Surprise can also develop suddenly. Below, a writer springs two stunners in the very first sentence:

> Renada Daniel-Patterson's relationship with her father began when she was 13 years old and he called from prison, offering her his kidney.
>
> (Evelyn Nieves, *New York Times*)[10]

Beginning a parental relationship at age 13? A kidney offer from prison? These tantalizing details are both surprising enough to hook you and also suggestive enough to plant a strong sense of what the story is about.

Some Ways to Surprise the Reader

Surprise stops the reader, makes the head turn, the brows raise. It commands attention. It makes the Writing Impact Meter needle leap. Here are some specific kinds of surprises writers can deliver.

The Unconventional

In the above article on the Webbs, Richard Leiby repeatedly catches us unawares with unconventional couplings: a woman named Eve/Fred; a couple divorced for a decade and still devoted; a writer unpublished for 14 years; a spartan lifestyle after giving away a fortune. These items run counter to our sense of what the norms are, and so they make us stop and think. They are like advertisements that catch our attention with unusual combinations of colors, words, or images. Media audiences tend to speed-read, and it sometimes takes an unconventional thought or phrase to slow them down.

Surprise sometimes strikes quickly. In the following magazine item, the first sentence sets you up for some unexpected revelations:

> Horse meat has never been America's idea of good eating.
>
> (Dan McGraw, *U.S. News & World Report*)[11]

The story goes on to report that horse meat is actually legal in every state, but that California is about to vote on outlawing it.

---

[10]   Evelyn Nieves, "Girl Awaits Father's 2d Kidney," *New York Times*, 5 December 1998, A1.

[11]   Dan McGraw, "A Horse Is a Course, of Course. or Is It a Pet?" *U.S. News & World Report*, 9 November 1998, 54.

The Unexpected

Drama sometimes derives from material that makes us view seemingly normal scenes in new ways. The *New York Times* piled one graphic detail upon the next in this article about young people and crime in a New Orleans housing project:

> Here, boys of 14 shoot grown men in drug deals gone bad, children of 11 tote guns too big for their hands, and old people and mothers with small children sleep under beds, because big children fire guns indiscriminately just to hear them go "bang."
>
> The most recent trend among the young criminals is to pre-pay their own funerals, because they do not expect to live past 16.
>
> (Rick Bragg, *New York Times*)[12]

The Extreme

Sometimes surprise comes from the sheer shock value of the material. Not every story lends itself to seeking extreme examples, but stories such as those trying to illustrate seriousness or excess often benefit from especially jarring examples, as in this lead:

> Kham Suk is 13 years old. She is a small child, with a delicate face. When she giggles, she sounds like any little girl at play. But Kham Suk doesn't have much time for fun. Three months ago, her mother walked her across the border from Burma into Thailand and sold her to a brothel for $80.
>
> (Sara Terry, *Christian Science Monitor*)[13]

The Ironic

Some words, images, and situations do not normally occur together, and when they do, readers will be surprised. Lorraine Ahearn began an article on the funeral of a beaten young drug user with this poignant sentence, drawing irony from the unexpected connection between the words "casket" and "mother":

> Leave the casket open, his mother decided.
>
> (Lorraine Ahearn, *Annapolis (Md.) Capital*)[14]

New Twists on the Ordinary

Many of life's routines chug along without much scrutiny. Good writers, however, should never take them for granted. What happens to a loved one after

---

[12] Rick Bragg, "Where a Child on the Stoop Can Strike Fear," *New York Times,* 2 December 1994, A1.

[13] Sara Terry, "A World Where Survival Is a Daily Battle," *Christian Science Monitor,* 30 June 1987, B1.

[14] Lorraine Ahearn, "The Cost of Drugs," *Annapolis Capital,* 11 June 1989, 4.

death, for example? That may be a question most of us do not think much about, trusting in others to handle things suitably. Walter F. Roche, Jr., of the *Philadelphia Inquirer* came up with a surprising answer. He reported that in 26 cases the local medical examiner's office "cut out the brains . . . and then—without informing the families or asking their permission—the city sent the brains to Penn Medical School."[15]

Drama from the Commonplace

From fiction writers, playwrights, and "new journalists" such as Tom Wolfe, among others, we can learn the value of finding meaning in everyday detail. Sometimes it is the accumulation of these details that brings a story or scene to life. Here, a Michigan State University student used a touching scene to help dramatize the plight of ordinary families coping with Alzheimer's disease:

> To get his false teeth back into his mouth, Marje sneaks up on her husband when he is sleeping in the chair. She places her knee on his hands, which are usually folded in his lap, and puts his plates in when he rears his head back to holler.
>
> (David Pierini, *Grand Rapids Press*)[16]

Unusual Juxtapositions

Remember those childhood puzzles where you looked at a set of objects and tried to find the one that didn't match? In a similar way, you can often surprise readers by creating a list or set and inserting something that does not seem to belong. A front-page *New York Times* article contrasted modern monks with their traditional lifestyles, ending with an unexpected combination. The article began this way:

> At Christ in the Desert, a Benedictine monastery tucked between stark mesas, 24 monks follow the routine of prayer and labor that has sustained their order for 1,500 years. They clean, chop wood, weave, carve icons, bake bread and design sites on the Internet's World Wide Web.
>
> (Elizabeth Cohen, *New York Times*)[17]

Striking Comparisons

Readers respond to metaphors, analogies, and similar helpful comparisons. David Finkel of the *St. Petersburg Times* described 891-pound circus per-

---

[15] Walter F. Roche Jr., "Relatives Learn the City Removed the Brains of Their Dead," *Philadelphia Inquirer,* 16 June 1994, A1.

[16] David Pierini, "Love Doesn't Forget," William Randolph Hearst Foundation Journalism Awards Program, November 1989.

[17] Elizabeth Cohen, "21st-Century Scribes: Monks Designing Web Pages," *New York Times,* 17 March 1996, 1.

former Fat Albert as weighing "more than twice as much as Sears' best refrigerator-freezer."[18]

At the other extreme, *Spokane Spokesman-Review* columnist Doug Clark observed that premature twins Justin and Joshua Kitt "together . . . didn't weigh more than a bag of sugar."[19]

WRITING WITH STYLE

Pardon a personal story. This morning I was revising a book review for a magazine when I faltered over a word that did not seem right. In summarizing someone's résumé, I had written that the person "produced live late-night TV for Boston's ABC affiliate before coming to CNN." The word *coming* made me stall. Wrong direction, tired sound, no sparkle. I changed it to *moving*. This seemed better but still too nondescript. I scanned my mental thesaurus. Then I struck *moving* and wrote in *migrating,* not perfect but certainly a more descriptive image to apply to a nomadic journalist.

Words are to writers as musical notes are to composers, as colors are to painters. Creative wordplay crowns a great writing project, imparting the artistic finishing touch that lifts the prosaic toward the sublime.

To readers, words are like snowflakes or seashells, ordinary articles with an incommensurate power to enchant. Reading the words is like being jolted over and over with tiny pinpricks. Weak, weasely words carry only a blunt thrust. Sharp, charged words sting and stimulate. Selecting words, fashioning phrases, and knitting them all into sentences are matters of both magic and craft.

Frequently, as with this morning's book review episode, I find that selecting the best word is a three-step process. First, you choose a word, such as *coming*. Most of us repeatedly overrely on a fraction of the words we know, so initial choices tend to be bland and obvious, creamed from the upper sections of our personal word lists. Then we strain to find a better word, such as *moving*. This step adds a layer of professionalism, a solid tone and feel. But it often does not entirely satisfy. It is the third step that often produces the niftiest word.

Writers tend to believe as an article of faith that awaiting them somewhere is the perfect word for every construction. In quest of a unique word, a writer will forge deep into the attics of memory, dusting off unremembered caches and reencountering neglected marvels and, occasionally, when lucky, exhuming words of such astounding grace and precision that it feels like discovering a Picasso hidden beneath some homely watercolor.

---

18 Carole Rich, "Tips for Better Writing," *Scripps Howard Editors/General Managers Newsletter,* October 1993, 5.

19 Doug Clark, "Joshua and Justin Struggle to 'Be People,'" *Spokane Spokesman-Review,* 23 March 1995, 1B.

These treasure hunts do not always pay off, but sometimes they produce a stage-three word, a word dazzling enough to redeem an entire article, to make a minor masterpiece of a single sentence, as in this lead from *Time* magazine's obituary for Sen. Everett Dirksen: "He had the rheumy eyes of a bloodhound, the jowls of a St. Bernard and a baldachin of white hair like that of an extra-ordinarily unkempt poodle."[20] A by-product, almost always, is a host of additions to the short list of interesting words that most writers lug around, looking for excuses to work them into their copy.

Annie Dillard tells an anecdote about how writers view their materials:

> A well-known writer was collared by a university student who asked, "Do you think I could be a writer?"
>
> "Well," the writer said, "I don't know. . . . Do you like sentences?"
>
> The writer could see the student's amazement. Sentences? Do I like sentences? I am 20 years old and do I like sentences? If he had liked sentences, of course, he could begin, like a joyful painter I knew. I asked him how he came to be a painter. He said, "I liked the smell of the paint."[21]

Writers like the sound of words, the ambrosia of language. A writer who does not like playing with words and sentences is like a tamer who hates the lions. You can keep trying, but it makes for a mighty dangerous livelihood.

Some Tips for Creative Wordplay

As you concentrate on word choice and placement, here are some devices to keep in mind:

- **Action words.** Nothing pumps energy into copy like hardball nouns and verbs. Here is a lead full of them. Do you think it has too many?

> An unemployed welder, enraged by his mother-in-law, axed a television set and held police at bay for seven hours Tuesday while he twirled a pistol cylinder and threatened to shoot himself.
>
> Tony Moiseenko, 44, finally staggered out of a tear-gas-filled bedroom . . . and was temporarily stunned by the electrically charged prongs of a Taser gun.
>
> (Doreen Carvajal, *St. Petersburg Times*)[22]

- **Descriptions.** Simple, relevant descriptions guide readers' senses. In this lead, Pulitzer winner Alice Steinbach comes near to poetry, fashions a per-

---

[20] "Everett Dirksen: American Original," *Time,* 19 September 1969, 25.
[21] Annie Dillard, "Write Till You Drop," *New York Times Book Review,* 28 May 1989, 23.
[22] Doreen Carvajal, "Man Destroys TV, Threatens Suicide Before Giving Up," *St. Petersburg Times,* 20 July 1983, 1B.

fect phrase ("the color of a robin's egg")—and never uses a word of more than two syllables.

> First, the eyes: They are large and blue, a light, opaque blue, the color of a robin's egg. And if, on a sunny spring day, you look straight into these eyes—eyes that cannot look back at you—the sharp, April light turns them pale, like the thin blue of a high, cloudless sky.
>
> (Alice Steinbach, Baltimore Sun)[23]

- **Vivid images.** Combine your powers of observation and your powers of language into vivid, original constructions. Pam Belluck described Pierre, South Dakota, in the *New York Times* as a city "which sits on a skinny elbow of the Missouri River . . . in the gullet of the Great Plains."[24] An *Ebony* article on dancing for fitness describes a "hot night spot" with "arms pumping, feet stomping, hips twisting, and of course sweat dripping" from "movers, groovers and shakers."[25]

- **Rhythms.** Techniques such as repetition and parallel form help make writing flow with rhythmic grace. Enjoy the cadences of this lead from the *Wall Street Journal:*

> MANILA—Filipinos staged a rebellion here, faced down an army, chased away a strongman, toppled a regime. And now, well, they're cleaning up the litter, doing a bit of sightseeing and going back to work.
>
> (June Kronholz, Wall Street Journal)[26]

- **Originality of expression.** Occasionally shoot for something a little more daring. Profiling conservative savant William F. Buckley Jr., a *Washington Post* writer captured the essence of both man and style in this bravura opening:

> NEW YORK—He has worn his gestures like a cassock and mitre, William F. Buckley Jr. has: the *haute* Tory leaning back in his chair at preternatural angles, his anteater tongue darting from his mouth as if for gnats, his mind clicking and whirring in wicked ratiocination . . . and his voice—a honking concoction of dislocation and breeding—whinnying and hooting after the Flaubertian *mot juste* . . . zeugma . . . sesquipedalian, perhaps . . . and then . . . gasp! . . . *pari passu* . . . some doughy liberal foe is pierced through his bleeding heart and pronounced DOA by the culture police.
>
> (David Remnick, Washington Post)[27]

---

[23] Alice Steinbach, "A Boy of Unusual Vision," *Baltimore Sun,* special reprint, 1985.

[24] Pam Belluck, "In Little City Safe from Violence, Rash of Suicides Leaves Scars," *New York Times,* 5 April 1998, 1.

[25] "Dancing Your Way to Fitness," *Ebony,* December 1998, 140.

[26] June Kronholz, "Filipinos Sweep Up," *Wall Street Journal,* 3 March 1986, 1.

[27] David Remnick, "Buckley, the Lion in Autumn," *Washington Post,* 5 December 1985, C1.

- **Plays on words.** Readers often appreciate clever twists on phrases or expressions they have heard before. *National Parks* magazine launched a report on global warming this way:

    In 1850, more than 150 glaciers could be found in what is now Glacier National Park in Montana. Today, that number is closer to 50. At this rate, within the next four decades, all 50 remaining glaciers will vanish . . . this harbor of ancient icefields will become known as "The Park Formerly Known as Glacier."

    (Lily Whiteman, *National Parks*)[28]

- **Alliteration.** In literature it is sometimes called *initial rhyming*, a technique by which writers use their senses of music and poetry to string together words with similar beginnings. Vivid images set up this triply alliterative passage in *USA Today:*

    MESQUITE, Texas—Louis L'Amour westerns in the paperback rack. A cherry pie in the glass pastry case. Reba McEntire on the jukebox. A pack of unfiltered Lucky Strikes on the diner counter.
    This is truckstop country, a coffee-stained crossroads where highway haulers climb down from their rigs for a steak, a song and a smoke.

    (L. A. Jolidon, *USA Today*)[29]

- **Playfulness.** Tone should match topic; on the right kind of stories, try a little friskiness. Here is an example from the front page of the *New York Times*, of all places:

    Tawk to a young New Yawkuh dese days and de foist ting you may notice is dat he aw she don't tawk like dis no maw.

    (Deborah Sontag, *New York Times*)[30]

SUMMARY

Superlative writing has three elements: a great idea (storyline), engaging content (surprise), and power-packed language (stylishness). From concept to completion, the writer must deliver on everything from the storyline through the material specifics to the component words, phrases, and sentences.

---

[28] Lily Whiteman, "The Heat Is On," *National Parks,* January/February 1999, 34.
[29] L. A. Jolidon, "Where the Trucks Stop, Bucks Start," *USA Today,* 29 August 1985, 1A.
[30] Deborah Sontag, "Oy Gevalt! New Yawkese an Endangered Dialect?" *New York Times,* 14 February 1993, 1.

None of the three ingredients of excellence necessarily comes easily, but craftwork and magic always help. Through craft, writers can lock in on the best available story idea, refine reporting techniques to gather the strongest possible material, and knead the words and phrases into fresh, stylish expressions. Through the magic of imagination and inspiration, they can lift their ideas and phrasing from the serviceable toward the sublime, from the physical to the metaphysical.

Practicing Craft and Magic

1. Put craft to work in your search for storyline and surprise. On an index card or sheet of paper, write a one-sentence storyline before your next assignment. Go through your notebook and circle information you think readers will find truly surprising; if it seems insufficient, do more reporting.

2. Call on magic. The next time you are unsure of a storyline or unsatisfied with your material, try this exercise: assign the problem to your brain, forget about it for a few hours, relax, and let your imagination run free. Chances are high that good new thoughts will soon come.

3. Sharpen your sense of style by compiling word lists. In your journal or notebook, keep an inventory of interesting words and look for opportunities to use them in copy. They can be exotic (one writer tells of encountering *compendious* in a John Le Carre novel and spending months looking for a chance to use it), but more often they will be of the hard-working ordinary variety, words that have fallen out of your immediate memory bank and are ready for a fresh start.

4. Conduct verb checks. Frank Barrows, an outstanding writer and editor at the *Charlotte Observer*, has described this technique. As a last step in polishing his work, Barrows inspects every verb in his copy in hopes of substituting something brawnier. Pep up just a handful of verbs in the typical article, and its vigor level will zoom.

5. Browse the dictionary. It is a splendidly generative hobby.

Part 2

Using Craft and Magic in Journalism

Chapter 5

The Very
Beginning: Ideas
and Reporting

Writing is an arrogant act, a projection of ego. We writers expect readers to drop everything, cancel all plans, and dedicate themselves to poring over our work. *Stop whatever you are doing and pay attention to me.* This is a supreme demand, and readers deserve much in return.

But if the act is arrogant, the actor is needy, a supplicant in humble quest of partners. Writers crave attention. Their writing is a transaction. It requires an audience. Without readers, writing is like dancing by yourself.

So writers should feel desperate: desperate for every second of every reader's time. Nothing can be taken for granted. Writers compete with every other possible use of a reader's precious moments. Their ardent hope is that reading their work bumps all other potential activities—eating and exercising, socializing and working, tending the kids and tilling the garden. "The only demand I make of my reader is that he should devote his whole life to reading my works," James Joyce once explained.[1]

Yet think of how most readers approach magazines, newspapers, and online information sources. Is their intention to read every article on every page from start to finish? Do they comprehensively complete every Web page before clicking onto the next one? Clearly not. Consider your own reading patterns. If you have read this far in this book, either voluntarily or on assignment, you probably have an above-average interest in reading and writing. But even so, you most likely do not read even half of your daily newspaper or favorite magazine, or a fraction of the material available to you electronically. Most people read selectively, and their decisions come swiftly and mercilessly. They read what grabs and holds them, and they quite willingly pass over the vast majority of texts aimed their way.

---

[1] "Hardcovers in Brief," *Washington Post Book World,* 28 June 1998, 13.

The lesson that should stick in every writer's head is this: most people have a predisposition *not to read,* and they dare writers to overcome it. Not reading is easy. From the start, then, writers must acknowledge the high demand being placed on the audience and the resistance barriers in their way. They must recognize the two-way nature of the fragile relationship they are building. The reader, often reluctant, tentatively yields the precious gift of time, expecting top return. The gift is temporary, withdrawable at any point the investment no longer seems rewarding.

Before they write a word meant for publication, writers should contemplate the bond they are trying to establish with the audience. How can they get and hold a threshold level of attention? Obviously, the earliest stages of a writing project can make or break the chances of snaring readers' notice. If you fail to produce compelling ideas and information, you forfeit a hold on the reader that is hard to regain.

You must never lose sight of the inescapable imperative of connecting with every reader.

Remember: writers begin writing at their point of maximum interest in a story, after researching it, thinking it through, drawing out its most intriguing aspects. Readers begin reading at a point of minimum interest, knowing almost nothing about the story's structure, drama, or uniqueness. The writer's responsibility is to quickly span this interest gap, to convince the reader that the story is worth following.

For the writer to compete successfully, the goal must be nothing less than exploring the best possible ideas, acquiring the best possible information, and arranging it in the best possible way. This chapter isolates the first few steps in the writing process and considers ways that both craft and magic can help achieve a propitious beginning.

WHY WRITERS WRITE

As first discussed in Chapter 2, media writers should ask themselves two pivotal questions at the outset of every assignment:

- What is my purpose?
- Who is my audience?

You write for many reasons. In media, the most common reasons are to inform and to entertain. When the primary purpose is to inform, you are writing news, which we can define as *current information of public value,* information that someone needs now. When the goal leans toward entertainment, you are writing *features,* which probe around, behind, and underneath the news, telling stories and developing narrative themes beyond their immediate urgency. There are many other potential purposes, including to persuade, to influence, to shock, and to educate, but the news and entertainment functions predominate.

In addition, writers serve an infinity of constituencies, from the heterogeneous mass audience viewing network television to the tiny band clicking on the Web site for tall people living in Oklahoma City.

Of course, various purposes and audiences are not mutually exclusive. For example, good news writing strives to entertain; likewise, as Chapter 13 will discuss in more detail, good features usually depend on good information. You may be writing for the science section of a news magazine but hoping also to attract attention from the larger potential audience of casual page-turners. A mixture of purposes and audiences is common.

Leaving literary aspirations aside for a moment, it can be said that the first job of any piece of writing is to achieve its purposes for its intended audiences. In that sense, a one-sentence bulletin reporting that a tornado is on its way can qualify as good writing. So can a 3,000-word magazine article explaining to teenagers the hazards of sexually transmitted diseases. And so can a Web site whose words and images effectively convey the shadings and subtleties of this season's hot fashion trends.

If you are covering the opening of a school year, you will view the assignment differently if you are writing for a community newspaper or the teachers' union newsletter or an online site directed toward high schoolers. Reviewing a popular movie, you will vary your style depending on whether you are employed by the *Wall Street Journal* or *Highlights for Children* or the *Playgirl* magazine Web site.

The key strategic imperative is *to pinpoint your reasons for writing and your principal target audiences.* Before embarking on a writing project, take stock of your goals. First, identify your purpose or purposes. The single best way to accomplish this step is to talk over the assignment with an editor or instructor. Relay your understanding of the purpose and make certain it squares with your assigning supervisor's goals; if not, negotiate or adjust as necessary. Second, develop a mental picture of your audience or audiences and make informed predictions of how they will likely access and use your material. Knowing (1) why you are writing and (2) for whom you are writing will affect every step from the idea to the research to the writing itself.

WHY READERS READ

Whether the genre is news or features, whether the audience is universal or localized, the essential first step in writing is deciding what to write about. No writer can afford to gloss over it.

The idea stage takes on special urgency in light of what is known about readership. Readers are an enigmatic crowd, sometimes fickle, occasionally loyal, often unpredictable. No one can forecast exactly where their eyes will land and their attention fix. But research tells us one central fact: the chief determinant in what readers read is *a topic that already interests them.* In other words, readers are temperamentally drawn toward certain favored subjects.

This is not to say that people never read about new things or that they cannot be enticed into the unfamiliar. But their natural propensity is to gravitate toward proven areas of personal interest.

For writers, the implications of this insight are gigantic:

- If topic selection is the single most important step in attracting an audience, then writers must first capture attention with a strong idea before the other elements of good journalism (including strong writing) even come into play.
- Writers need to frame story ideas in ways that play on intense reader interests, or present unusual or unfamiliar topics in ways that quickly spotlight their high-interest angles.
- The force of the idea must show succinctly and immediately, or else the potential reading moment will be lost.
- Even a beautifully produced package may barely be noticed if the overall idea fails to engage the reader.

All this can be sobering. Writers want to imagine their audience as a set of devoted fans eagerly scrutinizing the media for their bylines and, once spotting them, settling back with contented sighs to fondly devour every phrase. Something tells us, though, that we more often write for impatient skimmers hurrying through their reading, oblivious to authorship and resistant to all but the most compelling ideas.

To reach this audience, powerful ideas are necessary. Through both craft and magic, writers should use every available trick and technique to establish an initial beachhead in the reader's imagination.

FINDING IRRESISTIBLE IDEAS

I took my first newspaper job when I was 14, contributing articles to the twice-a-week paper in my South Carolina hometown. One day, the managing editor looked at me and said something like, "We need some copy for tomorrow's paper. Go downtown and come back with a story."

With no more guidance than that, I set off, and an hour or two later returned with notes for an article. I don't remember the specifics, but I think the story had to do with the local post office and how it served as a community gathering point and message center. It was not a memorable story, but the whole assignment taught me a lesson I have never forgotten. Any semicompetent writer can find a story. Walk down the street and you will bump into a dozen of them. Story ideas are everywhere. But great ideas are rare.

Too often, because of the pressure of time or the limitation of imagination, you settle for the first story you find. You set out on your rounds, worried as writers always are that today will be the day the creative well finally runs dry. Then you encounter something that has the look and feel of a story, you heave a sigh of relief, and you notify your editors that you are on the case. For their part, the editors are in their own frenzy, staring at their skimpy story budgets and besieged by the various exigencies of their trade. If your suggestion sounds vaguely like an acceptable story, they will gratefully accept it, check off one more writer as productively occupied, and turn to the next crisis.

This scenario helps explain how daily journalism—and to a disappointing extent even magazine and book production—tends to end up with a collection of good work but a dearth of the great. Journalistic systems and psyches are organized for speed and efficiency rather than excellence and wonder.

The last chapter outlined several ways that writers can refine their storylines, material, and words. But before you can work on any of those story qualities, you must have a basic beginning idea. In some ways, finding great ideas is just a broader version of selecting a storyline, and some of the same principles apply: look for larger themes, uncover the real meaning, locate metaphysical lessons within everyday physical situations, express the idea in an especially clever phrase or line. But these techniques assume that you have a body of material to work from. At the idea stage, you have not reached that point, and your operations require a higher level of abstract thinking.

With that in mind, here are some ways writers and editors can transcend their institutional limitations and generate better ideas:

- **Seek the best possible idea, not the first acceptable one.** The test is not, *can you find a story?* The test is, *what is the best story you can find in the time you have?* The goal is to so thoroughly canvas your territory that you identify a range of potential ideas and then select the top one. The trustiest way to achieve great ideas is to constantly pursue the best idea among many, rather than the first idea that meets the minimum standard.
- **Turn good ideas into great ones.** Think big rather than small—not necessarily big in the sense of long or complex, but big in the sense of high-impact. Push your ideas upward by asking questions like, What is the best story that could come from this? Is there a twist or angle that could make this truly unforgettable? What else would I need to make this a cover story or front-page candidate?

- **Answer the questions people ask you at parties.** Have you ever noticed how curious people become when they encounter a writer? They believe that writers have access to all sorts of inside secrets and special insights, and they fill the air with questions, in the earnest assumption that you know fascinating things they do not. If you cover city hall, they will ask you what the mayor is really like. If you cover sports, they want to know what goes on in the locker room. If you write about health and science, they like to hear about the newest frontiers. Unlike specialists who sometimes bog down in detail, lay people are generalists who home in instantly on the big, relevant questions. By listening to readers and potential readers, writers can get great guidance about story direction.
- **Schedule weekly brainstorming sessions with your editor.** Building regular "idea meetings" into your work schedule creates at least two positive effects. It establishes a routine that conditions you to think about ideas in advance of each meeting, an important way of engaging your magic-side creativity. And it gives you a disciplined way to test and flesh out ideas through conversation with an intelligent listener. Just 20 minutes of creative brainstorming almost always produces new and better ideas than you had before. Here is one simple goal for such meetings: to identify the best possible story you can do, under whatever practical circumstances apply, over the next few weeks.
- **Think future more than past.** At one time, the news media trafficked largely in the news of yesterday, providing regular recapitulations and summaries. More and more, the media are thinking "future spin": *what comes next* rather than what just occurred. As electronic media increasingly provide breaking news coverage, print writers are called on to push ahead with new angles and directions. A newspaper, for example, should be tomorrow's news, not just yesterday's. A magazine should advance issues far enough into the future to meet the shelf-life needs of nondaily publication. Good ideas must not only be relevant when you think of them; they must be relevant when the audience reads them.
- **Broaden your source networks.** Writers, especially those assigned to beats, tend to establish routines dominated by regular contact with a relative handful of sources, chosen because they predictably supply usable, reliable information under deadline pressure. Overreliance on this inner circle, however, breeds staleness. Writers need to stretch for diversity in every possible source category: age, gender, location, point of view. Make it a point to contact at least one new or unorthodox source every week. A helpful artistic approach is to draw or list as many interesting potential sources as you can think of, including some that at first may seem offbeat. A strong craft technique is to list, down one side of a page, your dozen or so key interest areas, then write beside each one the name of one or more new sources with special expertise or insight.

- **Get outside.** Telephones and computers, plus time pressures, tempt many reporters to hunker down at their desks for efficiency's sake. But beware of overly cocooning yourself. News never happens inside a newsroom or a writer's office. Move outside, look around, see things afresh, meet new people, change your vantage point. Visit new places, change the way you walk or drive to work, reexamine routine sites you have overlooked for years. Fresh perspective breeds better ideas.
- **Expand reader participation.** The interactivity of online communication makes it increasingly practical to tap sources you never even knew about before. Make it easy for readers to get in touch with you, by e-mail, fax, letter, or phone. Query relevant online communities for ideas and stimulation. Use news groups, listservs, and e-mail as two-way avenues to experts and lay readers across the street and around the globe. For too long, the media have stayed aloof from their audiences, rudely turning away most story ideas and timid approaches from readers. Now is a good time to reverse that trend and restore important relationships. Make the computer network a key part of your source network.
- **Kill dull ideas.** Finally, a negative point. Not every idea is a jewel, whether it comes from you, an editor, a source, or your audience. Your first step is to assemble as many ideas as possible from as broad a source community as you can. But the critical next step is to assay those ideas by the highest standards of journalism, to select and refine until you settle on the most compelling assignments. Here, you need the help of a constructive but tough editor who will push you away from the mundane ideas and toward the excellent. Sometimes writers and editors alight much too quickly on prosaic ideas, in a rush to move on to other duties. Both writer and editor may know full well, at that point, that the resulting story will be boring, but for reasons ranging from inertia to politeness they do not push hard enough for the highest possible ideas. Do not let this happen to you. Ask yourself the question, *why does this matter to anyone?* If you cannot answer it satisfactorily, then find a better story.

GATHERING COMPELLING MATERIAL

Writers depend on information. As we have repeatedly stressed, the biggest step toward improved writing is improved reporting. Good material triumphs over mediocre material.

Therefore, writers need a research strategy for every story. Ideally, they should push for the maximum allowable reporting time. Like detectives methodically building a case, writers need time to pursue, develop, digest, assimilate and revisit leads and sources. They should aspire to gain as often as possible the extended time necessary to research an issue in depth.

On many if not most occasions, however, media writers work under tough time conditions. Deadlines circumscribe their reporting time and flexibility. Under these conditions, they have only one choice if they want to grow and improve: they must become smarter reporters. They must learn to get better information without spending more time to get it.

Through improved reporting technique, and by enlisting the quantum powers of magic, good writers find ways to optimize what they obtain from whatever research period they have.

If two reporters receive the same assignment and the same deadline, one will invariably return with better material. Why? Obviously the variable is not time, since both reporters had the same amount. The variable is reporting skill. Some reporters secure better material than others within a given time. The question is, how?

As always, both craft and magic are involved. Using craft, writers can plan, organize, and conduct research in a disciplined manner, wasting a minimum of time and zeroing in on the key information. Concentrated efficiency is a matchless tool for improving reporting.

Using magic, writers can stretch for superior sources and material, abetted by the occasional inspired reporting master stroke. Intuition and native story sense inexplicably seem to lead some reporters directly to pay dirt while others are still plodding from one marginal source to another. As we have seen, these apparently capricious forces are not accidental. They come when conditions are right, to those who are receptive. Attentive reporters can find ways to summon, recognize, and apply these inspiring flashes.

The two most common ways media writers gather information are interviewing and using documents, databases, and records. The following subsections provide suggestions for improving the quality of your human and documentary sourcing and for energizing your overall reporting strategy. As always, you want to work along parallel tracks to upgrade reporting craft and to benefit from the marvels of magic.

Interviewing

In newsrooms of the past, reporters conducted almost nonstop reporting by telephone. They juggled scads of potential stories at once, spread telephone messages across the community like dragnets, and sometimes operated two phone lines simultaneously as they placed additional calls while fielding replies to earlier ones. At times they placed so many calls that they would lose track of whom they were calling. A reporter would realize what story was involved only when a source answered the phone and identified herself or himself. The result was that practically every interview was off-the-cuff and unprepared.

Through speed-dial reporting, these old-school reporters acquired a lot of information fast, but its quality tended to be rock-bottom. When they sat down to write, they were constantly kicking themselves for failing to ask key questions.

Modern journalists usually put a little more intelligence into their interviewing, but it remains a process open to great improvement. Time pressure is just one inducement to haste. Another serious drawback is that journalists tend to take interviewing for granted since they do it so much. Interviewing simply means conversing, right? And reporters, notorious schmoozers that they are, specialize in palaver, don't they?

Interviewing is the single most common act of reporting. But as we know, familiarity breeds laxness. Like so many acts of journalism, interviewing is trickier than it looks. What we may overlook in our nonchalance is the huge difference in outcome between a well-prepared, careful interview and a casual conversation. Attention to technique begets better interviews, and better interviews beget better material.

It would be impossible here to present a comprehensive manual on interviewing. Entire books are devoted to that topic. For now, we can focus on some trade secrets for increasing *interview efficiency:* your ability to maximize results from whatever time you are allotted.

Strategy

To squeeze more information from interviews without necessarily spending additional time, you start with a good plan. Almost every interview has a goal. You need to develop a plan most likely to achieve the goal.

Sometimes the goal is simple. You may want to know one exact figure, such as the salary of the local high school principal. Other times the goal can be broad. Maybe you want to see how local teenagers feel about a proposed weekend curfew. Occasionally the goal is more elaborate. You may be probing for sensitive financial information, trying to convince a reluctant source to become a whistle blower, or confronting a hostile bureaucrat.

Different goals require different approaches. What remains constant is the need to enter the interview with a plan:

- What do I need to know?
- What obstacles am I likely to encounter?
- What questions, in what order, delivered in what tone of voice, will most likely work?

A little pre-interview strategy and psychology can save immense frustration and haggling during the actual interview.

Preparation

Interviews require homework. Spend a few minutes learning about the person you will be interviewing and the topic under discussion. Scan relevant indexes (your publication's own library files, a good news database, a pertinent online site) for what is already on record about your topic. Anticipate points where the person you are interviewing might dissemble, and background yourself so you can challenge a less-than-forthcoming answer.

Devise a preliminary theme, write subject areas and even exact questions in the front of your notebook, set goals for what mixture of quotes and facts you want. For tough interviews, rehearse your questions, your phrasing, and your inflection. Imagine tactics that may be used against you (stalling, anger, refusal to answer, demands to go off the record), and prepare specific countermeasures. If you are prepared, you will probably control the interview. If you are not, your subject gains the upper hand.

Time Management

Most interviews require an ice-breaking stage, to let the interview subject relax and open up. What comes next is crucial. Interviewers often make the mistake of proceeding chronologically, an approach that at first seems logical but on reflection may waste time. For most interviews, the key material you want involves the present and the future, not the past—what is happening or about to happen, not what happened months or years ago. Early questions about the past often consume too much time, shortchanging the time you can spend on more important later material. If you are interviewing a candidate for mayor, for instance, you may be tempted to begin by asking how she got interested in politics, a question that can trigger lengthy reminiscences, when what you really need to concentrate is on her platform for now and the future.

Carole Rich, in *Writing and Reporting News,* proposes a formula to focus interviews on areas most likely to produce timely substance. She calls it the GOAL formula: Goals, Obstacles, Achievements, Logistics.[2]

Start by inquiring about goals, what your interview subject is trying to accomplish. Then move to obstacles, what stands in the subject's way. Under achievements, find out what the subject has done or will do to overcome the obstacles. Then, turn to logistics, or the chronological and other background material that rounds out your story.

By focusing early on goals, obstacles, and achievements, you raise the odds that most of your interview time will dwell on the most newsworthy points.

---

[2]   Carole Rich, *Writing and Reporting News,* 2d ed. (Belmont, CA: Wadsworth, 1997) 127–128.

Cumulative Interviewing

For most articles, you will do more than one interview. If you are pressed for time, you want to structure and order each interview to contribute something different and important. At the beginning, list the material you need. After every interview, reexamine your checklist. Notice especially what vital information you still lack. Use subsequent interviews to fill holes from your previous research.

For example, if Interview 1 produces great facts but poor quotes, then concentrate on obtaining succulent quotes during Interview 2. If Source 1 offers a clinical overview of damage from a local tornado, focus on obtaining compelling human interest material from Source 2.

Answers, Not Questions

Interviewing is not the science of asking good questions. It is the art of eliciting good answers. Posture and attitude can mean as much as chiseled questions. A good interviewer establishes rapport, listens respectfully, lets the subject discuss what is on her or his mind, uses nods and smiles and body language to encourage the person to speak freely. Asking clear, well-chosen questions is important, but so is the occasional nonsense nudge ("Um hmm" or "Really?" or "No kidding"). Sometimes silence is the best question; subjects almost always hasten to fill the emptiness. Repeating or rewording questions often works well, especially when you are trying to draw out a person, maybe because you are looking for good quotes; in general, the more times people are asked about a topic, the more they have to say about it.

Online Interviewing

Although a writer generally prefers face-to-face interviews, they are not always practical. Time and distance may not permit an in-person visit. Not surprisingly these days, more and more writers turn to online interviews, which have some special advantages and drawbacks.

A paramount advantage is convenience. Online interviews are inexpensive and easy. Many people who are nearly impossible to reach by phone will respond eagerly to an e-mail inquiry. Executives whose daily calendars are crammed with appointments and whose seclusion is enforced by officious gatekeepers will often log on to the computer while alone in their basements at night. For now at least, many of us are so enchanted with the Internet that we liberally grant access to one another.

Online interviews also have a dynamic that can engender especially rich dialogue. Typing at a terminal seems psychologically safe to many people. It creates a comfort zone that frequently leads to unexpectedly revealing, candid, and detailed comments. Back-and-forth discussions flow easily, follow-ups take place immediately, and, marvelously for a writer, everything is recorded into a ready-made transcript.

On the downside, online interviews can be stilted. They are not true dialogues and seldom produce the unrehearsed eloquence of human conversation. They often sound more like speeches than spontaneous comment. And reliability can be a huge concern. How do you know the unseen people across cyberspace are who they represent themselves to be? How do you measure their authority and veracity without seeing their eyes or hearing their voices?

Like any other technique, the online interview comes with risks and limitations. But it can infinitely broaden your source network over time and space, saving uncounted hours. It can offer speedy access to distant or hard-to-contact sources. And it can efficiently produce answers to questions that lend themselves to a quick written paragraph or two. It has rapidly become an irreplaceable tool for many reporting situations.

Magic Questions

Whether you interview by e-mail or phone, in a relaxed den or a frenetic meeting room, craft and discipline pay off. The more attention paid to the details of preparation, time management, and question choice, the better most interviews go. But do not overlook the power of magic. Try to treat an interview as a bit of an out-of-body experience, during which you observe yourself at work and monitor your progress. Are you friendly or remote, building a bond or putting off your subject? Pay attention to your intuition. Should you push harder, pursue an unexpected track, leave a topic and come back to it later?

Look for words and phrases that draw special response. Asking people to talk about "turning points" in their lives, for example, often prompts revealing disclosures. Lob the occasional change of pace or off-the-wall question. Ask politicians to tell you the nicest thing they know about their opponents. Ask scientists about their favorite poems. Ask a pro boxer what being a parent feels like. Be unpredictable. People make fun of television's Barbara Walters for asking questions like, "If you were a tree, what kind of tree would you be?" But a well-timed playful question can be stunningly disarming, disclosing brand new avenues into a subject's personality.

Imagine the best possible material you could hope to get from your source. Then be alert for those magic moments when you sense that the ideal material is within reach. Let your creative side help you close in on it.

Using Documents and Databases

Reporters live by two ironclad laws of document use:

1. Everything is on record somewhere.
2. It is then filed in a mysterious place and guarded by an overprotective bureaucrat.

While documents and databases seldom suffice for a story, they can add remarkable breadth and depth to both everyday and long-range articles. It is probably fair to say that reporters in general have long been more comfortable conducting interviews, which seem normal and undaunting, than searching records, a process that implies arcane research expertise. However, writers who skillfully mine the records quickly realize what great volumes of invaluable material lie very close at hand.

In tracing records, nothing beats tenacity. Some journalists devote years to the hunt for certain documents. If you know where a document exists and you want it badly enough, chances are good you can get it through persistence.

Luckily, not every record search takes years, or even days, since most writers cannot spare such time anyway. Today's writers have many options, starting with from-their-desk online retrieval that can provide swift access to data that once required laborious hand searching in faraway places.

To capitalize on today's opportunities and avoid spending an eternity tracking down records, reporters have to think strategically. What information do I need? Where can I most readily find it? Who can help me?

The First Steps

Steve Weinberg begins *The Reporter's Handbook,* his indispensable guide to using records, by citing what veteran investigative reporters call the "documents state of mind."[3] Good researchers assume there is a document or database for everything. They may not know the exact title of the file or the official number on the form, but they expect from experience that a golden documentary source exists somewhere. Their job is to find it.

A chief problem lies with the massive volume of available material these days. We are afloat in data, interconnected to a limitless array of online and offline sources around the globe. For a writer, locating the ideal source is like landing in New York City in search of one person, but without a name, address, or description to go on. Starting from square one is fruitless. You need systematic ways of closing in, of moving from a general topic to a specific source. Among the methods reporters recommend:

---

[3]   Steve Weinberg, *The Reporter's Handbook,* 3d ed. (New York: St. Martin's, 1996) 3.

- **Consult experts.** Ask yourself who would most likely know how to find the precise sources and data you need. Specialists who often can help include reference librarians, government archivists, attorneys and legal librarians, and college professors. There are people all over your community who specialize in research or who know far more about a given topic than you. Making friends with a friendly research librarian can be one of the best moves a writer ever makes.
- **Start with indexes.** Researchers talk about "meta-sources," which are sources that lead you to sources. Indexes, bibliographies, online search engines, and databases such as Lexis-Nexis are examples reporters frequently use. They let you legally piggyback on the work of someone who has already located, sorted, and processed the kind of information you need. Do remember your law and ethics, though: give proper credit to your sources, pay the appropriate fees, and never pass off someone else's work as your own.
- **Go online early.** To cope with the Internet's infinite supply of raw material, numerous online operators already offer useful information management services. Some organizations (Yahoo! was a pioneer in this group) classify information by topics that reporters can easily search. Individual and company Web sites collect information about every imaginable topic; *American Journalism Review*'s NewsLink, for instance, offered an early premier gateway to thousands of online sites and sources on journalism. Groups like ProfNet, a service putting reporters in touch with experts at universities around the country, let reporters reach sources that they could never track down alone. Individual sites will come and go, but good researchers always know to seek out the best current indexes and search sites.
- **Guard your standards.** When you follow an outside-in reporting strategy, moving from the general to the particular, you dredge a lot of information, and the quality varies. Online searches do not distinguish between hits that list Nobel Prize winners and oddballs-in-the-basement. No law of journalism declares that everything recorded on a document must be true. Documents and databases carry all the potential errors of any other sources (carelessness, dishonesty, incompleteness, outdatedness). Writers have to assume that all material gathered early in a documents search is raw and potentially unreliable. At this stage, you are seeking tips, direction, and guidance, not publication-worthy, final quality material.

How Records Help

A generation ago writers setting out on assignment were routinely advised to "check the clips." That task meant dropping by the "morgue" to sift through yellowing clippings inside metal file cabinets—at least the clips that had not been purloined by the last reporter burrowing through the file. Then writers would occasionally scout out a relevant paper document, say a court file or property record. Only rarely, on major stories and projects, did most writers undertake full-fledged document research, which inevitably meant inconvenient trips to the courthouse and tedious hand-sorting of mountains of material. The cost in time and effort was too high to expend on routine stories.

Today the same advice applies: "check the clips." But working conditions have changed dramatically. Maybe we should say "check the chips," since most clips now reside online on electronic chips, and finding them has become infinitely easier. The mildly productive visit to the morgue has been supplanted by the vastly more profitable—and quicker—session at the terminal.

Specific research sites come and go with such alacrity that listing them here would be futile: the electronic frontier changes so fast that locations, addresses, and vendors mutate overnight. A year from now, a map of the current online geography would be no more practical than a chart of today's cloud formations. What we can do, however, is consider what *kinds* of documents and databases are available and what *purposes* they can serve.

- **Basic name and topic search.** This is the equivalent of the old clip search, and it is hard to imagine any writing assignment where it should not be a standard starting point. Identify the key names and topics you are researching. If your organization maintains a library or database (or even, as is still the case in some places, an old-fashioned paper morgue), run the key terms through this internal resource first. Then plug them into a good mass media database to see what has appeared elsewhere. Finally, try an online inquiry using one of the many, generally free, electronic search engines. In most cases all this can be done within half an hour.
- **Official documents.** More and more local, state, and federal documents are available online. Many media organizations now routinely acquire various government databases (local property ownership records, for example) or set up phone links that allow direct searching of official records. Make certain you know what raw records are available to you and how to access them. Also, recognize that almost all government entities have online sites to publish meeting agendas, court transcripts, regulatory proceedings, contract and budgeting information, campaign contributions, and other material.
- **Full texts and archives.** Numerous services now provide or sell full texts of academic and scientific journals, court decisions, commission reports, television broadcasts, and the like, along with historical documents (such as speeches or treaties) that can be useful. Most such services provide free summaries that sometimes can provide the precise information a writer needs (such as the date on which an event took place).

- **Background and specialized help.** Thousands of commercial vendors now compile and sell information on a boundless variety of topics. The more sophisticated your story assignment, the more likely it is that these sources may repay their costs. Writers can also turn to public and private Web sites and discussion groups to obtain information ranging from gossip to expert sources. These sites are a particularly good way to locate real-life human examples illustrating a trend or issue.

Overall, conducting efficient document and database checks can geometrically increase your information base. Whether you are double-checking the spelling of a name, backgrounding yourself on a religious controversy, or downloading the full text of an arcane scientific report, access to records provides a harvest that redoubles your reporting power. It saves time, surmounts time and space barriers, and in effect turns researchers who have preceded you into your reporting assistants.

As a matter of craft, using records effectively is a procedural step that improves your information gathering. As a matter of magic, it is stimulating and invigorating to you as a writer. Every relevant record, every online hit, every creative inquiry feeds the part of your brain that is at work massaging your material and arranging it into potential themes and storylines. The spark from one successful document or database strike can be just enough to ignite a great idea that has lain dormant awaiting the right stimulus.

Energizing Your Reporting

Reporting is a never ending whirlwind. It requires energy and determination. As you move through your interviews, records research, and other information gathering, here are some hints to help guide and inspire you:

- **Set high goals.** Work toward obtaining the best possible information for the best possible stories. Keep standards high as to the number, range, and complexity of your ideas and the quantity, quality, and public value of your information.
- **Move fast.** As you work a story, keep housekeeping and delays to a minimum. Make rounds by telephone or e-mail, then get out of the house or office and meet as many sources as you can. Manage your time efficiently by planning and setting priorities.
- **Ask lots of questions.** Talk to everyone, from current sources to potential sources to people you meet while socializing. Stay curious.
- **Read.** Depending on your reporting interests, get yourself onto the relevant mailing lists and listservs. Keep up with magazines, trade publications,

online newsletters, government reports, and other published material of value.

- **Be openly competitive.** Thank sources for tips and helpful assistance. Let people know you want their suggestions. Make it easy for people to get in touch with you.
- **Use others' brains to enlarge your own.** Brainstorm regularly with friends, colleagues, teachers, and editors. Stay open-minded about ideas and information. Ask for help when you are stumped. Take advice and inspiration anywhere you can find them.

SUMMARY

Ideas and information drive writing. People decide to read largely because an idea appeals to them. Once they start an article, they stick with it only if the material proves surprising and absorbing enough to overcome their natural inclination to move on to something else. So writers must be both confident and humble—confident enough to contend for the reader's time, humble enough to recognize the size of the challenge: *A sense of urgency has to underlie every writer's petition to attract readers.*

From the outset, writers owe it to themselves and their audiences to push for the best possible ideas and to filter out the weak ones. Through their craft, they cast broad and diverse news nets; brainstorm and interact with editors, sources, and readers; and apply their training as critical observers. Step by step, they identify and refine their ideas. Always receptive to the magic of inspiration, they also think big, visualizing the ultimate possible story and stretching with assurance toward that ideal.

They report thoroughly and imaginatively to amass a wealth of information from which to select. They master techniques of efficient interviewing and records searching to make the most of scarce time and to gather choice data and details. Primed with these fruits of craft, they deploy their writerly antennas in the direction of excellence, trusting that instinct and inspiration will crown their efforts.

Practicing Craft and Magic

1. Examine the cover story in your favorite magazine. From the writing and presentation, try to decide what the writer's major purpose was and what audience the writer had in mind. How well did the writer succeed in matching purpose, audience, and final result?

2. For your next assignment, list several different ideas and approaches before you settle on the final one. Work to make this your standard procedure.

3. Once you have selected an idea, visualize the best possible story you could hope to write. Organize your reporting to come as close as possible to the ideal.

4. On your next assignment, consult at least one human source and at least one document that otherwise might seem unfamiliar to you. Constantly stretch your reporting in this way, expanding your range of contacts and resources.

Chapter 6

Beginning to Write: Leads

In the beginning wasn't the word.

There sits the problem. Words do not exist until a writer creates them. The writer is god of the words. No matter how much time has been devoted to planning and research, every author eventually confronts that dreaded blank screen and the implacable demand to fill it. The moment comes to write the lead. You can put it off, but you cannot avoid it. "The last thing we decide," said French philosopher Blaise Pascal, "is what to put first."[1]

For most writers, the lead is the hardest trial. The stakes are self-evident. Nothing except the topic itself outweighs the lead. If the lead misfires, the article crashes. Without a good lead, few readers will get to paragraph 2, much less paragraph 10.

The pressure can seem paralyzing. Writing coach Don Fry talks about "lead anxieties" that cause writers to "suffer at their terminals, clutching their heads and chewing on themselves."[2]

So the lead is a big deal. But at the writer's side as always stand those trusty allies, craft and magic. Through craft, writers can undertake a series of orderly steps that remove much of the panic and strain from beginning to write. Preparation and technique can help abate even the apprehensions of the lead. Through magic, writers can invoke the mightiest powers of their creativity at lead-writing time. Luckily, this is one of the moments when coveted inspiration is most likely to strike.

This chapter considers what makes a good beginning and how craft and magic can help writers organize their material and shape their leads.

---

[1] Jon Winokur, ed., *Writers on Writing* (Philadelphia: Running Press, 1987) 94.
[2] Don Fry, "Helping Your Writers with Lead Problems," *ASNE Bulletin,* March 1994, 17.

WHAT MAKES A GOOD LEAD

A good lead should *inform, underline,* and *stimulate.* Those virtues hold whether you are writing news or narrative, 200 words or 200 pages, on paper or online. Whether you call it a lead, lede, opening, beginning, or intro, the initial salvo should achieve these three goals:

- **Inform.** A good lead keys the reader to your main point and demonstrates that the point is fresh and compelling. Obscure leads drive away busy readers.
- **Underline.** A good lead aims its spotlight on the vital points of interest. Its wording should reinforce in the reader's mind the impact, significance, or drama of your topic.
- **Stimulate.** A good lead makes the reader react and want to know more. It should arouse some emotion, like surprise, anger, fear, sadness, humor or just plain curiosity. Flat leads offer no reward for continuing.

Here is an example:

> Dental surgeons said yesterday they had discovered why snoring can kill sometimes: It can damage the arteries. [3]

The lead is informative; it conveys a concrete fact. It underlines the point, succinctly drawing attention via the setup–punch line construction. And the lead stimulates curiosity. How does snoring affect the arteries? Am I at risk?

No one can dictate precise specifications for a lead, and brave writers would resist even if someone tried. Personal tastes affect how writers create leads and how readers respond. About the only certainty is this: *a good lead is one that gets the most readers to the next paragraph.*

Still, it is possible to identify some common characteristics of successful leads, and it can be useful to match what you write against them. In general, strong leads share many of the following qualities:

- They are short, consisting of one sentence of 25 words or less.
- They are surprising, delighting us with the unexpected.
- They are focused, expressing one main thought in concentrated form. While limiting the number of words in a lead is important, limiting the number of ideas is vital. One powerful idea comes across far more effectively than several ideas jammed together.
- They are direct, conveying the main point in a robust independent clause. Its subject and verb are the two most important words in the article.

---

[3] "Research Reveals Why Snoring Sometimes Kills," *Washington Post,* 16 August 1998, A12.

- They are front-loaded, featuring the dominant point as near the beginning as possible.
- They are active, reflecting movement and change. For a lead to hold the reader, something must happen or change, or be about to happen or change. Stay away from "to be" verbs and most passive constructions.
- They are clear.
- They are stylish, sealing their point with some literary flair.
- They are electric, containing words, images or thoughts that spray little jolts up and down the reader's intellectual spine.

Good leads also steer clear of certain common pitfalls:

- They don't serve as roundups. Roundups confuse people by throwing too much information into play at once: "The City Council today fired the city libraries director for allowing excessive overdue books, raised next year's target for parking fines by 10%, ordered wholesale revisions in the city purchasing system, and agreed to make a tentative offer for two blocks in the southeast section for a new park and athletic complex." Whew! Better to focus on one of those developments and list the others later.
- They avoid unnecessary peripherals like overblown titles ("The deputy assistant secretary of state for hemispheric affairs said Friday"), needless scene-setting ("at a press conference in the State Department's main auditorium"), and complicated numbers ("that 15,617 of 22,943 applications for political asylum have been approved this year, 16.3% more than last year"). Streamline it to the essentials, then build in details later.

Finally, good leads are unique to their particulars, breaking any of these rules if the occasion commands. An all-time favorite lead snubs many of them. It appeared on a *Life* magazine article by master writer William Zinsser:

I've often wondered what goes into a hot dog. Now I know and I wish I didn't. [4]

SOME LEADS WITH AMBITION

In classrooms, newsrooms, and conferences, writers commonly share examples of leads they like or dislike, and quibbling inevitably follows. No two writers, editors, or teachers, it seems, can agree on which are the best examples. This happens in part because journalists are natural contrarians. Tell them something is good, and they dig for its vulnerabilities. Journalists operate this way all the time—testing sources, weighing evidence, seeking out

---

[4]   William Zinsser, *On Writing Well*, 5th ed. (New York: HarperPerennial, 1994) 143.

other sides—so it should surprise nobody that they also turn their skepticism on claims about writing.

Yet their reactions illustrate another simple but important point. Different readers like different leads. A writer's audience is not homogeneous and mono- lithic: it comprises many subsets with varying tastes and interests. It no more makes sense for every reader to like the same lead than for every motorist to prefer the same car.

One morning, I received a note from a former student who copyedits for a well-known newspaper. One of his paper's top writers had just won the Pulitzer Prize. The ex-student was puzzled because the same series had not even placed in the top two in an earlier regional contest. He wondered if there are any con- sistent standards.

It is a good question. Must we slump into literary nihilism, an endless rela- tivism that mocks all standards? Not really. Most writers, editors, and readers can distinguish very good leads from very poor ones, and we often achieve con- sensus on these matters. It is simply worth issuing a gentle warning against becoming too dogmatic about what is "good" and what is "bad." Three or four judges in one contest almost inevitably reach different verdicts than three or four different judges in a different contest do. Writers should applaud this diversity of taste. It greatly expands the range of writing that will win appreci- ation.

The following sections provide some examples of leads you may find intrigu- ing for a variety of reasons, from their literary merit to the audacity of their aspi- rations. Resist if you can the impulse to expound on their flaws. Instead, look for something positive about each lead, something about the content, wording, pace, or tone that can help tune your own writer's ear. The point is not to imi- tate but to assimilate. The more you study the styles and approaches of other writers, the richer your storehouse of writing techniques will become.

As you read the following leads, ask yourself these questions:

- What was the writer's purpose?
- How does the lead help achieve the purpose?
- Does the lead inform, underline, and stimulate?
- Can you think of alternative leads that would have worked better?
- Under what circumstances would you try a similar approach?

The Standard

Men have landed and walked on the moon.

(John Noble Wilford, *New York Times*)[5]

---

[5] John Noble Wilford, "Men Walk on Moon," *New York Times,* 21 July 1969, 1.

This understated lead topped one of the biggest stories of all time. Interestingly, the second paragraph of Wilford's story served almost as a second lead. The first paragraph has both poetry and potency, and the second paragraph expands on it. Here is the second paragraph:

> Two Americans, astronauts of Apollo 11, steered their fragile four-legged lunar module safely and smoothly to the historic landing yesterday at 4:17:40 p.m., Eastern Daylight Time.

The Snappy

> The vote was unanimous. Kill him.
> (Bill Harmon and Neil King Jr., *Tampa Tribune*)[6]

One handy rule of thumb is that the stronger the material, the simpler the style should be. The writer makes the point and gets out of the way. This little dagger of a lead is a good example. It begins a story telling how four children and their mother agreed to kill their father-husband.

The Whimsical

> BREEZEWOOD, Pa.—On the baseball diamond of life, a place like Breezewood is second base. You don't want to get stranded here, but you have to stop.
> (L. A. Jolidon, *USA Today*)[7]

In this story about the impact of holiday travelers passing through a small town, the writer links the ordinariness of Breezewood to a larger point. Life, like a weekend journey, has its way stations. The analogy is well-founded, the tone is agreeable, and the reader is quickly lured in with a strong hint of what will follow.

The Shocker

> The secret to diving under a moving freight train and rolling out the other side with all your parts attached lies in picking the right spot between the tracks to hit with your back.
> (Roger Hoffmann, *New York Times Magazine*)[8]

---

[6]   Peter Bhatia, "Super Starters: Some Appetizing Leads," *ASNE Bulletin*, March 1992, 32.
[7]   L. A. Jolidon, "Breezewood," *USA Today*, 27 August 1985, 1A.
[8]   Roger Hoffmann, "The Dare," *New York Times Magazine*, 15 March 1986, 70.

Few examples better illustrate the key principle of lead writing: make them want to know more. This piece does indeed describe the breathtaking childhood stunt of leaping under a moving train. The first line hooks you.

The Play on Words

> On a baseball field in Maryland's green hills Sunday, God and the First Amendment are scheduled to clash. This one could go extra innings.
>
> (Richard Willing, *USA Today*)[9]

Writers often select words that metaphorically play to both the literal story (here, a legal case involving baseball) and its larger meaning (constitutional issues of church and state). The words and ideas work together to underline the meaning.

The Suspenseful

> It was New Year's Eve in the shark-inhabited waters off Hawaii's Kona Coast, and Hal Corbett was preparing to die.
>
> (Mary Ellen Corbett, *Fort Wayne News-Sentinel*)[10]

Suspense leads are among the riskiest. They taunt busy readers with a tease and hope it will lure them. To succeed, they should be used sparingly and they should bristle with anticipatory energy. Here, the writer effectively uses foreshadowing and the potency of words and images. Notice especially a small touch here: the way she nimbly substitutes the similar but fresher phrase *shark-inhabited* for the clichéd *shark-infested.*

The Impressionistic

> KOREM, Ethiopia—The first thing that struck me was the sound. Except it was not sound. It was the absence of sound. People everywhere, and so little sound. Starvation does make a noise. It is silence. And it is very loud.
>
> (Mark Patinkin, *Providence Journal-Bulletin*)[11]

---

[9] Richard Willing, "God, First Amendment in Pitch Battle," *USA Today,* 28 August 1998, 3A.

[10] Mary Ellen Corbett, "Features," in *Best Newspaper Writing 1979,* ed. Roy Peter Clark (St. Petersburg, FL: Modern Media Institute, 1980) 45.

[11] Mark Patinkin, "They Flee from Hunger but Keep Their Humanity," in *Best Newspaper Writing 1985,* ed. Roy Peter Clark (St. Petersburg, FL: Poynter Institute, 1985) 187.

Once again, in this lead a writer seizes on a physical reality (the absence of noise) and connects it to a metaphysical truth (the horror of starvation), surprising us with the contrast of expected noise and eerie quiet. The short, staccato sentences show how the writer, and by extension the reader, can take in and process these quick sad impressions.

The Casual

> SOMEWHERE IN SICILY, Aug. 11, 1943—Probably it isn't clear to you just how the Army's setup for the care of the sick and wounded works on a battlefront. So I'll try to picture it for you.
> (Ernie Pyle, Scripps-Howard Newspapers)[12]

Legendary combat correspondent Ernie Pyle wrote this lead during World War II. Pyle's dispatches, with their simplicity and informality, read more like columns or letters from a friend than news articles. Like this example, they tend to be straightforward and concise in summarizing their topics, but they have an ingratiating quality that encourages you to keep reading.

The Eloquent

> If baseball could speak, it would have sounded like Red Barber.
> (Martin Merzer, *Miami Herald*)[13]

It may seem odd, but obituaries often produce some of the best writing in print. Writers seem to dignify them with more care and tenderness than a city hall story receives. Obits also provide a chance to write large, to meditate on someone's broadest contributions.

Whatever the reasons, obituaries often radiate good writing. In this example, the writer captures the essence of eminent sportscaster Red Barber, "whose melodious Southern voice evoked memories of peanut shells and cigar smoke and long drives to deep center field." How did Merzer manage this effect? He, too, found a physical image (a familiar voice from radio and television) that connected perfectly with a larger story (fans' love of baseball). The matchmaking between specific material and grand theme is frequently a key to great lead writing.

---

[12] Ernie Pyle, "As Proficient as a Circus," in *Ernie's War,* ed. David Nichols (New York: Simon & Schuster, 1986) 146.

[13] Martin Merzer, "Voice of Baseball Silenced at Age 84," in *Best Newspaper Writing 1993,* ed. Don Fry (St. Petersburg, FL: Poynter Institute, 1993) 105.

The Rule-Buster

> The nation's major airports, a vast, varied and aging collection of former farm fields and swamps that funnel more than 450 million passengers into high-flying aluminum capsules to travel the annual equivalent of 76 round trips to the planet Pluto, are rapidly approaching gridlock.[14]

Care to guess where this flowery specimen appeared? On the lead story on page 1 of the *New York Times* itself, a sure sign that every now and then a writer is permitted to let it all out. Is Andrew H. Malcolm's lead too far over the top? Some readers think so. But it also mingles a dash of literary swashbuckling with a solid theme and pertinent facts. If every lead were this elaborate, readers would be exhausted, but we should cheer for the occasional experiment that enlivens the media with novelty and derring-do.

ORGANIZING AND OUTLINING

Where do good leads come from? Assuming you have compiled strong material, the first step toward writing a good lead is deciding what the point should be. The worst way to approach this decision is by staring at an empty screen. This is a little bit like gazing blankly at a garden in hopes a flower will sprout. You have to prepare the ground first.

The best approach is to work your way systematically toward a lead by organizing your material, pinpointing the key angle, and testing potential phrases and formulations that can crystallize your angle.

Like good poems, good leads look simple once they are written. Achieving that grace and elegance, however, can be fiendishly difficult. A major reason is that writers too often rush to write before adequately organizing their material and locating the main points. Editors and coaches say that busy writers are more likely to shortchange organizational steps than any other part of writing. Yet a few extra minutes invested in organizing and outlining will multiply geometrically in value as the writing progresses.

As we have already discussed, organizing is not a one-time effort. It applies throughout a writing project. Choosing an idea, collecting information, and selecting a storyline all require thought about focus and order.

Writers should be encouraged to think about focus at every step: focusing the idea, focusing the reporting, focusing the storyline, focusing the lead, focusing the full article. The major organizational effort, though, comes just before approaching the lead. This is the climactic moment, the point where

---

[14] Andrew H. Malcolm, "Aviation Experts Warn of Gridlock at U.S. Airports," *New York Times,* 19 June 1988, 1.

the assignment and material and theme must transmute into the discrete words and sentences of an article—an article that requires a lead.

If you want to find an individual planet, you do not start by peering aimlessly into the heavens. You determine its coordinates or at least its general position in the sky. Locating a lead is analogous. You do not stare randomly. You organize, to limit the area that must be searched.

Organizing is a process of reduction and selection, as discussed in Chapter 2. The goal is to narrow your material from (1) an undifferentiated mass to (2) a series of related groupings to (3) a list of topics to (4) a one-sentence theme. Once you have a theme, the lead search is simplified: you select a lead from the material most pertinent to your theme.

Generally, the lead escorts readers to a second paragraph that amplifies the lead and often to a *nut graf*, a paragraph that puts the story in perspective. Those concepts will be discussed further in the next chapter.

For now, concentrate on choosing an organizing procedure that is compatible with your work style. *No method fits everybody, but everybody needs a method.* The following paragraphs examine some typical ways writers work toward focus.

- **Sorting.** Organizing almost always begins with examining the material and classifying it by topic. Some writers use labeled folders or envelopes; some color-code using highlighter pens; others create computerized indexes. My personal method is to start by reading through my research material and listing on a legal pad every germane point. Then I try to consolidate that long list into a shorter one, with three or four major headings, and I write those headings on a second sheet. As I go, I constantly think about leads and endings, and I keep separate running lists of possibilities.

- **Ranking.** However you choose to order your material, the next step is to set priorities. In my case, I take my short list of major headings and rank them in the order they should appear in print. Now I have the makings of an outline. A comparable, but nonlinear, approach is followed by Rick Bragg, a Pulitzer honoree for the *New York Times*. Bragg envisions a set of five boxes in the sky. "I just imagine it like a little bubble over a cartoon," Bragg says. "You know your lead is going to go in the first box, your nut graf in the second. You begin a chronology in the third and continue it in the fourth, and the fifth is your kicker."[15]

- **Finding a theme.** A list of topics is helpful, but an article should not read like a sequence of separate subjects. It needs a theme that integrates all the topics into a meaningful whole. You will remember from

---

[15] Rick Bragg, interview with the author, 16 April 1998.

Chapter 3 that a great theme and storyline are hallmarks of excellent writing. If you have not already settled on a theme, you should do so at this stage. Try putting the theme into words (no more than one or two sentences), and writing those words at the top of your list of topics. Once that task is completed, here is what you usually have: a sheet of paper with a theme at the top, a list of topics in the order you want to present them, and some ideas for leads and endings. The mass of material is now scaled to workable size.

- **Mulling.** So far, organizing has been thoroughly linear and craftlike. Now, call on some magic. At this point, intimately familiar with the material and the emerging outline, many writers take a break. They apply the "release" part of the WRITE formula. They release, or detach, from the work, occupy themselves with something else, and leave the subconscious on automatic pilot, still sorting, shuffling, and sensing. They let things percolate for a while. Chances are extremely high that some welcome new thought, idea, or phrase will soon explode into view—a fresh way of viewing the material, a connection that had been overlooked, a word or image that captures some essence of the story. Staring into space, a wasteful procrastination earlier, can now be most profitable. Some writers spend hours or even days in this stage, but media writers generally face harsher deadlines. Even so, a few minutes of detachment at this point can actually save writing and revising time. Take a quick stroll around the office, get a sip of water, let ideas float in your mind for a few moments. Imagine a small icon on your computer screen that reads, "One moment . . . writer downloading," or one of those blinking buttons that tells you your browser is away doing vital off-screen work for a little while. Properly fertilized in whatever way, the mind can be readied to respond. Nourish this moment as much as possible. It is prime time for taking the great leap toward excellence. What is the best possible story you can stretch toward? What is the most extraordinary lead? Immersed in your material, you try to will it to the next level of excellence. Often, though not always, the magic side will respond.

- **Troubleshooting.** But what if the muse abandons you? What if your material foils all attempts to order it? What if you simply cannot close in on a suitable shape for your article? If you feel frustrated at this stage, consider two options. First, do more research. The most common reason that writers have trouble focusing their material is failure to report comprehensively enough. They lack sufficient information to see a complete picture. A writer's axiom: *if you cannot make sense of your material, you need more material.* Second, experiment with different ways of kneading the material you do have. Chapter 3 listed several methods writers can use to locate a storyline. At this point, you can use similar means to help turn your storyline into a structure that best conveys it. Mix craft and magic as you proceed. Here are some ideas.

1. Write about your topic as fast as you can without notes; the result may be a kind of nonlinear outline, a set of impressionistic ideas that can be adapted into a list of topics.
2. Talk aloud about your material, with a companion or even alone, if necessary, and listen for potential themes and structures.
3. Envision using your material for an alternative literary form. If it were a book, what would be the chapter titles? If it were a term paper, what would be the research question, the findings, and the conclusion? If it were a speech, what would go into the introduction, middle, and ending? Shifting focus in this way will sometimes give you new insight into the points you need to make and the best way to order them. It will reconnect you to the muse. Many writers, when stuck, pull out a favorite book and read for a while. "I find that reading is critical for me," says Alice Steinbach, a *Baltimore Sun* Pulitzer winner. "Reading good writing is a great tonic. It reminds me of how great good writing can be."[16]   .

- **Moving ahead.** You may need an interlude of inspiration before you proceed, and you may have to circle back and repeat some reporting steps. Eventually you return to focusing. Put ample mental energy into this stage, and do not give up until you produce a plan of organization. For many writers, the plan takes the form of a simple sheet containing a theme statement, an ordered enumeration of topics, and rough ideas for the lead and ending.

Some variation on list making is the most common organizing device encountered among writers. But other writers produce classic outlines, complete with Roman numerals, large and small letters, and so forth. Some writers assign labels to each part of their outline; for example, see two-time Pulitzer winner Jon Franklin's excellent exegesis of organizing in his book *Writing for Story.*

It is probably unwise to be doctrinaire about something as personal as writing, so you should go forward with whatever works for you. But heed this caveat: whatever system of organizing you choose, do it in writing. Too many writers organize in a hurry in their heads, and the outcome too often is less-than-ideal focus.

If you are not accustomed to producing a written plan of organization, try it faithfully for six months. Good results can almost be guaranteed.

---

[16] Alice Steinbach, interview with the author, 26 March 1998.

SELECTING BETWEEN NEWS AND NARRATIVE

Too much folderol is written pitting hard news leads against narrative leads, as if they were gladiators only one of whom could be left standing. Do not trap yourself in this snare. Hard leads and narrative leads should coexist in any writer's repertoire. You need to master both forms.

Neither is inherently superior. The relevant question is: which kind of lead fits a writer's purpose?

Hard leads present the main point directly and succinctly. The most common type of hard lead, the *inverted pyramid*, begins with the most important information and adds secondary material in descending order of importance. Hard leads work best when you are offering important information the audience does not yet know.

Narrative writing lends itself to storytelling. The *narrative lead* is a hook that grabs readers and leads them into a tale with strong character, plot, and depth. Narrative leads work best when you are dramatizing a topic beyond its immediate informational urgency.

Today, however, you should also consider a third style of lead: the *news-plus lead*. Fewer and fewer print articles actually present brand-new information. It is through radio, television and online newswriting that you are most likely to divulge information for the first time. By the time they encounter print sources, today's audience members most likely know something about most major stories and issues.

The news-plus lead incorporates the main theme but adds some important new dimension. Its goal is to add value for readers who already know the outlines of a story, while conveying basic information for readers who do not.

News-plus leads resemble what writers for afternoon newspapers used to call *second-day leads.* These were leads in which the evening paper's writer would seek a new angle on a story already covered in the morning competition. Given the speed of today's media, however, it no longer makes sense to think of the news cycle in terms of the first day and the second day. News now changes by the hour if not the minute, and broadcast and online sites are live or updated on the fly. Often, because of the volume of information already in circulation, a news-plus lead is indicated for the very first written version of a story.

How do you decide between the hard lead, narrative lead, and news-plus lead? You ask yourself what your purpose is and what your audience likely already knows.

Suppose, for example, you were sitting in a meeting room, and you suddenly looked out the door and saw that the building was on fire. How would you break that news to your colleagues? Would you choose a compelling storytelling intro ("Things seemed deceptively normal when Hank Snurdly arrived at work

Thursday. No odd smells from the basement. No hint of raw electrical wires rubbing each other the wrong way. . . .")? Of course not. By the time you reached your nut graf, everyone in the building might be in flames.

Instead, you would organize your information into a classic inverted pyramid pattern, most important information first, followed by secondary material. "There's a fire in a hall," you might say. "Everybody needs to leave right now."

However, if people in the room already know the building is ablaze, a simple fire alarm no longer helps. In that case, you would choose a news-plus announcement. For example: "Let's head for the second door on the right. That's the nearest exit that will take us away from where the fire is burning."

Here is an example of a news-plus lead, showing how a local newspaper both reported the outcome of a court case and added an intriguing angle:

> Confessed killer James Elledge was sentenced to death yesterday, hours after telling a jury that "there is a wicked part of me, and this wicked part of me needs to die."
>
> (Rebekah Denn, Seattle Post-Intelligencer)[17]

Sports writers often use news-plus leads. Because most fans will quickly learn whether their team won or lost, the sports writer must offer new information or analytical insight. Here is an example:

> Number 1 Ohio State unveiled its Swiss Army knife offense in its 35-14 victory over Missouri. . . . Name the tool—speed, strength, running, passing, depth—and the Buckeyes flipped it out.
>
> (Ivan Maisel, Sports Illustrated)[18]

Narrative leads apply when the stress is on story rather than newsiness. These accounts usually have some larger theme that expands beyond the immediate breaking news event. In the fire example, narrative writing might be used to dramatize some special element in the story: a heroic rescue by a passerby, a pattern of malfeasance that led to the tragedy, a backstage examination of modern fire-fighting techniques. Your purpose in those cases would not be to notify people of the fire but to satisfy their curiosity. Numerous questions always surround important episodes, and once readers have slaked their most pressing notification needs, they want more depth and explanation.

Narrative leads take numerous forms. They can be anecdotal, descriptive, or expository. They can follow a problem-solution or complication-resolution model. They can be conventional or experimental. But the best narrative leads consistently have three qualities:

---

[17] Rebekah Denn, "Murderer Elledge Is Sentenced to Death," *Seattle Post-Intelligencer,* 22 October 1998, 1.

[18] Ivan Maisel, "Jacknifed," *Sports Illustrated,* 28 September 1998, 82.

- They introduce the central character or main idea.
- They illustrate the main theme.
- They make the reader want to know more.

An important caution: writing in narrative style is not a license for fancy word usage or meandering indirection. Narrative leads should be calculated to achieve their impact quickly and dramatically, by illuminating their main theme in an arresting way. Book writers may be allowed a chapter or so of introductory material, but media writers cannot be permitted that luxury. With only a few seconds to seize reader attention, you should avoid unnecessary scene setting or throat clearing, the kind of material that leads up to the point but is not the point. The best narrative leads do not prepare readers for the point; they immediately demonstrate something vital about the point.

Here is an example of a narrative lead, from a magazine profile showing the high-charged personality of computer entrepreneur Bill Gates:

> Bill Gates rocks. Literally. When his brain cells really start firing, Gates has a habit of leaning forward in his chair, putting his elbows on his knees, interlocking his fingers, and pumping the balls of his feet against the floor, going at it like Grandma Moses on a triple espresso.
>
> (Russ Mitchell, *U.S. News & World Report*)[19]

Leads should be like lasers—powerful, concentrated beams of thought that project readers straight to the center of something important. Reading the lead should be akin to slipping on ice: readers should find themselves sliding halfway into a story before they know what has happened.

Chapter 13 will discuss narrative writing in greater detail. For now, the relevant concern is that writers should select which style lead—hard news, news-plus, or narrative—best fits the story at hand.

DRAFTING A LEAD

Few sights are more nerve-racking to writers than a vacant screen. Staring into the emptiness, they begin to twitch and squirm. Their minds race into overdrive, fast-forwarding through their mental notebooks, ideas tumbling in their brains like soggy clothes in a dryer. Lead possibilities race past their eyes like credits scrolling by too fleetingly at the end of a movie. All is a blur, nothing stands still, the page remains maddeningly word-free.

If the computer prodigies at Microsoft, IBM, and other such havens of genius were really on the ball, they would pour their brainpower into pro-

---

[19] Russ Mitchell, "Microsoft's Midlife Crisis," *U.S. News & World Report*, 19 October 1998, 44.

gramming a Lead Search key, a saving piece of software for those of us who are lead-challenged.

Until its discovery, you have to make do on your own—but maybe you can come closer than you think. If you take care in the organization stage, you can create a simulated human version of a Lead Search key. By organizing and ranking material, you evaluate each major point, a process somewhat equivalent to a computer's giving an electrical rating to each data byte. If a computer's Lead Search key were scanning such material, it would jump to the point with the highest rating, highlight it, and blink proudly over the lead it had found. When your brain scans your plan of organization, a similar marvel occurs. It comes to a stop at the point you want to emphasize most.

The effect of all this work is to funnel your thinking from a hazy blur to a pointed focus. By spending some time organizing the material and considering what style lead is needed, you limit the number of ideas tumbling in your head and reduce distraction. Drafting the lead becomes easier, especially if you follow through in an orderly way.

Follow Your Focus

Discipline yourself to stay on point. A common lapse is for a writer to laboriously produce a complete outline, decide on an approach . . . and then inexplicably sit at the keyboard and write something entirely different. If your lead clashes with your outline, rethink both until you can reconcile them. But if you are confident in your focus, craft a lead that stays true to it. Whether you choose hard news, news-plus, or narrative, hold firm to your dominant point as you write the first few words.

Write Several Leads

Even if you adore the first lead you produce, write two or three more. If nothing else, the exercise loosens your writing muscles and inspires creativity in general. But often you will unearth words or phrases that improve the good lead you began with, and on rare but blissful occasions you will amaze yourself by stumbling onto a super lead on the fifth try.

Think Subject-Verb-Twist

For all their infinite variety, stories often boil down to two recurring formats:

1. Somebody Does Something Interesting.
2. Something Happens That Is Unusual.

The most powerful way to convey such thoughts is to fuse content and format so they reinforce each other. That is, you want to arrange your material so that the major points of emphasis occupy the strongest positions grammatically. For instance, you do not want to bury your key point in a secondary clause or muffle it with superfluous modifiers. Most often, the strongest setup for the lead is as follows:

- Put the *main doer* or *main idea* in the *main subject* of the lead sentence.
- Put the *main action* in the *main verb.*
- Add the *main twist,* the reason that your topic compels attention, immediately after the main verb.

Here is an example of a *subject-verb-twist* lead:

> Mail is being stolen so frequently from blue street collection boxes in Seattle that the U.S. Postal Service is advising customers not to use them.
>
> (Jane Hadley, *Seattle Post-Intelligencer*)[20]

Another caution: nobody likes formulaic writing. Not every lead or every sentence should follow the above format, or any other rigid formula. Use subject-verb–twist thinking as a starting point, not as a required template. Follow it when it works; abandon it when you can do better.

Make a Literary Leap

Recall once more those three qualities of excellence: storyline, surprise, and stylishness. Scavenge everywhere for at least one splendid word in every lead—something playful or eye-popping, a mind-opener or neck-snapper, some word, phrase, or image that inspires a frisson of delight in the grateful reader. Here's an example from an everyday story. Notice the fresh verbs (mastered, mortared) and the unadorned imagery ("a great hush of snow"):

> The elements mastered Maryland yesterday as they seldom do, as a great hush of snow mortared over the state with accumulations of 22 inches. . . .
>
> (Tom Horton, *Baltimore Sun*)[21]

SUMMARY

Not long ago I was watching a huge marching band at a football game, when suddenly the performers broke ranks and began milling around the field in

---

[20] Jane Hadley, "Master Key Stolen, Then Checks Are Forged," *Seattle Post-Intelligencer,* 22 October 1998, A1.

[21] Tom Horton, "Airport Closed, City Buses Halted," *Baltimore Sun,* 12 February 1983, 1A.

seeming anarchy. Then on cue the marchers halted as one, and the chaos instantly converted into a precision formation.

The whole scene reminded me of the challenge of writing a lead. It forces you to corral ideas that swirl tumultuously in your head and to arrange them on demand into a specific word formation.

For all the apparent confusion on the football field, the band members knew where they wanted to go. Lead writers need the same sense of direction and planning.

Good leads inform, underline, and stimulate. They tend to be short, direct, focused statements, whether newsy or narrative, that pique reader curiosity with interesting material and stimulating words.

Most often, good leads flow from solid work: strong reporting followed by careful organization, topped at just the right moment with inspiration. As artisans, writers need a disciplined system for selecting, ranking, and ordering their material into a logical plan of execution. As artists, they also need a dash of detachment, a nice setting in which to think and perhaps talk about their material and to stretch toward its highest meaning. Leads test all writers, but a combined linear-nonlinear approach usually pays off.

Practicing Craft and Magic

1. For your next assignment, take extra time to try the steps mentioned in this chapter: (1) produce a written outline or game plan; (2) narrow your focus to a one- or two-sentence main theme; (3) crystallize that theme into your lead. Keep practicing this system, adapting it as you see fit to your own working style.

2. Write three separate leads for your next assignment: a news lead, a news-plus lead, and a narrative lead. Think about how the various approaches can be used to achieve differing purposes.

3. Build magic into your lead-writing system. As you begin organizational work, give an "assignment" to your imagination to help with the breakthrough idea, the focus, and the wording. Release yourself from direct contact with your story, for a few minutes or hours as you are able. Then stay alert for the insights or inspirations that will result from your right brain carrying out its assignment.

Chapter 7

Managing
the Murky
Middle

Writers reap honors for intrepid reporting, praise for great headlines, and kudos for winning leads. But no one wins awards for writing a great middle.

Middles probably get less attention from writers and editors than any other part of writing. Drained by the concentrated effort required to produce a compelling idea and an enticing lead, writers tend to speed through the body of their copy, surging toward the end. The middle barely gets a notice.

The consequences can be calamitous. Stories drift and meander, focuses blur, wordiness spreads. People stop reading.

A good middle holds the audience won by a great lead. It moves readers to the meat of the material. It keeps them on the page. A poor middle drives them away, even when they do not realize why.

Editors, coaches, and teachers hear many recurring comments from writers. High on the Top Ten list would be this one: "I often spend half my writing time on the lead. Once I'm satisfied with it, the story just seems to flow from there."

Many of us nod in agreement when someone makes that point. After all, as earlier chapters have discussed, a hefty investment at the front end of the process (spending ample time organizing and getting started, for example) does accelerate the whole creative enterprise.

It might be good, however, to entertain some second thoughts about the implications of writers' preoccupation with leads. The more carefully and thoughtfully you read various articles, the more you notice that a big complaint is their disorganization—lack of direction, lack of cohesion, lack of the kind of structural integrity that defies a reader to stop reading. Too many stories seem some sort of miscellaneous collection of marginally related tidbits and factoids, rather than a unified narrative or news tale. To use the wonderful old phrase, they consist of "a beginning, a muddle, and an end."

Granted, the topic and the lead are vital, and we should never begrudge the time and effort expended on them. But true craftspeople also recognize that the beginning is simply that—just the beginning. Lots more work comes afterward.

This book will not propose that you spend less time at the front end, but it will advocate giving more time and attention to the secondary stages of writing.

It is always risky to recommend anything to writers that costs them time. Time is their most precious asset. Virtually every writer yearns to spend more time reporting, organizing, writing, and rewriting. But deadlines loom. Today's production demands make it seem naive to propose spending more time on much of anything.

Much of this book dwells on ways writers can save time or use available time more efficiently, but here we can consider three reasons for spending extra time on the body of a story.

First, the ideal. Our first goal is to consider ways to improve writing. Taking more time is one important stride. Time alone never guarantees excellence, but in most cases the quality of the final product relates to the time and effort spent. Writers should not become defensive about that fact. Great writing tends to take more time than you think—more time than publishers, editors, and readers think too. If writers do not defend that position, who will?

Second, the practicality. Writers do have power to redistribute their time. They should look for ways to save time elsewhere that can be applied to the act of writing. If you cannot expand the gross amount of time devoted to a single story, then your only solution is to rearrange your use of existing time. Better time management helps. Becoming a more skillful interviewer, for instance, means you can acquire more and better information in less time. Becoming a more efficient outliner means you can organize your stories more quickly. Organizing better means you spend less time sweating over leads. And so on. If you constantly improve at each stage, you should find yourself saving some time.

Third, the most pragmatic point of all: pick your shots. If you cannot spend more writing time on every story, then do so on some stories—on the most important ones, the most sensitive ones, the ones where extra writing time matters most. Not every writer can spend extra writing time on every story, but every writer should be able to spend extra writing time on some stories.

This chapter establishes the importance of maintaining focus, order, and clarity throughout the body of copy. To do so is part craft, the devotion of meticulous, linear attention to building a logical, coherent story. And it is part magic, calling for a panoramic vision of the story and the arrangement of various elements, like symphonic instruments, to promote overall harmony and grace.

WHERE TROUBLE BEGINS

Assume you have a strong idea and an engaging lead. Trouble often erupts right there—at the second paragraph.

The second paragraph is the most neglected single aspect of writing.

Writers bleed over the lead, sometimes for hours, occasionally for days and even weeks. Then they write it and roll. It is as if a notebook-dam bursts, and words come flooding out. That super-important second paragraph washes by in an eye blink. It may not get a second thought.

But you need to slow down. The second paragraph plays a crucial role in maintaining readers' interest and escorting them into the body of the story. A lousy second paragraph—one that lets go of a reader who has been grabbed by the lead—can undo all that effort invested in an exemplary project.

Read some newspapers and magazines, and you will find several recurring problems with second paragraphs.

Problem: The Second Paragraph as the Runner-Up Lead

Writers have an innate desire to tell everything first. They fall in love with their material and breathlessly want to deliver it all, or they cannot decide whether the main point is that the City Council fired the police chief or raised fines for parking tickets. The easy way out seems to be putting one point in the lead, the second one in the next paragraph.

To a writer, this makes sense. To a reader, it is a logic killer. By definition, a reader who gets to paragraph two has been engaged by paragraph one and wants to find out more. By changing the subject, the writer breaks the connection that has been established and provides a splendid opportunity for the reader's eye and mind to wander elsewhere.

Problem: The Second Paragraph That Repeats the Lead

Writers also sometimes become infatuated with different ways of wording things. So they use one phrase in the lead and a synonymous formulation in the second paragraph. Or they inject a direct quote that merely retells the lead in different words. It is okay to repeat main points in paragraph two; in fact, you should do that as a logical linking device. But you need to be careful that you add important material and do not just rehash what the reader has been told already.

Problem: The Second Paragraph That Drops Back to Background Too Soon

A newspaper printed a story about police storming into a government meeting to arrest and haul off an elected official. Wonderful lead. The second paragraph, instead of building on that dramatic confrontation, went immediately to background, way back to the beginning of the dispute that led to the arrest. What readers surely wanted to know was what happened. Did the official resist, depart silently, apologize contritely, blurt a confession, exit with dignity and a witty retort? Did the police use handcuffs, shove the official, behave like intruders at the opera? Did the audience react, gasp with shock, shout insults? The background is needed, and fairly soon, but not in paragraph two. The second paragraph needs to stay with the action.

Solutions: Second Paragraphs That Sizzle

To avoid problems like these, strong second paragraph have several key characteristics.

First, *they should build on the most compelling point in the lead.* They should amplify, with additional insight and detail, the point that most engages the reader in the first place. Build on the hook that first attracted your audience. Following this logic, we can sometimes call the second paragraph the *amplification graf.*

Second, they often add the essential *how and why* to the story. As early chapters discussed, leads tend to focus on who and what, on the fact that someone has done something important or that something dramatic has occurred. A logical next step for readers is to learn how it happened or why it matters.

Third, second paragraphs need a *structural connection* to the lead. The grammar of the two paragraphs should link smoothly. For example, in the second paragraph a writer might repeat the name of the key person from the lead, employ a pronoun with a clear reference to the lead, or use a synonym that refers to a key idea. You should not merely rephrase the lead; rather, you should use form (that is, grammar) to connect content from one paragraph to the next.

Here is an ineffective second paragraph:

> A County Circuit Court judge has allowed the owner of a condemned apartment building to seek compensation for lost income from the property.
> Edgar F. Williams, who owns the eight-unit apartment complex, is seeking $157,000 from the city for lost rent. . . .

The problem is that the second paragraph offers only background. What readers need to know at this point is the judge's rationale. Knowing that, they can understand the story's impact.

Here is an effective second graf. It supplies specifics to build on a teaser lead:

> Mosquito stories are sometimes like fish stories. Except this time, you should believe them.

Thanks to heavy rains, mosquitoes are so bad this summer that in some areas, you can get bitten an average of 10 times a minute, officials said this week.

(Debra Shimanski, *Annapolis Capital*)[1]

NUT GRAFS: WHY ARE WE AT THIS PARTY?

Read the following lead, and then take the short quiz that follows:

Arlene Davido dropped her maternity pants, sat at her kitchen table and leaned with difficulty over her pregnant belly.
Then she injected heroin into her right calf.

(Loretta Tofani, *Philadelphia Inquirer*)[2]

Here is the quiz:

1. Does this story have a strong lead?
2. Does it have a compelling second paragraph?
3. What is the story really about?

For many readers the answers might be (1) yes, (2) yes, and (3) I'm not sure yet. The graphic opening scene grabs attention, and the second paragraph is a shocker. But they could be introducing any of several different story-lines: an in-depth profile of one addict, a look at the problems of addicts in general, a story about complicated pregnancies, an investigation of the welfare system.

The problem: the writer knows the theme but the reader does not; the writer knows where the story is heading but the reader does not. The solution: a nut graf, an early paragraph that crystallizes the theme, gives readers context, and highlights the story's significance.

Here is how the writer then presented the nut graf:

This is the story of Arlene Davido, a heroin addict, and her frantic daily search for the drug during her pregnancy. This is also the story of Cheryl Anne Davido, who lies in a Thomas Jefferson University Hospital nursery. . . .

---

[1] Debra Shimanski, "Mosquitoes Are Back, and Worse Than Ever," *Annapolis Capital,* 28 June 1989, A1.
[2] Loretta Tofani, "Addict Gives Birth, Addict Is Born," *Philadelphia Inquirer,* 13 March 1988, 1A.

With this strong nut graf, readers become oriented. They now know what the overall story is about. The scenic opening is fitted into its larger framework in a way that furthers reader understanding.

Not every story requires a nut graf. Breaking news stories, for example, generally do not. Their significance should be obvious. If a plane crashes or a president is elected, the news itself is the "nut." But complicated articles such as profiles, investigations and trend stories need nut grafs. Sometimes labeled "why are we at this party grafs," they should appear within the first three or four paragraphs and orient readers to the article's overall scope.

Here are two more examples:

Lead

A Roman Catholic priest from Minnesota died of AIDS late last year after isolating himself from the church and concealing his lifestyle and illness from all but a few close friends.

Nut Graf

The privacy surrounding the priest's death is typical of similar cases that are surfacing nationwide. Such secrecy underscores the dilemma that AIDS poses for the Catholic Church, which demands its clergy be celibate. . . .

(Jacqui Banaszynski, *St. Paul Pioneer Press Dispatch*)[3]

Lead

It should be enough to drive the Coors boys to drink. Workers at the beer company run by the Coors family, longtime funders of the political right, now attend a diversity workshop and get training on sexual harassment. . . . The company sets aside a specific share of purchases each year for minority-owned firms . . . the brewer has sponsored . . . a marathon gay dance party. . . .

Nut Graf

Coors Co. isn't alone. The company's socially progressive policies are part of a larger trend. Call it corporate leftism: businesses are adopting policies considered wildly liberal in the political arena. . . .

(John Cloud, *Time*)[4]

THE MIDDLE BECOMES MUDDLE

Now where does your article stand? It has a good idea, a strong lead, and a compelling, amplifying second paragraph. A solid nut graf provides significance and perspective. Typically, the first few paragraphs will also include

---

[3] Jacqui Banaszynski, "Priest Dies; Church Dilemma Growing," *St. Paul Pioneer Press Dispatch*, 8 February 1987, 1A.

[4] John Cloud, "Why Coors Went Soft," *Time*, 2 November 1998, 70.

the best quote on the main point and perhaps one or more paragraphs of detail supporting the lead. All this constitutes a strong introductory section.

Here, if you are not careful, the middle begins to muddle. Afloat in mid-story, having spent most of their thought and energy on the lead and its ancillaries, writers have a tendency to write faster and faster, dropping in thoughts as they occur. What began as a well-focused story can quickly turn into a jumble.

Two techniques to help stay on track are the *interior outline* and the *refocusing paragraph*.

I once attended a church where the minister began every sermon, after a brief introduction, with the words, "Point number one." His sermons always had three points and he unfailingly introduced them as "point number one," "point number two," and "point number three." You could not get more organized than that.

Most of us write stories that have several points, even if we do not announce them with the preacher's wording. Most but not all writers prepare some sort of beginning outline, whether it takes the formal shape of Roman numerals and letters or the more common form of a list of points. Often this outline stands up throughout the writing. But sometimes, after the lead, the outline needs revisiting. In those cases, an interior outline may come in handy.

Interior outlines, often written after you have completed the introduction, organize the body of the story. Typically, they comprise three to five points, ordered logically and arranged in blocks.

Even if you have a strong main outline before you begin writing, my experience is that it helps to return to outlining after you have completed the lead and introductory segment. Having written the lead, you will probably now see the story differently. You have overcome what most writers feel is the hardest writing challenge—the lead—and are free to concentrate on the story's innards.

The process should not take much time. Consider how you have framed the story in the lead, and then determine what major points need coverage and in what order. Jot them down, in order, with any subpoints or supporting matter that you need. And decide, if possible, on your ending. Some writers have trouble conceiving the actual ending at this point, preferring to let it emerge during the momentum of writing. That's fine. However, even if you do not want to settle on an exact ending, you do need to know the overall point you are heading toward. Otherwise, you fly without direction.

Interior outlines can be simple. Here is an example. The topic: how newspapers have changed over the past generation. The focus of the lead: they have changed in many ways that will seem obvious but in other ways that will be surprising and perhaps even alarming. Once these decisions are made, the interior outline helps guide the writer in explaining and corroborating the focus. It looks something like this:

1. Overview of changes, documented with statistics
2. Changes in looks, content, and tone, documented with examples
3. One specific comparison: a paper in 1964 and 1999
4. Main reasons for the changes
5. Ending

Once you have an interior outline, you can craft your refocusing paragraph. Think of it as the lead to the body of the story. It is transitional in nature, linking the main section to the middle and ending. To use a more right-brain metaphor, the refocusing paragraph—sometimes called a *refocusing graf*—is also umbrellalike; it spans the whole project in a way that helpfully orients the reader.

Refocusing paragraphs can be written in many styles, but all generally share certain virtues. They move from what is *already known* to what is *new and upcoming;* they specify or at least hint at every major point that is to come; and they present points, usually in summary, in the same order as they will be developed in the body.

Take the common example of a school board story. The lead isolates the main point. Let's say it is a story reporting that anti-drug programs will begin in local elementary schools next year. The introduction will deal with the decision to institute these programs, the pros and cons, quotes from those who favor and oppose them, and so forth. Then, a refocusing paragraph can lead readers into the rest of the story.

Typically, a school board story might cover several other points. If the story has multiple points, the refocusing paragraph should become a roundup. It should begin with the known, perhaps something as simple as, "Besides the new anti-drug program. . . ." Then it itemizes the remaining key points the story will cover. For example:

> Besides creating the new anti-drug program, the board also raised teachers' salaries by 5 percent, adjusted boundaries for two middle school districts, and rejected a citizens' challenge to current high school history textbooks.

Perhaps the story is not a roundup. If the entire story is about one main action, such as the controversial anti-drug programs, then the refocusing paragraph might take a different form. For example, it might introduce a contextual look at how the new program came about:

> The decision climaxed a six-month controversy during which some parents' groups lobbied for the anti-drug education and others resisted imposing it on tender elementary pupils. Board members personally visited dozens of classrooms in nearby school districts using similar programs.

Refocusing paragraphs remain important in non-news articles as well, such as feature stories or profiles. They tend to come shortly after the nut graf and, as always, to preview in order the points to come. Let's say, for instance, that you have profiled a local professor whose research wins a major prize. The lead might focus on the turning point, the moment the professor realized her central experiment had paid off. By paragraph four or five, the nut graf would summarize the story's thrust, perhaps that a lifelong devotion to science, sometimes at the risk of ridicule and frustration, underlay the professor's triumph. The introduction completed, the refocusing paragraph then might signal the rest of the story as follows:

> For Prof. Blithers, passion for science began with the tiny bottles of chemicals she bought with her childhood allowance. It drew her through graduate training under the masters, a frustrating stint in private industry, and a second career as a professor that almost aborted during her first ill-fated research project.

Refocusing paragraphs launch the reader on the main stage of the journey. Their goal is to send the reader off both organized (knowing what points are to come) and interested (roused by the drama about to unfold).

FROSTY

Developing a story's architecture seems mostly an artisan's process. You are drawing on your capacity for orderliness and logic. But here, too, you should not forget to invoke some magic.

Consider the concept of Frosty. Imagining a snowman can apply your visual sense to organizing a body of copy. Almost universally, I suspect, people have similar mental images of Frosty: an affable snowman made of three large snowballs, a smallish one on top, a larger one in the middle, and the largest of all at the base.

Good stories are often created with a shape similar to Frosty's. They have three snowperson-like sections: a top that is usually relatively small, a transitional middle section that expands on the lead, and a bottom that is half full of detailed elaboration.

Each section serves a different purpose:

- **The top, the lead section, should be the clearest, most direct, most accessible portion of any article.** Think of Frosty's friendly face, the first sight that greets the viewer, establishing tone and personality and conveying the most notable impressions. This section, typically composing about a fourth to a third of the story, should be aimed at the most general segment of your target audience. It should touch on the most important point and every vital subtheme.

- **The transitional middle supports the lead section but adds to it.** At this point, a writer can assume that those audience members still reading are fairly committed to the story. They have digested the early summations, and now they want more. Here you can raise the level of complexity, both of ideas and language.

- **The final section welcomes a devoted set of readers, obviously deeply interested and thirsting for detail and depth.** Of course the writing should remain clear and lively at this stage, but the density level of information can increase, and the accrual of detail, which can drive off readers if it occurs too soon, becomes far more desirable here.

Now, please do not take this model too literally as a left-brain outline. As you can see, it is a kind of fattened-up inverted pyramid, and it does not necessary encourage a smooth narrative flow. Instead, look on Frosty as a useful artist's way to envision what many stories generally look like and to frame a mental image of what you want to accomplish at various points. Envisioning a three-stage, gradually intensifying story can help prevent you from letting everything after the first few paragraphs mix into a blur.

INTERCONNECTIONS AND TRANSITIONS

Another image that can help unify the artist's and artisan's approaches is that of a linked chain. Think how its pieces interlock. Each one physically connects to the piece before it and the piece after it, forming a whole that is difficult to break.

You can apply a comparable principle to writing. An article is like a chain in that it is strongest when each part connects firmly to those parts before and after it. Specifically, you want to give each paragraph some grammatical connector to its predecessor and its successor. We can call these devices *interconnections*. Because they help create a seamless and logical flow, interconnections make it harder for people to stop reading.

Among the best interconnecting devices are pronouns, synonyms, oppositional words, and repeated key words. Consider how one writer used each of these in the following article. The interconnections are capitalized:

> The first time Lanette Anderson left her daughter, Lindsay, at a day-care center, she was the one who CRIED.
> "I CRIED all day. I had to get used to leaving her," said Ms. Anderson, a nurse at Cabell Huntington Hospital. "I still feel guilty just because my MOM was always home with me. . . .

Ms. Anderson is one of a growing number of MOTHERS returning to work.
. . . And more working mothers are feeling GUILT over leaving their children
with others.

"I think the GUILT is there, and it's hard to resolve those feelings, . . ." said
Natalie Schneiderman, a psychologist. . . . "Their parents are saying, 'I stayed
home with you. Why don't you STAY home with your child?'"

Lindsay was 6 weeks old when Ms. Anderson LEFT. . . . She missed the first
time her daughter rolled over, and the baby sitter was the one who discovered
Lindsay's first tooth.

"THEY were the little things . . . but I was devastated. . . ."

(Rose Roccisano, *Huntington Herald-Dispatch*)[5]

Transitions serve a slightly different but related purpose from interconnections. Transitions help readers switch smoothly from one topic to another.
Instead of establishing a connection between ideas in adjacent paragraphs, a
transition helps hold the reader's attention by providing a logical bridge when
the subject changes. In general, interconnections are used within main sections of an article, and transitions occur between the sections.

Most of the time, simple transitions work best, one or two words when possible. In magazine-length articles, more-complex transitional sections, of a
paragraph or two in length, may be needed.

Here are some ways to create transition:

- *Linking words* signal the continuation or accumulation of a point—words
  such as *and, also, in addition, for example, similarly.*
- *Contrasting words* indicate a change of direction—words such as *but,
  however, on the other hand.*
- *Chronological words* show progression in time—words such as *next, then,
  a few hours later, the following day.*
- *Locator terms* show shifts in place—words such as *next door, a few miles
  away, elsewhere.*
- *Logical devices* prepare readers for a summation, conclusion, or effect—
  words such as *consequently, because, what it all meant, they now realized
  that.*

On the craft side, writers can anticipate the need for strong transitions by
considering them during the outline and interior outline stages. Once you
have an outline or a list of your four or five main points, you can plan your
transitions, note them on your outline, and place them as you write.

On the magic side, you can imagine your articles in web or flowchart form,
thinking of the transitions as the lines linking the panels or sections. Visually,

---

[5] Rose Roccisano, "The Day-Care Dilemma," *Huntington Herald-Dispatch,* 28 May 1989, 1D.

it is easy to see the impact of transitions. Without connecting lines, the panels simply float separately, like a group of helium balloons released into the air by schoolchildren. But once connected, they gain a unity that transcends the independent parts. Instead of seeing a series of individual and unpatterned objects, you find yourself picturing a single integrated structure made up of multiple related parts.

SHOWING CONSIDERATION FOR THE READER

So far, so good: great topic, lead, second paragraph, interior outline, refocus, and connectors. Even with this strong foundation, you still do not necessarily avoid the muddle.

Here, you might imagine two visions of the writer. One is from the realm of craft, the other from magic. First is the writer as mechanic or construction worker, lugging a toolbox or wearing one of those holster belts with assorted wrenches and pliers dangling from the pockets. This is, of course, a linear kind of writer, a writer as professional technician, certified to operate a set of tools and techniques and employ them as needed to fix the copy. This is nitty-gritty craftwork.

A second, more artistic concept is the writer as tour guide. Here we have a knowledgeable and personable companion, always ready to offer an observation or suggestion and constantly on duty to keep us fellow travelers on the proper course. Thinking of themselves this way, writers should act as the readers' friend, or at least ally, in a kind of host's role that requires good manners and helpful service.

Bear in mind these two concepts—the mechanic and the tour guide—as we examine some ways writers can tune their copy and assist the reader toward an orderly, rewarding excursion through the middle of a story:

- **Previews.** If a section or subsection will take more than a handful of paragraphs, then write a preview paragraph that introduces it and makes clear its range and scope. A preview works like a paragraph's topic sentence. It introduces the main point and establishes direction and tone. Readers need these paragraphs to help them see the general boundaries of the territory they are entering.
- **Wrap-ups.** Wrap-ups are the opposite of previews. They come at the end of a long or complex section and offer readers an opportunity to pause, catch up and take stock. Wrap-ups function like subtotals in a mathematical report. They sum up one section, fix it in the reader's mind, and give necessary perspective from which to evaluate upcoming information.

- **Signposts.** When you drive through unfamiliar landscapes, you regularly encounter helpful signs: "slippery when wet," "watch out for falling rocks," "don't feed the bears," and the like. Readers, like motorists, benefit from such guidance. One of the most functional things you can do is to share with your readers the intelligence you have about what is coming up. In a phrase or a sentence, you can signal that a key turning point is about to befall your protagonist, that the next section is complicated and full of statistics, that the tone of the adventure is about to change dramatically. The longer the story, the more signposts you should erect along the trail.

- **The buddy system.** Ever been on a hike or a field trip with a bunch of kids? Then you know the value of the buddy system, where individuals share responsibility for one another, and the expedition occasionally comes to a halt to count heads. Writers should consider themselves as readers' buddies, and should pause from time to time so everyone can regroup. Here is where we have been, here is where we are heading, here is a review of the story so far. When you think of it, neither writing nor reading can be truly solitary. Writing vanishes without a reader, and reading is impossible without a writer. In view of this mutual dependence, writers should project a strong sense of helpfulness and concern.

- **Scenes and connections.** A classic organizational device is to use scenes to slow the action and show your points. Scenes are often presented in present tense, a semblance of real time, with a minimum of writer intervention. For clarity, they are interspersed with connections. Connections speed things up, by summarizing, condensing large gaps of time between scenes, and letting the writer intervene with material the reader needs in order to appreciate or evaluate the scenes. We will discuss scene-setting in more detail during the chapter on feature writing, but it certainly belongs on any list of reader-service devices.

GOOD WRITING AT THE CORE

No matter how well an article is organized, it ultimately comes down to a series of words fit into sentences. As craftspeople, writers recognize the cumulative importance of perfecting this infrastructure. Good words make good sentences, and good sentences make good stories. A strong story tends to be a collection of good small parts assembled with care.

Focus, organization, and transition are imperatives of readability, but the importance of clear sentences cannot be overlooked. No matter how well-organized, an article will descend into murkiness if readers cannot make sense of its individual sentences.

In constructing clear and interesting sentences through the middle portion of copy, here are some guidelines writers find helpful:

- **Keep most sentences short** (under 25 words), but vary the pace and use short and long sentences for different effects. In general, use shorter sentences when explaining complex material. Use longer sentences when the going is not too tough. A common aphorism applies here: The more complicated the material, the shorter the sentence. Shorter sentences slow the reader and drive home meaning in a point-by-point fashion. Longer sentences supply variety and rhythm. They work best when the material is not heavy with data, for example in quotes where someone is expressing feelings or in a preview paragraph where general concepts, rather than precise details, are presented.

- **Limit most sentences to one main idea.** It is not really the number of words that makes a sentence difficult, but the number of ideas. The clearest sentences drive home one main point. A good rule of thumb is to limit most sentences to one main clause and no more than two subordinate clauses. Writing in this way is not a matter of "dumbing down" your copy but of respecting the cognitive processes all readers follow. It is easier for readers of all intellectual abilities to understand material that is presented one idea at a time, in orderly fashion. Stories that throw out too many ideas at once can confuse us all.

- **Stash the hot words in the hot corners.** Main points of emphasis of sentences and paragraphs are their corners—the beginning and the end. Concentrate your most potent words there, and you maximize their firepower.

- **Express main concepts in the main subject and verb of a sentence rather than in clauses and phrases.** Form and content need to work together. Central characters and important actions are the most important ingredients of most writing, so it follows that they should occupy the most important positions grammatically. Main characters should show up in the subjects of your sentences, key actions in the verbs. Avoid burying main points in secondary grammatical positions, such as in prepositional phrases or subordinate clauses.

- **Begin sentences and paragraphs with familiar ideas and references to what has already been written.** End sentences with new information or more-complex data. If you are changing the subject, do so toward the end of a sentence or paragraph.

- **Place quotes strategically.** They are most valuable when they accompany the dramatic high points of an article. Even a great quote can go to waste if it doesn't attend one of the article's major points.

- **Use details and examples to clinch points, not simply for decoration or because you are proud of finding them.** Attach them to the most significant points you want to make.

A TOUCH OF MAGIC

Writing is in part a craft, and thus it profits from attention to detail and from laundry lists like the one above. Bringing your artisan's discipline to bear on an article's middle will result in a better story. Middles are so often overlooked that even modest attention tends to improve them noticeably.

But, as you know, writing is also in part magic, the bounce that comes from free thinking and inspiration and bolts from the great beyond. So let your creative side help too. Think about the body of your story. Imagine what you want it to become. Draw diagrams to help you discover, and connect the points like branches to a tree trunk. Devote a portion of your noodling time to your interior outline, your refocusing paragraph, the components of the body of your copy.

As you visualize your story, stretch for the most creative ways to express the main points, dramatize the action, humanize the characters. The occasional flashes of magic that result can lift copy from the ordinary to the inspired.

SUMMARY

Shopping for a sweater not long ago, I spotted a handsome wool pullover. Like many browsers, I have my own ways of evaluating a potential purchase. I like to handle an item, hold it up, stare at it from different angles. When I looked closely at the sweater, something about the shoulder stitching caught my eye. Many of the threads seemed loose and off alignment. It made the sweater seem not quite fully finished. I didn't buy it.

Maybe the sweater had a murky middle. Maybe painstaking attention went into the overall design and coloring, but someone neglected the detailed follow-up.

Shopping for the sweater reinforced, from a different direction, a lesson the writing life is always dealing out. Attention to detail does matter. An article, like any other creative project, will suffer if the writer lets down. A murky middle can estrange readers just as fast as a dull topic or confusing lead.

To avoid murky middles, articles need a logical interior outline, orderly and interconnected paragraphs, and good transitions. The writer needs a controlling vision of the whole story, its component sections, and the best ways to tie the sections into something unified.

Both craft and magic apply. Through craft, the writer bears down on planning and executing good writing technique, making each section, paragraph, and sentence flow and connect. Through magic, the writer arranges these story parts with creativity and imagination and enhances them with inspired artistic touches. When all goes well, the outcome is writing that is both well-organized and exciting.

Practicing Craft and Magic

1. Select the front page of any newspaper and run the following tests on each major article:

   - Compare the leads and second paragraphs. Do the second paragraphs amplify the leads or stray in new directions?
   - Circle the nut grafs. Is any story missing a needed nut graf?
   - Underline transitions. Are they effective? What would improve them?

2. Run the same tests as above on the cover story of your favorite magazine.
3. Run the same tests as above on the next article you write.
4. Imagine the format of your next story as a set of shapes. Picture what each shape should contain and what the best arrangement of the material would be. To apply both craft and magic, blend your imagined story form into a written outline and then an interior outline.

Chapter 8

Writing
for
Clarity

When was the last time a reader complained that something you wrote was too clear?

The very idea seems laughable. Imagine angry phone callers venting their vexation at your ultraclarity . . . an e-mail bin brimming with messages assailing your accessibility . . . strangers accosting you at parties to protest your precision.

If this happens to you, it should make news. Criticism of clarity is a problem most writers never face. The problem lies at the opposite end of the clarity-obscurity continuum. We regularly discover that our writing has confused someone. Just the other day, a colleague commented on a review I had published of a well-known author's book. "Wow, you really let him have it," the colleague said. I was dismayed. I thought I had written a positive review.

Heed the lesson. Writing clearly is one of our greatest challenges, and we fail more often than we realize. The goal seems simple enough: to transmit a message from the writer's brain into the reader's with as faithful a reproduction as possible. But it is like being asked to carry a bucket full of water across a rickety bridge without spilling a drop. The execution is harder than the concept.

The preceding chapters have traced the writing process through several stages, from the idea through reporting and focus to the writing itself. The previous chapter ended with a look at the importance of sustaining quality throughout the body of copy. This chapter and the next one will elaborate on the two central challenges writers confront in constructing complete and compelling stories: making them clear and making them interesting. We will call these challenges writing for clarity and writing for drama.

Start with this declaration: *there is no such thing as too much clarity.*

Media writers deal with readers in a hurry. By definition, mass media audiences are large, diverse, often underinterested, and lacking in background. To confuse them is to lose them. As a writer, you are in the service business.

Your goal is to convey information accurately and accessibly. To achieve this goal in the face of all the obstacles to reading these days, you need to make it as easy as possible for people to start reading, to keep reading, and to understand what they read.

Why some writers resist this truth is something most teachers and editors cannot fathom. Countless times we hear writers cling to obscurity as a virtue and sneer at plain prose as "dumbing down" the copy. Let us be clear: there is nothing dumb about writing clearly. There is never anything to gain by confusing a reader. Readers are often turned off by overwriting, but few of us have ever seen a reader who felt insulted by clarity.

Still, we should not equate clarity with superficiality. Clarity does not enslave every writer to an unremitting diet of inverted pyramids and single syllables. Complex composition and varied structures have a noble role in narrative writing. Dramatic tension in storytelling often depends on a buildup of subtle points leading to a cumulative payoff at the climax.

Even in the most elaborate media narratives, however, clarity of purpose and expression should prevail. Each sentence should clearly connect with the harried reader. Every paragraph should communicate plainly. Writers should never embrace obscurity in some misplaced infatuation with pseudo-sophistication. Sophistication does not equal complication. On the contrary, the genius of great writing often lies in the ability to make difficult topics seem less complicated.

Here is the crucial point: a writer's themes can be complex, but the exposition should be simple. The ideas can be dense, but the articulation should be lucid.

Simple writing does not equal shallowness—it does not require forsaking serious journalism. Quite the contrary. Clarity is a tool that makes it possible for writers to undertake serious work. Making sense out of the complex lies at the very heart of the writer's art. Media writers struggling to remain relevant in a changing world cannot afford to sidestep the serious. Entertainment will always be a pleasurable part of the news media, but information is its soul. To renounce the obligation to guide readers through life's increasingly labyrinthine corridors would be a mortal miscalculation.

The object is not to avoid serious subjects but to make them accessible. The more demanding the subject matter, the more vital is clarity. Consider this question: which article would necessitate clearer writing, a report on tomorrow's weather forecast calling for rain or an analysis of the threat of global warming? Readers probably will understand even a mediocre article imparting the rain prediction, but a murky report on global warming will chase them off the page.

Clear writing begins with clear thinking. To write with clarity requires mastering the material. It is one thing to research a topic to the point where you generally comprehend it, but it requires far greater effort to reach a depth of understanding that lets you explain something to others.

Let me offer a personal example. When *USA Today* was created in 1982, I was one of its editors. With its colorful format, bold personality, and space-age vending machines, it immediately became popular with readers. Staff members found themselves invited to speak to audiences, who always wanted to know about the then-innovative practice of transmitting pages by satellite to printing plants around the country.

The first time I was asked about this process, I mumbled something about beaming pages to satellites that beamed them back down to the production sites. I realized that while I vaguely understood the concept, I was in no position to put it into words that others could grasp.

So I asked the paper's technicians to delineate the process for me in detail. I needed a deeper level of understanding before I could explain it to others. With their help, I developed a satisfactory explanation that went something like this:

> Every newspaper page is composed of thousands of dots. By designating which dots receive ink and which do not, we determine what any given page will look like.
>
> Imagine a simple code: If a dot is to receive ink, its code is a one; if it does not get ink, its code is a zero. Presses read the code for each page, apply ink to the appropriate dots, and the page emerges.
>
> For satellite transmission, a computer scans a page, determines its code, and converts the code into a simple electronic signal: one beep for dots with ink, no beep for dots without ink. It transmits that coded signal to a satellite. The satellite can then beam the signal to any printing plant anywhere. Once the plant has the code, it can print the page.

I learned something from this experience. It is hard to write clearly about things you only half-understand. Clear writing grows out of thorough reporting and processing. It is a virtue of all media writing, and its value skyrockets with the increasing degree of difficulty of an assignment.

To help you enhance your concentration on clarity, this chapter will first offer a test, then outline an overall strategy, and finally list a range of specific techniques.

A SIMPLE TEST FOR CLARITY

A clear sentence is one that readers understand. How do you know when a passage is clear? Try this test: ask someone to read a passage you have written and then to paraphrase it aloud.

If the writing is sufficiently clear, readers should be able to rework the material into their own words in a way that is accurate and understandable. If they cannot paraphrase correctly, then you have not yet clearly communicated.

Let's try an experiment. Read the following lead, adapted (mainly by changing the names) from an actual daily newspaper article:

> The $50 million Urban Arts Campaign may become a $30 million arts campaign. Reginald McGraw, cofounder of the two-year-old arts drive, has changed the conditions of his commitment.
>
> In April, the McGraw family and Wilde Industries pledged $2 million, up to $20 million, for every $3 million raised in the community toward the drive's $50 million goal. Now McGraw has tied this pledge exclusively to the construction of a proposed auditorium downtown.
>
> McGraw said yesterday, however, that "I believe that the possibilities of the auditorium happening are nil. . . . My commitment is moot."
>
> He said he would not redesignate his previously pledged $20 million toward the $30 million of the drive that is being raised in the community. . . .

Now apply the test: Try to summarize out loud what you have just read.

Does the lead pass the clarity test? Hardly. It has too many numbers, too many convolutions, and too many negatives. It lacks an overview sentence that crystallizes the core point. To effectively paraphrase it requires several very close readings.

How can you clarify a confusing lead? Try this three-step procedure:

1. First, *locate the meaning.* Read the entire article and determine the central overriding point.
2. Second, *express the meaning within the subject, verb, and object of the lead.* Use the strongest available grammar to convey the strongest point you want to make.
3. Third, *create a logic chain* that deals with the key points one at a time.

Let's try a rewrite:

> Local business leader Reginald McGraw may withdraw his $20 million pledge toward the Urban Arts Campaign.
>
> McGraw said yesterday that his pledge depends on a new auditorium being built downtown. But he predicted prospects for the auditorium are "nil."
>
> If the auditorium isn't built, he said, "My commitment is moot."
>
> McGraw's stance throws into question the entire $50 million campaign. In April, McGraw and his company, Wilde Industries, had pledged to contribute $2 for every $3 raised in the community. The goal was to raise $20 million from McGraw and $30 million from the community. City officials had hoped

that even if the auditorium were not approved, McGraw would designate his contribution for other arts purposes. . . .

Is the new version easier to understand and paraphrase? It seems clearly so, largely because the meaning now resides in the heart of the lead sentence. The subject *(McGraw)*, the verb *(may withdraw)*, and the object *(his pledge)* team to spotlight the main message.

STRATEGIES FOR CLARITY

Mainly, clear writing hinges on clear words and sentences. But you should not wait until you are at the keyboard to begin thinking about clarity. Clarity is cumulative. You should build it into your overall philosophy and approach, from the assignment stage through reporting and focusing. The precision of your sentences will be directly proportional to the clarity of thinking in your ideas, reporting, and story planning.

Think of it this way. Landing an airplane requires the execution of precise last-instant maneuvers with scant margin for error. But pilots set up a successful landing with a careful approach, completing a series of sequential operations that are prerequisite to touchdown. By applying an overall strategy that emphasizes clarity, writers too can improve their approaches. The more you concentrate on clarity throughout the process, the less prone you are to stray into the clouds and fog of murky writing.

Here, then, are some guidelines as you move through the writing process.

Don't Avoid Complex Subjects—Master Them

Clarity is not achieved by ducking tough topics and settling for the superficial. The writer's role is to tackle challenging subjects on behalf of readers who gladly pay for the service of explanation.

Sometimes the process resembles a trip up one side of a mountain and down the other. Writers, like readers, begin at ground level, with modest knowledge of the subject. Writers then undertake the arduous climb to the summit, learning all the way, until they stand triumphantly atop the mountain and the material. But they do not write from this remote Olympian peak. They travel with their newfound knowledge back to ground level, where they use their expertise to explain to others what they have learned.

Even when a topic is not overly complicated, writers must endure the tedium of thorough reporting before they can convert their knowledge into crystalline prose. For example, suppose your community hospital is one of three candidates for funds for a coveted new emergency room offering state-of-the-art trauma care. You cover an all-day meeting where the medical board debates all the proposals, in exhaustive technical detail, and selects a winner. Think about what you will hear: hours and hours of procedural deliberation, followed by an all-important vote that may take only a minute or two. Think about what your notes will show: page after page of preliminary process discussion, a recording of the final vote, and the few quotes you can gather as participants depart from the meeting.

If you rely unthinkingly on your notes, your story will mirror this ratio of process to substance. It will dwell on the complexities of the process (after all, that is what you spent all day listening to) rather than on the impact of the outcome.

What readers need, however, is an article stressing the decision and its consequences. As you sit through the deliberations, then, you must be absorbing the material to the point that you can condense the process into a tight summary and spotlight the decision. But you must also act affirmatively to get additional information to show the effect on readers. Clarity in this case will rely on your ability to transcend the potential pitfalls of the reporting system itself.

Think of Yourself as a Translator

One big reason so much writing seems unclear is that writers often reproduce the language of their sources too faithfully. Here is an actual example:

> Determination letter requests for certain defined benefit and target benefit plans will be considered by the IRS once the agency has settled on fixed safe harbor rules under Section 401(a)(4), an IRS official tells the Enrolled Actuaries meeting.

This lead appeared in a newsletter aimed at pension executives, so the writer presumably was dealing with a knowledgeable audience. Even so, the language bears little resemblance to English. It is bureaucratese, the lingo of the administrative class.

The problem here, it should be emphasized, is not with the sources. Specialized groups all tend to speak in their own technical language. Doctors, lawyers, athletes, musicians—and even journalists—rely on a professional shorthand easily understood by insiders. It saves them time.

Writers covering these groups also come to understand the jargon, as they must in order to understand their beats. Where they fail is by passing such language into their copy, inflicting it on lay audiences unfamiliar with the baffling codes and parochialisms.

It is barely an exaggeration to say that many sources speak what amounts to a foreign language. The writer must be a translator. To produce clear prose, writers must break down off-putting terminology into plain language, all the while (like any good translator) maintaining strict fidelity to the original intent and meaning.

The More Complicated the Subject, the Simpler the Form

When you think of complex writing forms, certain writers frequently spring to mind: William Faulkner, James Joyce, Isabel Allende. Why novelists? Novelists get away with complex structure, in large part, because they are not loading up their sentences with masses of fact. A Faulknerian paragraph may be entangled, but it is seldom dense with data.

Complicated form works best when a writer deals with feelings and overall themes. Simple form works best for facts and details requiring close attention and memorization.

Media writers need a balance of short and long sentences, simple and complex formulations. Not everything need be written in staccato fashion. For example, quotes can frequently run long because they tend to transmit ideas and feelings rather than hard particulars.

It may seem ironic, but the time to simplify form is when complications of content set in. A good strategy is to view the onset of a complicated topic as a yellow traffic signal: a warning to slow down. Short sentences, simple language, and one-idea-at-a-time exposition all increase in value as the topic grows more difficult.

Simplify Without Oversimplifying

Nothing that has been said so far gives writers a license to oversimplify. The clarity imperative never excuses inaccuracy and imprecision. Writers and their editors must be mad dogs for accuracy. Nothing is more important.

For that reason, achieving clarity is harder than it looks. Shortcuts with the facts are not allowed. To simplify is to help people understand the difficult. To oversimplify is to mislead and misinform.

How do you stay on the proper side of the line?

We can try the notion of *concentric circles* to illustrate the many ways of expressing a point. Think of it like layers of an onion. In the smallest inner circle, you start with the simplest possible explanation of a complicated concept. Gradually, you expand outward to larger and larger circles, adding information as you go. The writer's job is to select which circle, or level of explanation, best fits the story at hand.

For example, consider the theory of relativity. In the innermost circle, it could be described as a scientific explanation of the relationship among mass, motion, space, and time, represented in part by the familiar formula $E = MC^2$. In a short article, or if the theory is simply mentioned in passing, this explanation might be adequate.

Moving out to the second circle, you would add further details, maybe reaching a paragraph or so in length. In a magazine-style article, this level of explanation might suffice.

In each larger circle, you would add elaboration, until by the fifth or sixth circle you would have a definitive explanation, suitable for, say, a textbook. Each circle should contain precise and accurate information, but the larger circles will offer more detail and amplification. Writers select the appropriate level based on how much space they can devote.

If writers master their material at a fourth- or fifth-circle level, they can work backward toward the center in their efforts to simplify. As long as each circle contains precise and accurate information, you can simplify without oversimplifying.

Strive to Make It Easier Rather Than Harder for Your Readers

An editor once challenged a writer to explain an especially convoluted paragraph. "I don't know what it means," the writer confessed. "It's what the source said, and I decided to quote it exactly rather than risk getting it wrong."

The writer had succeeded in part of the job, getting the facts right, but had ultimately failed in the overall quest of helping the reader understand. As a writer, your role is to handle the hard work on behalf of readers, not simply to transfer the raw material to them for processing.

As petitioners, intruding on readers' time and patience, writers should feel an urgency about good service. It is easy to find parallels with other service professionals: teachers who can explain the mysteries of math, doctors who can describe each step of a complicated procedure, coaches who can articulate the steps to a good tennis serve. And it is easy to recall poor examples. Think of how annoying it is when you buy some new gadget and confront incomprehensible assembly instructions, or when an uppity car mechanic veers into technobabble to justify your $1,000 repair bill. Consumers respond to clear explication, and so do readers.

Clear writing is a vital competitive courtesy. It means extending a helping hand to hesitant readers, going out of your way to make it as easy as possible to read as much as possible of your work. Every writer has a selfish interest, if nothing else, in achieving that goal.

When in Doubt, Err on the Side of Clarity

This is a writer's foolproof mantra. You will never make a mistake by choosing clarity over confusion.

Many writers fear devolving into some sort of empty Dick-and-Jane kindergartenese, but in truth we all know how to stop short of that extreme. The problem is situated at the other end, the confusion extreme.

If the question of unclearness even occurs to you (or, yes, to your teacher or editor), take it as a warning. Err toward clarity. You will seldom regret it.

25 TRADE SECRETS FOR CLEARER WRITING

1. **Stress substance over process.** A key to clarity is cutting through the clutter and isolating the message your readers need most. As discussed above, writers spend a lot of time watching processes like meetings and hearings that take a long time to produce results. The results, not the processes, must drive the writing.

   CLOUDY: Expansion of the Water Reclamation Facility can be deferred at least 10 years, members of a citizens advisory committee concluded at a meeting Wednesday.
   CLEARER: Local taxpayers will save millions because reduced development and increased conservation are cutting water demand, a study group reported Wednesday.

2. **Install the main message in the main subject and main verb of a sentence.** Once you decide what you want to say, say it directly, by using the subject and verb of the sentence to convey the main point. Don't bury your action in a secondary phrase or clause.

   CLOUDY: The owner of vacant property on Highway 41 plans to lease the building to one of several interested businesspeople, with plans for an under–21 nightclub the leading candidate to fill the void.
   CLEARER: An under–21 nightclub could open within weeks in a vacant building at Highway 41 and Third Avenue.

3. **Choose concrete words and images.** Think of words such as *prison, sidewalk,* or *shark*. These are sometimes called *banana words* because, like the word *banana*, they conjure up specific, shared images for most of us. By contrast, consider words such as *proposal, facility,* and *problem*. These are sometimes called *fuzz words, blob words,* or s*econd-degree words* because they convey only abstractions. Readers can understand banana words standing alone, but fuzz words require other words before making sense. Especially in the first few sentences of an article, strive for the highest possible percentage of banana words and images.

   CLOUDY: Officials today will consider the city's proposal for tackling increasing traffic problems in school zones.
   CLEARER: State senators will decide whether to slap $250 fines on drivers who speed through school zones, where cars have hit three children this year.

4. **Go easy on the numbers.** Many articles require numbers, but good writers avoid tossing around too many figures at any one time. Some good rules:

- Avoid more than two large numbers in any one sentence.
- Do not bump paragraphs that contain heavy doses of numbers.
- When you can, display numbers in charts and tables rather than in copy.
- Tally totals first, before listing individual figures. Once readers know the bottom line, they can make better sense of its parts.

CLOUDY: The State Power Authority yesterday raised its pending $241 million rate increase request by an additional $16.2 million or about 30 cents a month per customer, to a total of 11%, saying that a 17% increase in fuel costs could produce third-quarter losses of $194 million.

CLEARER: The State Power Authority yesterday raised its rate increase request to 11%, blaming rising fuel costs. If granted, the hike would cost the typical customer $96 a year.

Follow this paragraph with a quote, not containing numbers, and then return to the numbers.

5. **Shorten sentences.** Try for an average sentence length of 15 to 20 words. For rhythm, some sentences should be shorter and some longer, but most should be under 25 words. Rule of thumb: use more periods, fewer commas. A good test: when you are tempted to insert a comma and keep a sentence going, try ending the sentence and moving to a fresh one for your next thought.

CLOUDY: Mayor Marquita Romano told City Council members Friday that her recent remarks about "crazy overspending" and "out-of-control give-aways" were not an attempt to intimidate the council, but rather were an effort to concentrate public attention on the importance of this week's budget hearings.

CLEARER: Mayor Marquita Romano denied Friday that she meant to intimidate the City Council with her recent remarks about "crazy overspending" and "out-of-control giveaways." Instead, she told council members, she was trying to focus public attention on the importance of this week's budget hearings.

6. **Limit the number of verbs per sentence.** Verbs are like chocolate eclairs: one or two are sublime but too many upset your system. Anytime you add a verb, you add an idea, something else for the reader to chew on. If a sentence contains more than three verbs, consider dividing it in two.

CLOUDY: Judge Adam Robinson ruled Monday that a local man who refused to stop mowing his lawn even after neighbors complained he was disturbing a pool party did not violate city noise ordinances.

CLEARER: A local man didn't violate the law by mowing his lawn during a neighbor's pool party, Judge Adam Robinson ruled Monday.

7. **Keep subjects close to their verbs.** A subject and verb beside each other make maximum impact, like two hands clapping together. The more words you put between the subject and verb, the more you muffle the force, like adding layers and layers of gloves.

   CLOUDY: A new pill, approved by the federal government after seven years of testing and costing about $10 per treatment, could reduce baldness by half, scientists said yesterday.
   CLEARER: A new $10 pill could reduce baldness by half, scientists said yesterday. It has been approved by the federal government after seven years of testing.

8. **Limit the number of clauses and prepositional phrases per sentence.** Adding phrases and clauses is a common way that writers, and also editors, try to cram too much detail into one place. Avoid overwhelming readers.

   CLOUDY: Smith said he decided to leave at this time because he believes the election of the next president "is critical to the future of this nation" and that it was important to make a commitment to the candidate at an early stage.
   CLEARER: Smith said he decided to leave now because the next election is critical and he wanted to commit early.

9. **Avoid multiple layers of modifiers.** Sometimes, in the eagerness to explain and attribute, writers overload sentences with parenthetical qualifiers.

   CLOUDY: No prison employee has contracted the human immunodeficiency virus as a result of a job-related incident, according to Lucille C. Rangers, the author of a series of reports on AIDS, done for the National Institute of Justice, a division of the U.S. Justice Department.
   CLEARER: No prison employee has contracted the human immunodeficiency virus as a result of a job-related incident, according to Lucille C. Rangers, the author of a series of reports on AIDS. The National Institute of Justice, a division of the U.S. Justice Department, sponsored the studies.

10. **Avoid stacked modifiers.** Placing too many modifiers before a word clutters a sentence, slows the reader, and muddles the message.

    CLOUDY: The towering, 18-story, 47,000-square-foot, $27.4 million, cross-walk-connected bank will dominate the city's skyline.
    CLEARER: The 18-story bank will dominate the city skyline. The $27 million tower will have 47,000 square feet and connect by crosswalk to nearby buildings.

11. **Use active voice to stress the main actor or action.** In active voice, the subject of the sientence acts; in passive voice, the subject is acted on.

Active voice has more clarity and vigor because it parallels how we think. "I played the piano" is a more natural expression than "the piano was played by me." Most sentences benefit from active voice.

CLOUDY: The loss of power and phone service in more than 50,000 homes was caused when lines across the region were blown down by winds.
CLEARER: More than 50,000 homes lost power and phone service when winds blew down lines across the region.

12. **Use passive voice to downplay the actor or to spotlight the recipient of action.** Beware a blanket ban on passive voice. Passive sentences serve well when you want to fudge on who the actor is. For example, in crime stories you often do not know or cannot say who committed the act. "A prominent business executive was murdered, and her husband was arrested" is an example; using active voice could make that sentence libelous. Passive voice also suits when the recipient of action outweighs the actor and needs to come earlier in a sentence.

CLOUDY: Electors chose George Washington as the first president of the United States.
CLEARER: George Washington was elected the first president of the United States.

13. **Limit *to be* verbs.** In good writing, energy hinges on power-packed verbs. Forms of the verb *to be* (*is, are, was, were, will be*, and so on) sap a sentence's life force. They express being rather than doing, rest rather than motion. Replace most *to be* verbs with action words.

CLOUDY: The new program will be of special benefit to the elderly, who are now less likely to use public transportation.
CLEARER: The new program will especially benefit the elderly, who ride public transportation less than younger people.

14. **Zap weak verb constructions.** If it takes several words to form your predicate, consider whether one word would do. Lock on to the word in the predicate with the most power, and build from there. Watch for such constructions as "took the witness stand to testify" (try "testified"), "engaged in heated verbal sparring with" (try "yelled at"), or "is in the process of cutting the staff" (try "is cutting the staff").

CLOUDY: Police Chief Martin Garcia held a press conference Thursday to announce the firing of his top deputy.
CLEARER: Police Chief Martin Garcia fired his top deputy Thursday.

15. Root out nominalizations. Look out for words ending in *-ion,* known as *nominalizations* because they are nouns made up of verbs with suffixes. Examples include "make a decision," "reach a conclusion," "take action." Using the root verb will power up your sentence: "decide," "conclude," "act."

CLOUDY: The judges have reached an official determination as to the winners of this year's local music awards.
CLEARER: The judges have determined the winners of this year's local music awards.

16. Cut down on jargon. As we have already discussed, jargon and insider language require translation. Political scientist James David Barber once watched an evening newscast and identified 31 expressions he found confusing to viewers, including "cottage industry," "most-favored-nation trade status," "tariff concessions," "cold shutdown," "Republican conference leader," and "long-range facility plan."[1] Where possible, replace jargon with clear, accurate wording; where jargon seems necessary (for example, when sources are using it so often readers cannot avoid it), then explain it.

CLOUDY: Police said Jones was treated for contusions and abrasions suffered during an altercation preceding his apprehension.
CLEARER: Jones was treated for bruises and scrapes suffered during a fight with police, authorities said.

17. Purge tag-along words. Tag-alongs hop onto a sentence for a free ride but contribute nothing. Notice how you can strike the last word in each of the following constructions and lose nothing: "traffic conditions," "thunderstorm activity," "canned food items."

CLOUDY: The school board has proposed more counseling activity by teachers to combat low enrollment problems.
CLEARER: The school board has proposed more counseling by teachers to combat low enrollment.

18. Curtail clichés. Clichés begin as fresh phrases, then become so overused that they bring no specialness to a thought. Writing coach Paula LaRocque lists two kinds, the old, common clichés like "sharp as a tack" or "slept like a log," and newer "fadspeak," like "deal with it," "are we

---

[1] James David Barber, "Not The New York Times: What Network News Should Be," *Washington Monthly,* September 1979, 19.

having fun yet?" or whatever expressions are hot on TV or in the movies.[2] Replace clichés with original phrasing.

CLOUDY: The governor today appointed a blue-ribbon commission to consider a full range of options for dealing with whopping increases in the state's budget.
CLEARER: The governor today appealed to three business executives and two consumers for ideas on reducing state spending, which has risen 12% this year.

19. **Banish euphemisms.** A euphemism is a deliberate obscurity, meant to lessen impact. In today's culture, many sources and spinmeisters specialize in manipulating language to sway the message. This can be subtle (talking about "reforming" a less-than-loved institution like the IRS, for instance) or brazen (referring to declining test scores as "negative gains"). In dirty politics, attack ads are labeled "comparative ads." In government, tax increases are called "revenue enhancement." In business, bad debts are referred to as "nonperforming assets." Amusement parks supposedly use terms like "protein spill" or "green alert" as code when someone throws up on a roller coaster.

CLOUDY: Mathers admitted in the interview that he "got too physical" with his 4-year-old son.
CLEARER: Mathers admitted in the interview that he beat his 4-year-old son with a leather belt.

20. **Clarify ordinary words used in overgeneralized ways.** Confusion can occur with common words as well as with exotic ones. What is an "above-average student," "an overwhelming majority," "a heavyset woman," or "a well-to-do family"? Writers usually mean something specific (a student with a 3.4 grade average, a candidate who won 73 percent of the vote, and so on), but readers do not necessarily share the definitions.

CLOUDY: The tornado touched down in a well-to-do neighborhood, injuring several people and moderately damaging a corner shopping center.
CLEARER: The tornado touched down in a gated neighborhood of $500,000 homes, injuring at least nine people and ripping the roof off a corner jewelry boutique.

21. **Provide direction before detail.** Especially when dealing with procedural matters (such as in covering government meetings), try to precede new material with an overview sentence giving readers a sense of the direction, effect or outcome. For example, before describing a complex

---

[2] Paula LaRocque, "Time to Banish Worn Cliches from Writing," *Quill*, March 1997, 31.

parliamentary move by a school board, let readers know that its effect was to delay the school superintendent's plan to merge school districts. Before detailing a multicar pileup on the highway, let readers know no one was seriously hurt. If readers know the general direction you are heading, then the details make more sense to them.

CLOUDY: The House Rules Committee, in an emergency meeting May 3, passed by voice vote a rule calling for a floor vote on a concurrent resolution that would scrap provisions in the transportation budget bill that allegedly discriminate against smaller counties.
CLEARER: The House Rules Committee gave a victory yesterday to those who oppose a transportation bill they say hurts smaller counties. In an emergency meeting, the committee passed a special rule requiring a floor vote on the issue.

22. **Establish a thought before modifying it.** Beware of introductory clauses and phrases that qualify a point the reader has yet to encounter. It is wiser to make the point first, then modify it. Veteran writing coach Roy Peter Clark recommends using the "right-branching sentence," in which the subject and verb come first (on the left side of the page), followed by the rest of the sentence (branching to the right).[3]

CLOUDY: Despite state laws and court decisions that seem to invalidate unannounced sweep searches on school property, a state court has refused to throw out evidence obtained when officers searched a teacher's car in the high-school parking lot.
CLEARER: A state court will let prosecutors introduce evidence obtained from a teacher's car, despite laws and earlier decisions that seem to prohibit unannounced searches on school property.

23. **Slow down.** When the going gets tough, good writers slow things down. Use some of these common methods to slow down your text. Present ideas one at a time instead of in bunches. Supply needed background. Define unfamiliar terms. Insert preview and summary paragraphs. Try an *outreach paragraph*, a readers' courtesy device by which writers bring a complicated article to a pause and provide helpful background, context, or explanation.

In the *Wall Street Journal*'s 1997 Pulitzer Prize–winning series on combating AIDS, Michael Waldholz reported on a key discovery. Doctors had found that AIDS resists treatment in part because the virus produces billions of new and different viruses every day. Then he offered this outreach paragraph:

---

[3]   Roy Peter Clark, *The American Conversation and the Language of Journalism* (St. Petersburg, FL: Poynter Institute, 1994), 8.

That meant that new mutant copies of HIV, some of them possibly drug resistant, were being produced every few minutes—and that the only chance of subduing the virus was a combination of several drugs attacking different parts of the virus, all at once.

(Michael Waldholz, *Wall Street Journal*)[4]

24. **Think ahead.** An article is necessarily a snapshot, fixed in time, but the topic at hand usually has a past and a future that readers need to understand. Many writers do better covering what has already happened (background) than what is coming (future spin), because covering the past is easier. After all, it has already happened and information is available. Covering the future calls for informed speculation and can be riskier. But because readers have a stronger interest in the future than in the past, writers must do their best to look ahead.

For example, suppose scientists announce a potential breakthrough in treating an affliction like breast cancer. The development is clearly newsworthy. The background is important (how was the treatment developed?). But questions about the future overshadow all else: when will the treatment become available, how much will it cost, who will have access, how should a potential patient sign up . . . ? Clarity requires answering as many of those questions as possible. When the answers are unavailable or speculative, at least share with your audience the best available information on when answers may come.

CLOUDY: Mayor O'Leary said that her proposal should eventually provide local citizens with "a tax decrease of some magnitude."
CLEARER: Mayor O'Leary said that her proposal would cut local taxes by 2% this year and 3% next year. City Council will vote on the proposal March 15.

25. **Use metaphors and comparisons.** As every teacher or poet knows, a central method of explaining the complex is to relate it to something the audience already understands. Consider the clear and powerful comparisons in the examples that follow.

Ambika Narula weighed just 11.3 ounces when she was born five months ago. She was 11 weeks premature, slightly bigger than a Snickers candy bar and three ounces lighter than a normal daily edition of the *Washington Post*.

(Marcus E. Walton, *Washington Post*)[5]

---

4 Michael Waldholz, "Drug Withdrawal: Dr. Ho's Next Step," *Wall Street Journal*, 17 December 1996; available from http://www.pulitzer.org/year/1997/national-reporting/works/9.html; Internet; accessed 10 November 1998.

5 Marcus E. Walton, "Tiny Md. Infant Shows She Can Beat the Odds," *Washington Post*, 7 August 1998, B1.

Because the brain exhibits such unpredictability, physicists refer to it as a chaotic system: While the overall pattern may be as predictable as the autumn leaves falling from a tree, the behavior of specific components remains as unpredictable as the precise path of descent taken by a specific leaf.

(Richard Restak, *Washington Post*)[6]

Finally, in all your writing, pay attention to the fundamentals. Careless mistakes undermine clarity. Do you notice dumb errors in magazines, newspapers and newscasts? We all do. Lazy errors probably outnumber ignorant ones, and they cause at least as much damage to clarity and credibility. Double-check your grammar, spelling, punctuation, usage, and logic, and you will reduce mishaps like the following:

- The *Washington Post*'s obituary describing a woman as "the owner of Norwich and Norfolk Terrier dogs who also did figure skating and played piano."[7]
- The *Wall Street Journal*'s front-page item noting that "the administration had become ensnarled in an flap . . . ."[8]
- The *Boston Globe*'s book review that resurrected the dead: "Bad health resulting from sheer overwork . . . killed him when he was only 58. Still, he carried on."[9]

SUMMARY

There is no such thing as too much clarity. A writer is a translator, who undertakes to master complicated topics and explain them to lay audiences, to simplify the complex without oversimplifying it, to err on the side of clarity rather than confusion. As topics grow more convoluted, the writer's form should grow simpler. Make it as easy as possible for readers to grasp your meaning. Do not memorize the list of strategies for simplifying. Internalize it, by constantly thinking about clarity as you conceive, report, write, and revise. Too many rules create potholes on the road to good writing; they rattle your brain. You should not try to apply every prescription as you go.

Instead, start by committing yourself mentally and emotionally to the primacy of clarity. Through craft, writers can apply a variety of clarifying techniques, many of which are listed above. Think of them as a tool set, and grab the ones that may help you. While writing, devote yourself to clarity without trying to recall every single rule. As you revise and edit, match your copy

6   Richard Restak, "The Endless Levels of the Mind," *Washington Post,* 2 November 1986, C3.
7   "Patricia Quigley Paige," *Washington Post,* 4 June 1996, B7.
8   "What's News," *Wall Street Journal,* 28 March 1991, 1.
9   Richard Altick, "Dickens: His Life and 'Hard Times,'" *Boston Globe,* 23 October 1988, 103.

against the guidelines. Move step by step in the direction of clarity, and your work will shimmer with precision.

Through magic, writers can summon help in moving toward understanding. As you walk or drive, shower or exercise, think about the complicated points you are trying to express. Talk them through with others or even with yourself. Strain to imagine fresh phrases, metaphors, or comparisons that will resonate with readers. Knead your explanations through increasing levels of clarity, seeking to produce irreducible meaning. The more you exercise your magical side, the more likely you are to receive the impulses of inspiration.

I will never forget the first time I saw the crystal-clear waters of the Caribbean, sparkling and limpid. Who could predict the joy of such a simple encounter? Perhaps readers feel a dash of the same delight on those rare occasions when they address copy of comparable purity.

Practicing Craft and Magic

1. Make a list of your favorite trade secrets from this chapter. Post it on a bulletin board or wall near the place where you write, and glance over the list before your next writing assignment. When you run across other tips for clarity, add them to the collection.

2. Analyze your writing, looking for patterns that reduce the clarity of your work. For example, perhaps you tend to overuse passive voice or jargon. Make a list of three recurrent problems. When you revise your next story, concentrate on reducing their incidence.

3. Keep a notebook with you at all times. Set your artistic side to work on finding clear and original ways to express complicated points. Record words, images, metaphors, phrases, and any other helpful ideas as they occur.

Chapter 9

Writing
for
Drama

At night, thieves play hide-and-seek on the rooftops of Los Angeles' warehouse district, a hidden corner of the city where disparate worlds collide and
Darwinian laws prevail.

Ill-bred wraiths, the burglars clamber from one building to the next in search
of air vents, attic doors, any place they can break in. There are petty bonanzas
to reap: stereos, shoes, tomatoes and oranges by the crate. . . .

When alarms go off, they scatter like wharf rats, shimmying down drainpipes
and disappearing through trash-strewn streets—gone before the police can get
there.

(David Ferrell, *Los Angeles Times*)[1]

Writing for drama means making and keeping things interesting. In this example David Ferrell piques interest by achieving the three qualities of excellence described in Chapter 4. He stakes out a strong *storyline*, an inside look
at an underworld few of us know about. He *surprises* us with an inventory of
unexpected specifics (the young thieves come down air vents, steal crates of
oranges). And he *stylishly* arranges the words (*clamber, shimmying*) and
phrases ("ill-bred wraiths," "petty bonanzas").

Leading us through the story, Ferrell sustains the drama beyond the first
few paragraphs. Throughout the piece, he unveils one nice writing touch after
another, applying a variety of devices that help hold readers: *scenes*, which
transport readers, via their imaginations, and imprint them with a strong sense
of place; *details*, which convey reality and surprise; *rhythm*, which provides
appealing literary quality; *quotes*, which add human voice; and *haunting
images and insights*, which help seal the meaning.

---

[1] David Ferrell, "Life in the Underbelly of L.A.," *Los Angeles Times*, 9 November 1992, 1.

Scenes

Rollie's nights are spent cooking on open grills and smoking crack, plotting warehouse raids or worrying about intruders. A religious man, he also has ample time to think about his soul. Before he moved from the bridge, he often bowed to pray with a lay minister who came to the bridge Tuesday evenings to lead the transients and crack addicts in Bible study.

"I believe in God," Rollie said one day under the bridge. But he lives by his own set of commandments. Sitting in his hooch, Rollie explained how he reconciles his religious convictions with his damned life as a thief and addict.

"Thou shalt survive," he said. . . .

Details

Startling tales abound: The warehouse that lost $80,000 in goods in a single night . . . break-ins accomplished with blow torches, or by ramming stolen vehicles into loading dock doors . . . $20,000 rooftop air-conditioning systems laid waste for $200 in trade at nearby scrap-metal yards. . . .

Rhythm

Here, weary truckers from across the country disembark for a few hours before gearing up again—their rigs often plundered by transients. . . . Here, intravenous drug users inject themselves in alleys while prostitutes troll for lonely drivers. Here, walled off from persistent thieves and intimidating beggars, a dwindling artist's colony holds on in paint-stained lofts once heralded as the vanguard of the city's artistic renaissance.

Quotes

Barbed wire is almost useless. "If they had an Olympic event for barbed-wire climbing, I've got some guys who could win," said land owner Howard Klein. "Not only can they get over the fence . . . but they can get *back* over the fence, with the batteries out of the trucks. . . ."

Haunting Images and Insights

To enter this domain, to roam the streets of the warehouse district as it spins through its hyperkinetic 24-hour dance of trucks and human jetsam, is to undergo sensory bombardment—to be assaulted by the pungent odors of vegetables, urine, beer, sawdust and diesel fumes; to feel the shuddering gears of the city. . . .The fallen are everywhere—ghost men, phantom women, drifting through the district's ravaged tableau as if time and memory mean nothing. . . .

In a "how I wrote the story" memo written for Bob Baker, an editor at the *Los Angeles Times,* Ferrell described an archetypal process of craft and magic. After months of reporting, filling 14 notebooks, he faced a mass of material and observations. How could he make sense of it all?

"It was difficult conceptualizing how all these elements fit together," Ferrell wrote to Baker. "An important insight was to realize that this was really a land of outcasts. That theme guided many of my latter interviews and became a subtle but, I think, critical element in tying the story together and giving it a focus.

"Often, on long and complex features or profiles, especially when there is no real news hook, I find myself going through this mental ordeal, trying to understand the subject at its most fundamental level. And if I'm lucky, after some days of introspection, the subconscious mind coughs up an answer."

In this case, Ferrell said, it took "three or four days" to hit upon his lead. "The 'hide-and-seek' line seemed somehow perfect," he said, "adding a touch of the surreal while accurately conveying the activity I was describing. It was probably one of the few inspired insights of my life."[2]

From overall concept to line-by-line phrasing, Ferrell combined hard craftwork and the magic of inspiration. He reported thoroughly, combed his material for larger truths, and called on his subconscious for the all-important boost at writing time. His story illustrates an abiding principle of writing for drama: the writer strives for drama in both the overall approach to a story and in the individual sentences that bring it to life.

With that canon in mind, this chapter will examine some attributes of dramatic writing, some steps writers can take during reporting and focusing to heighten drama, and some specific techniques writers can apply in the sentence-by-sentence final round.

WHAT MAKES DRAMATIC WRITING?

Strong writing grabs readers and won't let go. Writers use numerous instruments and effects to vitalize their work. The common goal is to make things interesting, but there is no single guaranteed route to the reader's fancy. Drama comes from the impeccable detail as well as the big idea, from the bombshell revelation as well as the accumulated weight of the whole. One constant is the effort to keep the work interesting.

Before turning to operational specifics, then, a writer might ask a strategic question: what kinds of things do readers find interesting? If you can pinpoint some properties of dramatic writing, then you can strive to assimilate them into your thinking and writing.

Dramatic writing does tend to exhibit certain qualities. You can remember them by using the acronym SIFT:

---

[2]   David Ferrell, "How I Wrote the Story," included in material received from Bob Baker, *Los Angeles Times,* 11 October 1993.

Surprise
Impact
Force
Tension

Surprise

Chapter 3 discussed surprise in a somewhat larger context, noting that great stories need to be full of surprises. Here we have in mind something similar but narrower: the simple word, sentence, or paragraph that involves readers in a process of discovery. In this context, surprise tends to come from the unusual (something new, unexpected, unknown) or from new insights into the usual (something revisited, challenged, seen in a different light). A good surprise is a reader stopper. It halts the momentum sweeping the eyes across the page, and it flicks a switch in the reader's imagination.

It the excerpts that begin this chapter, for example, Ferrell achieves surprise from the very beginning, by showing us Los Angeles night life in a new and different light. The biggest surprise in his story, you might say, is the idea itself.

Impact

Dramatic material should stand out. It should not be buried, muffled, or muddied. Writers want to wring the maximum punch out of every point. In conceptual terms, and sometimes literal ones, good material should be spotlighted, underlined, or italicized. It should build into peaks or punch lines. It should fix in readers' minds visions or images or impressions. It must get their attention.

Look back at the paragraph from Ferrell's story labeled "Details." Notice how he achieves impact by assembling several pointed specifics into one powerful paragraph.

Force

If you have ever ridden a roller coaster, then you know about force. The train rumbles up the hill, straining and grunting with unmistakable eruptive buildup, and in the dizzying moment of release you are flung forward with heart-pounding power. Dramatic writing needs a comparable propulsive force. It will not actually sweep readers over hills and through loops, but it should generate a parallel form of mental motion, a dynamic steeplechase through a theme park of ideas.

Force tends to come from a blend of material and writing. In the Ferrell story, re-read the paragraph labeled "Haunting Images and Insights." The language itself seems to have energy (notice phrases such as "its hyper-kinetic 24-hour dance" or "the shuddering gears of the city"), and its power is magnified by the force of the human drama being described.

Tension

Dramatic tension makes readers want to know more. It gives them an intellectual or emotional stake in how things play out. Like a well-plotted novel, dramatic media writing attaches itself to universal themes such as life and death, winning and losing, alienation and reconciliation, challenge and triumph. Some line of narrative tension should throb just underneath every piece of dramatic writing, prodding the reader forward toward resolution.

In Ferrell's story, a central tension surrounds the rather appealing characters and their outlaw lifestyles, a troubling conflict Ferrell captures in the section labeled "scenes."

No formula will completely explain the mysteries of dramatic writing, but the SIFT model can help by making the goal less abstract. By associating the notion of "interesting writing" with a definite set of attributes, writers can create targets on which to concentrate. The targets give writers' minds some direction, in both conscious and subconscious realms. They are then ready to apply both craft and magic in the service of drama.

STRATEGIES FOR DRAMATIC WRITING

During my short career helping coach kids' baseball, I learned a lot. One day I shouted out to my team's pitcher, who had walked several batters, "Just throw strikes." I vividly remember his look of disgust as he yelled back, "You think I'm trying to throw all these balls?"

In writing as in baseball, figuring out what you want is the easy part. Just as every pitcher wants to throw strikes, every writer wants dramatic copy, which is not hard to recognize or to describe. Producing it, however, challenges the best writers every time they step up.

Craft and magic can help. Through craft, writers can apply tested techniques that enliven their work. Through magic, they can open themselves to the mighty artistic leaps that give stories extra gusto.

Imagine the following continuum:

Reporting ⟶ Seeing ⟶ Understanding ⟶ Communicating

Writers glean drama from their material, so good reporting is essential. But reporting cannot be passive and mechanical. It requires a constant processing and reprocessing of the intake. The cozy routines of asking questions, jot-ting down answers, and collecting the paperwork yield data but not drama. Writers need to surround a story with observational intensity, to probe every angle, peer into every cranny, penetrate toward the innermost layers and deepest waters. They must see as much as possible because eventually seeing leads to understanding, to epiphanies of insight that drive stories upward. By achieving breakthroughs in understanding, writers position themselves to communicate higher truths.

Here, craft and magic work in tandem. Craft, as usual, leads the way. You can actively work at reporting in-depth, analyzing information, and searching for insights. The more energy you devote to craft, the more open you become to flashes of magic, to moments when the subconscious suddenly forges together some chain of specifics, rewarding you with unexpected completion.

Denise Reaman, a reporter for the Allentown, Pennsylvania, *Morning Call*, once described how much of herself she puts into her research. On one story, reported over several weeks, she returned time and again to a graveyard where a murder victim had been buried. Often, she simply sat, watching, listening, concentrating, a process she called "sensory reporting."

"The best work I do," Reaman said, "is when I really open up not just my ears but my eyes and my nose and my sense of touch. You have to take the story on a more personal level so you are actually living it or experiencing it. It inspires me to write because I actually feel like I'm living in the story."[3]

As writers progress through these intense reporting and planning steps, it is important to keep good records. Unless you store it somewhere, the germ of an idea that skitters across your brain on Monday will be forgotten by Wednesday. Many writers block off a section of their notebooks to record words, phrases, or images that occur to them. Almost all keep pads or tape recorders in their cars, near their beds, and in other locations where ideas might occur. At least one keeps at bedside a pen equipped with a small flashlight. Many use an open-ended computer file where they simply type in words, phrases, and ideas that happen to strike them. Others use handheld computer units that allow for recording or keying in messages.

The reporting-to-writing process is seldom seamless, but the earlier stages undoubtedly feed the later ones. At whatever point in the process you happen to be working, the writer part of you needs to stay alert for the key ingredients of drama. Dramatic material can arrive in many ways. Sometimes it comes in direct revelations to the writer: driving to work you may think of a good example for a pending article. Sometimes the revelations come to your sources, and you must uncover them through reporting.

---

[3]   Denise Reaman, interview by the author, 23 March 1998.

Sometimes you know exactly what your article lacks. Some writers compile a written list of items that they need (for example, a strong quote to back up the main point or a graphic phrase to describe a key scene). Wherever they go, they carry on an ongoing scavenger hunt for these elements.

At other times you cannot reduce your needs to such a neat checklist. Perhaps you simply feel vaguely dissatisfied with a project but do not know why. Writers frequently find themselves feeling that they have not quite arrived at their writing destination, even though they cannot pinpoint where they fall short. In those cases, they revisit areas where drama tends to reveal itself. The process is a little like what you do when you misplace your television's remote control. You know its three or four favorite hiding places, and you search there first. This may seem simpleminded but it helps. When you are stuck, return to the most reliable sources you know. Among the prime points of origin for drama are the following:

- **Clicks of insight**—instants when something suddenly takes on a wholeness or a new meaning, as if an all-powerful focus knob had magically been adjusted
- **Crossroads or turning points**—places where your source or your story moves irreversibly in some important new direction
- **Crises or climaxes**—points where thought and action reach highest pitch and utmost drama
- **Solutions and resolutions**—actions that bring closure or at least presage an outcome

Through some or all of these methods, the writer's objective is to collect material that moves toward meaning. The next step is to communicate the best material in the most meaningful way.

25 TRADE SECRETS FOR DRAMATIC WRITING

Raw material is not finished goods. Once writers have collected their gems and jewels, they need to show them off, to bedazzle the reader with polished finery. Here are some ways to do it.

1. **Feature real people doing real things.** As Tom Wolfe and others have often reminded us, people enjoy reading about other people, especially the real-life trials and triumphs that at times engulf us all. Here is a simple but power-packed "this could happen to anybody" example, which opens a window into what we all recognize will be a harrowing world. Notice the blow delivered by the electric phrase "pea-sized lumps":

Dee's life changed one morning in the shower as her hand moved over three pea-sized lumps in her right breast. Nothing that followed was as simple.

(Delia M. Rios, *Newhouse News Service*)[4]

In the next example, a University of Missouri student writer uses strong words and everyday detail to show with excruciating ordinariness how an illness disrupts life:

Forrest Rose's eyes opened wide for the first time in more than two weeks . . . . He was tired, disoriented and the place on his shorn head where they had cut into his brain hurt like hell. It was a warm spring day, 16 days after a brain aneurysm slammed him against a wall and dropped him to the stage of a Nashville bluegrass parlor. He was in the middle of playing a solo to "Sweet Georgia Brown" on his stand-up bass.

(Brian Wallstin, *Columbia Missourian*)[5]

2. **"Let's go to the videotape."** When television producers want your attention, they speed you directly to the action. Good writing makes readers see what is happening, through the power of imagination. Here is a gripping episode from "South of Heaven," a detailed look at one year in a local high school:

John is walking through the neighborhood . . . carrying some schoolwork—he has already retrieved the .32 from its hiding place and has it inside his pants, just in case—when he runs into the dealers. . . .

"What you all waiting for?" [one dealer] says to the others. "Let's get him. . . ."

Suddenly John hears these sharp pops, like firecrackers going off. At his left side,where he's carrying the textbook for Mr. Feazell's history class, he feels the impact of something hitting the book. . . .

There is no other way to look at it. He has been saved by history. Spared by a book. Protected by Mr. Feazell, who always manages to look out for him, even from a distance.

(Thomas French, *St. Petersburg Times*)[6]

3. **Create storylines.** Earlier chapters have stressed the importance of an overall storyline. Sometimes writers can snag attention simply by making

[4] Delia M. Rios, "This Is What Breast Cancer Looks Like," series reprint (Washington, DC: Newhouse News Service, 1994) 4.
[5] Brian Wallstin, "From the Bass to the Basics," *Columbia Missourian*, William Randolph Hearst Foundation Journalism Awards Program, January 1992, first place.
[6] Thomas French, "The History Lesson," *St. Petersburg Times*, 19 May 1991; special reprint, Day 5, page 6.

the storyline explicit in a phrase or two. Sarah Pekkanen, writing in the *Baltimore Sun* about one weekend at a group's beach house, announced her storyline as "twenty- and thirtysomethings about to converge in a swirl of booze, junk food, sun and seduction."[7]

Sometimes storylines are more elaborate. Consider this tour de force by a Pulitzer Prize–winning reporter, who evokes the soul of New York City in his first nine words:

In a city of disconnected lives and romantic possibility, it was hardly a remarkable beginning: a wine tasting on a spring evening, a swirl of Beaujolais and conversation, a lovely separated woman and a lonely divorced man, strangers with savoir faire and talent, bruised but still open to a relationship.

(Robert D. McFadden, *New York Times*)[8]

Introducing a magazine-length report on the San Francisco earthquake of 1989, writer Gary Blonston combines mundane daily routine and historic sweep into a panoramic storyline:

It began 11 miles beneath the surface of a nearly anonymous hump in the Santa Cruz Mountains, at 5:04 p.m. on a bright Tuesday afternoon. It happened as the Bay Area's workday was coming to an end, as people across the nation were tuning in for the third game of the World Series at Candlestick Park, as traffic was mounting on Interstate 880 in Oakland and life on Santa Cruz's Pacific Garden Mall was easing into evening. It happened just as the experts said it would, give or take a few decades.

(Gary Blonston, *San Jose Mercury News*)[9]

4. Take people places they have never been. Take readers new places, tell them new things. This is the essence of surprise. In a Pulitzer Prize–winning effort cited below, Tim Weiner broke through layers of bureaucratic concealment to introduce readers to the Pentagon's supersecret "black budget":

That [budget] includes some of the most expensive and fantastic projects on the Pentagon's books, including expanding plans for World War III and World War IV—that's right, World War Four. The plans include robots stalking radioactive battlegrounds, satellites orchestrating nuclear attacks and generals speeding along in lead-lined trucks, ordering warheads fired from faraway

---

[7] Sarah Pekkanen, "Beach House Blitz," *Baltimore Sun*, 6 September 1998, 8F.

[8] Robert D. McFadden, "Brief Romance, Growing Fears, Then 2 Deaths," *New York Times*, 9 April 1994, 1.

[9] Gary Blonston, "We Will Never Forget," *San Jose Mercury News*, 22 October 1989, 1B.

silos. . . . Its scope ranges from multibillion-dollar Air Force bombers to a project aimed at training dolphins as underwater saboteurs.

(Tim Weiner, *Philadelphia Inquirer*)[10]

5. **Foreshadow.** You cannot tell readers everything at once, but you can
   leave clues that signal tone and direction. In this article about child
   molesting, the writer chills us with bare-bones description and an omi-
   nously off-kilter point of view:

> He first saw the boy riding a bike in the warm air of spring, pedaling past
> the small, identical houses with the small, identical lawns in their suburban
> neighborhood.
> The boy didn't notice the man, who sat in a rocking chair on his front
> porch. But the man followed the boy's every move, smoking one Marlboro
> after another, draining glass after glass of Pepsi.
> He could not take his eyes off the child.

(Frank Bruni, *Detroit Free Press*)[11]

6. **Bridge from the specific to the universal.** An earlier chapter stressed
   the impact that comes from moving from the physical to the metaphysical.
   Below are two examples in which writers show a specific physical scene,
   then connect it to a larger thematic insight. Their technique is first to
   accumulate meaningful details and examples from a single case and then
   to construct a sentence or so showing how the individual case links to a
   more universal point.

   First, Laura Blumenfeld writes about the life and death of Teresa
   McGovern, daughter of onetime U.S. senator and presidential candidate
   George McGovern:

> The battle for Terry began at age 13, when she drank a Colt 45 with a cou-
> ple of friends. She stood on her head, for a bigger rush. Giggling, she did a
> cheerleading jump off a ledge but forgot to put her feet together. She landed
> on her back and chipped her tailbone.
> For the rest of her life, the pattern held: a moment of soaring, a backbreak-
> ing crash.

(Laura Blumenfeld, *Washington Post*)[12]

In the second excerpt, the writer portrays a typical domestic scene, then
zeroes in on what makes it so precious to a mentally retarded couple who
almost lost their children:

[10] Tim Weiner, "A Growing 'Black Budget' Pays for Secret Weapons, Covert Wars,"
Philadelphia Inquirer, 8 February 1987, 1.
[11] Frank Bruni, "Twisted Love," *Detroit Free Press,* 31 August 1991, 1.
[12] Laura Blumenfeld, "A Death in the Cold," *Washington Post,* 5 February 1995, F4.

Randy Travis is on the radio, singing about unrequited love, but nobody in the house on Coalbrook Street is listening.

Radiant in her frilly pink dress from Sears, 5-month-old Jessica forms a toothless smile and looks into her mother's eyes.

Veronica Hornbeck gives the girl a playful squeeze.

"Mommy loves you," she coos. "You're my little one."

These are the moments Ralph and Veronica Hornbeck almost never had.

(William Miller, *Spokane Spokesman-Review*)[13]

7. **Frame the point for the reader to see.** If you own a painting master-piece, you display it on a prominent wall and illuminate it with distinctive lighting. If you serve a magnum opus to readers, give it the equivalent special treatment. Make it stand out.

The *Huntington Herald-Dispatch* opened a story about a deadly lovers' quarrel with several paragraphs of description. Then came this plain but memorable framing sentence: "This is the story of Tracy and Stephen and what happened when their love died."[14]

The Economist, a serious but at times puckish magazine, used a tongue-in-cheek tone plus quotes and details to frame an unusual news development:

On August 15th, Timothy Boomer fell out of his canoe. Naturally, he cursed, using "loudly and repeatedly . . . a most offensive vulgarity." . . . He was in the middle of nowhere at the time, in a wilderness area of the Rifle River near the Jack Pine Trail in Michigan. Imagine his surprise, therefore, when a deputy sheriff . . . promptly issued him with a ticket for swearing.

(*The Economist*)[15]

8. **Don't mince words.** When your material speaks for itself, stay out of the way. The most potent messages often need nothing more than plain English. Below, two writers summarize a lengthy investigation into child abuse with piercing bluntness:

It is easy to kill a child and bury the secret.

Throughout America, poorly trained coroners and shoddy death investigations are helping mothers and fathers get away with murder.

(Rochelle Sharpe and Marjie Lundstrom, *Gannett News Service*)[16]

---

[13] William Miller, "Family Finds Hope," *Spokane Spokesman-Review,* 11 April 1994, H1.

[14] Jeanne Curry and Mickey Johnson, "A Day of Rage," *Huntington Herald-Dispatch,* 29 May 1988, 1A.

[15] "Incident at Rifle River," *The Economist,* 2 January 1999, 29.

[16] Rochelle Sharpe and Marjie Lundstrom, "Getting Away with Murder," in *Best of Gannett 1991* (Arlington, VA: Gannett, 1992), 26.

9. **Show through scenes.** Scenes help readers experience material directly, without the writer's intervention. In most writing, the writer is telling a story to the audience; when scenes are used, the audience at least simulates the feeling of seeing for itself. Here, *Rolling Stone* takes us behind the curtains with the rock group Aerosmith:

> Backstage, Steven Tyler is getting ready to go on, meticulously applying cake eyeliner to his lids and blowing it dry with a Conair 1000. His mirror has a sticker on it that says: STEVEN TYLER KICKS ASS. While he's putting on his makeup, he's listing complaints to his stage manager: the monitor mix is lousy, there's a light missing. . . .
>
> "The problem with rock & roll today," Tyler opines, putting the final touches on his eyes, "is that nobody wants to move. . . . Onstage they just stand there. . . ."
>
> He shakes his head, bewildered. Moving is the thing that Tyler does best.
>
> (Daisann McLane, *Rolling Stone*)[17]

Radio writing often depends on scenes because of the medium's need to help listeners "see" with their minds. In a report on a trend toward do-it-yourself funerals, Jacki Lyden of National Public Radio used simple understatement to describe this moving scene:

> Last summer, George Foy stood in a crematorium in Cambridge, Massachusetts, clutching a small, white box. Inside was his month-old baby's body. It was the final moment for father and son. From the time the child had died two weeks earlier, Foy decided he wanted to take care of the baby's body himself. . . . He held his son's coffin until the last possible moment before placing it himself on the crematorium's roller. . . .
>
> (Jacki Lyden, "Morning Edition," NPR)[18]

10. **Find the "significant trifle."**[19] Media writing is reductive; because writers cannot publish everything they know, they have to simplify. So they seize on self-contained episodes, anecdotes or vignettes that carry larger meaning. George Plimpton, alluding to Ernest Hemingway's style, called them "small details, intimately preserved, which have the effect of indicating the whole."[20] Perhaps the most heralded example in literature

---

[17] Daisann McLane, "Aerosmith's Train Keeps a Rollin'," in *The Best of Rolling Stone* (New York: Doubleday, 1993), 266.

[18] Jacki Lyden, "Do It Yourself Funerals," "Morning Edition," National Public Radio, 8 December 1997; available from http://www.npr.org/programs/death/971208.death.html; Internet; accessed 5 June 1998.

[19] I have seen the phrase "significant trifle" attributed to John Galsworthy and used without reference by numerous writers, but I have not found the original reference.

[20] *Writers at Work: The Paris Review Interviews,* 2d series (New York: Viking Press, 1963), 236.

comes from Marcel Proust's *Remembrance of Things Past,* in which the narrator tastes a small pastry and is overwhelmed (for the next 3,000 pages) with sensory memories of his childhood, all touched off by the flavor of the pastry.

Significant trifles often draw a gasp or a "wow" from readers. Some examples:

- In a *Sports Illustrated* profile detailing the relationship between Muhammad Ali and his best friend Howard Bingham: "he even went along on one of Ali's honeymoons . . . at the invitation of the bride."[21]
- In an investigative article on the government's war on drugs: "Florida lawmen say they don't want to be transferred to Miami because all the drug money circulating there has driven the cost of living too high."[22]
- In a *Washington Post* report on children's reactions to their father's imprisonment: the children "sprayed his cologne on the pillows before climbing into bed."[23]

An all-time favorite example comes from a *Tulsa Tribune* look at evangelist Oral Roberts and his fixation on finances:

When Oral Roberts was elected king of his sixth-grade class in a rural school near Ada, he sold newspapers to earn $2.16 for a shirt, overalls and tennis shoes for the coronation.

The youngster, wearing his brand-new outfit, was stunned when his teacher suggested he go home and put on his good clothes.

. . . the incident made a lasting impression.

"He hates poverty like he hates sin and the devil," asserts Harold Paul, longtime Roberts friend.

(Mary Hargrove, Grant Williams, and Pam Infield, *Tulsa Tribune*)[24]

11. Create clever metaphors. Inventive wordplay can both charm the reader and impart meaning. Writing about Frank Sinatra, Richard Harrington of the *Washington Post* observed that the singer's aging "made no difference, because fans always heard him with the innocence of yesterday's ears."[25] Profiling a far different vocalist, the *Toronto Globe and Mail*'s Jan Wong termed Raffi the "troubadour to the thumb-sucking set."[26]

---

[21] Frank Deford, "The Best of Friends," *Sports Illustrated,* 13 July 1998, 85.

[22] Sharen Johnson, "Signposts of Failure Measure the Problem," Gannett News Service, in *Best of Gannett 1983* (Rochester, NY: Gannett, 1984), 12.

[23] Hanna Rosin, "Unfinished Parable," *Washington Post,* 15 November 1998, A1.

[24] Mary Hargrove, Grant Williams, and Pam Infield, "Evangelical Empire," *Tulsa Tribune,* 3 February 1986, 2.

[25] Richard Harrington, "Sinatra, On the Record," *Washington Post,* 17 May 1998, G1.

[26] Jan Wong, "Troubadour Raffi," *Toronto Globe and Mail,* 23 January 1997, C1.

And in an award-winning piece for the *Louisville Courier-Journal*, C. Ray Hall found these words to describe a bounty hunter:

Ray Meredith has the perfect face for a bounty hunter.
It is absolutely unmemorable. Superior in its averageness. . . .
Meredith stands 5 feet 8 inches tall and weighs 195 pounds, with the inevitable puffiness that comes to 43-year-old men who work too much and work out too little. He wears a hearing aid. He looks like the kind of person who vacations in a Buick, stopping at cider stands.

(C. Ray Hall, *Louisville Courier-Journal*)[27]

12. **Choose comparisons that carry the spirit as well as the content.** The last chapter discussed how using comparisons can help make copy more understandable. Here's an example of how comparisons can upgrade the voltage of writing, and add edge to your point:

The nation's war against narcotics traffickers has been waged the past 10 years with all the success the previous decade's soldiers enjoyed against the Viet Cong.

(Sharen Johnson, *Gannett News Service*)[28]

13. **Scatter tidbits and jellybeans.** Readers appreciate the small rewards that writers can bestow throughout copy. Like encountering the prize in the Cracker Jack box, nothing jostles the reader forward like the occasional bonus-at-the-bottom. Chancing onto one of these nuggets is like catching a foul ball at the stadium.

In a magazine profile discussing how muckraker Jack Anderson doted on his children, for example, Walt Harrington offered this trinket: "He'd always stop whatever he was doing when a child entered his office at home. . . . He once put President Kennedy on hold."

The *Anchorage Daily News* wrote about a U.S. boat crew held for a week after straying into Russian waters. Deep into a description about the rigors of captivity came this winning change of pace: "The Soviets also ate all their candy. . . ."[30]

14. **Use quotes to add fact or feeling, especially at the high points.** Quotes, like jokes, can beguile or land with a thud. Placing them well is an art. First, a good quote must *add* something—some information or point of

---

[27] C. Ray Hall, "The Life of a Modern-Day Bounty Hunter," *Louisville Courier-Journal*, in *Best of Gannett 1990* (Rochester, NY: Gannett, 1991), 38.

[28] Johnson, "Signposts of Failure Measure the Problem," 12.

[29] Walt Harrington, "The Making of a Muckraker," *Washington Post Magazine*, 10 June 1990, 46.

[30] Ronnie Chappell and Richard Mauer, "Curiosity Led Frieda K. Crew into Captivity," *Washington Post*, 21 September 1984, A2.

view or emphasis. Avoid quotes that merely state the obvious or recap previous information. Second, a good quote should illustrate an important point. Pass up quotes, even lively ones, that stray off topic. Third, a quote should be catchy, phrased with some elegance, bite, or wit. Reject quotes that meander. Here are some examples of well-chosen quotes:

- **Clinching the point:** In a *New York Times* article on overcrowding, following the description of a tiny room that is home to four people: "At night," she said . . . , "when the mice crawl over us in bed, it feels even more crowded."[31]
- **Providing passion:** In a *Detroit News* report on how a daughter responded to a 911 operator's reprimand for repeat calls pleading for an ambulance: "I said I don't care if this is the 20th time," said Jody. "My father is dying here in the kitchen. He's dying on the floor. What the hell are you doing?"[32]
- **Capturing mood:** In a *Washington Post* story on a baby born in a parking lot: "The baby just flew out," Mrs. Fasick said yesterday. "He just torpedoed right out. I just reached down and grabbed him like a football, scooped him up and wrapped him in my skirt."[33]
- **Adding spice:** In a recollection by veteran UPI reporter Helen Thomas, quoting President Jimmy Carter's mother "Miss Lillian": "Sometimes when I look at my children, I wish I had remained a virgin."[34]

15. Use specifics and details. Relevant details help readers answer the primary question: what is this really like? They make the abstract seem real. In the example below, Indiana University student writer Lori Michele Nickel converted a routine assignment to cover football practice into a graphic and unexpected inside view:

> He sits soaking his foot in a pail of iodine to clean a raw, infected, oozing blister the size of a quarter on his big toe. A large bag of ice is wrapped to his left shoulder. He has scars and scratches all over his stomach and chest. The inside part of his arms, near the biceps, [is] a mass of black, blue and burgundy bruises.
> And he hasn't even played a game yet.
>
> (Lori Michele Nickel, Indiana University)[35]

---

[31] Deborah Sontag, "For Poorest, Life 'Trapped in a Cage,'" *New York Times,* 6 October 1996, 1.

[32] Cindy Loose, "EMS Crew Sits Idle in Crisis," *Detroit News,* 7 May 1987, 1A.

[33] Charles Fishman, "Baby's Arrival Rivals Mother's Speedy Entrance," *Washington Post,* 19 September 1984, C1.

[34] "Helen Thomas of UPI Remembers Times to Laugh, Times to Cry," Editorially Speaking, *Gannetteer,* April 1985, 5.

[35] Lori Michele Nickel, "A Day with the Team," William Randolph Hearst Journalism Awards Program, February 1992, fourth place.

Describing a teenage couple's elaborate preparations for prom night, Jeanne Curry sprinkled familiar details throughout her piece. "It took Gene Romero four months to save $650 waiting tables at Mr. Steak," she begins. All those earnings and more, she writes, will go toward his attire ("a rented black tux and tails, complete with white gloves and top hat"), dinner ("Anthony's at the Delta, 23 miles away . . . lobster AND escargot"), and deluxe transportation ("a chauffeured limousine at $50 an hour"). Why is the night so important? Two weeks after the dance, Romero leaves for the Army.[36]

16. **Provide vivid examples.** Make a point and illustrate it. That principle applies in writing as well as many other areas. Some of the best sentences in journalism begin with the words, "For example." For example, reporter Mary Bishop's investigation of the extermination business was rife with explicit for-instances:

Marcelle and Joel Gabrell of Prince Edward County have been sick since an exterminator illegally sprayed chlordane, a now-banned pesticide, under their house two years ago. A scientist determined the house was ruined. . . .

[Another company]—with a string of crimes in other states—bilked hundreds of elderly Virginians of $400,000 by taking bugs into their homes and selling unneeded treatments. . . .

Chlordane dripped from the basement ceiling after an exterminator treated the Grayson County home of Maxie and Steven Stone. In a lawsuit, they said they had to destroy 300 cans of food that had been splashed by chemicals. . . .

(Mary Bishop, *Roanoke Times and World News*)[37]

17. **Create unexpected pairings of words and ideas.** Advertising copywriters routinely startle us by coupling images and words from different worlds. News and feature writers can perform a similar feat, by creating odd alliances that make readers do a double take or murmur to themselves, "I never thought about it like that."

The effect often occurs quickly, as when John P. Wiley, Jr., in *Smithsonian*, labels brushes between underwater divers and manta rays as "close encounters of the graceful kind."[38]

Writing about two young drug users, Lisa Petrillo of the *San Diego Union-Tribune* offered this jolting observation: "So Mike, like Nick, was stoned before he had all his permanent teeth."[39]

---

[36] Jeanne Curry, "They Could Have Danced All Night," *Huntington Herald-Dispatch,* 12 May 1989, D1.

[37] Mary Bishop, "Bad Things Can Happen When the Exterminator Visits," *Roanoke Times and World News,* 21 August 1988, 1A.

[38] John P. Wiley Jr., "Dance with the Devilfish," *Smithsonian,* July 1998; available from http://www.smithsonianmag.si.edu/smithsonian/issues98/jul98/devilfish.html; Internet; accessed 2 July 1998.

[39] Lisa Petrillo, "A Second Chance," *San Diego Union-Tribune,* 16 June 1996, 5.

In a magazine essay, Henry Louis Gates, Jr., used a disarmingly simple device to compare Michael Jordan the basketball and marketing colossus with Michael Jordan the real person:

> The first thing you notice when you sit down with Michael Jordan is how very much like Michael Jordan he is. The resemblance is uncanny, and not incidental to his success.
>
> (Henry Louis Gates, Jr., *New Yorker*)[40]

18. Use pointed words. Every paragraph needs a zinger, a luminous word or phrase, a speck of muscle. Nothing deadens writing faster than vapid language. Notice how many meaty words propel the following story:

> Ternae Jordan Jr. heard a whistling sound in his right ear before suddenly sinking to his knees in the lobby of the YMCA in Fort Wayne, Ind.
> "I felt real hot. I couldn't move any part of my body," Jordan, 15, recalled. "I remember dropping down on my knees. I started praying right there."
> The aspiring musician later woke up in a hospital with a bullet lodged in the side of his head. A 17-year-old had sprayed two bullets into the lobby—aimed at someone else.
>
> (Deborah Barfield, *Albuquerque Journal*)[41]

In a second example, a writer picks aptly spiritual terms to evoke the anguish of parents whose three small sons all drowned together in a frozen pond:

> Thus began the agonizing pilgrimage of Charles and Mary Gragg, two ordinary people who now stagger in the footsteps of Job.
>
> (Tad Bartimus, Associated Press)[42]

19. Use playful words. Readers enjoy a sporting good time as much as anyone, so writers should serve up the zesty when the theme permits. Writer Joe Klein, for example, describing a scene in which politician Alfonse D'Amato tries to make friends with some demonstrators, writes that D'Amato "decided to love-bomb the protesters."[43] Sports writer Bob Parasiliti had some appropriate fun with a boxing match televised at a local arts center:

---

[40] Henry Louis Gates Jr., "Net Worth," *New Yorker*, 1 June 1998, 48.

[41] Deborah Barfield, "America's Culture of Violence," *Albuquerque Journal*, 6 February 1994, 1B.

[42] Tad Bartimus, "Family, Town, Grieve Three Drowned Brothers," Associated Press, in *The Editors' Choice* (New York: Associated Press, 1989), 8.

[43] Joe Klein, "The Soul of the New Machine," *New Yorker*, 1 June 1998, 42.

The posh, red velvet seats and soothing cultural surroundings of the Maryland Theatre—which usually houses the tweets and tones of music and motion of Maryland Symphony Orchestra—gave way for at least one night of thuds and pops of leather and bobbing and weaving of prize fighters.

(Bob Parasiliti, *Hagerstown (Md.) Morning Herald*)[44]

20. **Compress material for impact.** Facts are like fuel: the faster you inject them into your story, the faster it accelerates. Not every story lends itself to compression. You need to avoid overly dense writing in stories that are complicated, heavy with numbers, or bulging with confusing new concepts. But trend stories, profiles, and descriptive efforts, among others, provide an opportunity to serve a full banquet of tastes and flavors.

In a *Wall Street Journal* profile of the head of CBS entertainment, the writer delivers a truckload of information in a single paragraph:

The son of a Brooklyn plumber, he has lived in only New York and Beverly Hills, except for a year in Texas for Army duty. He earns about $300,000 a year. And in a country where the average household has 1.79 TV sets, Mr. Shephard and his wife and four children have only one—a 21-inch Sony that sits on the living-room rug. Although they have lived here for five years, the Shephards have yet to buy a TV stand.

(Bill Abrams, *Wall Street Journal*)[45]

21. **Highlight irony and contrast.** Life often runs counter to expectations, and so do good stories. Irony and contrast can provide little jabs of surprise that draw readers into an article. Paula LaRocque, a leading editor and writing coach, cited two excellent examples in a column in *Quill* magazine. Both come from the Associated Press:

Middleweight "Sailor" Danny Grogan, who never has been anywhere, is making a comeback.

(Ed Tunstall, Associated Press)

Rama Dama Rau, Premier Ky's personal astrologist who predicted five years ago that the [Vietnam] war would be over in six months, was drafted today.

(Hugh Mulligan, Associated Press)[46]

[44] Bob Parasiliti, "Local Fans Enjoy Fight in Comfort," *Hagerstown Morning Herald*, 13 June 1989, D1.
[45] Bill Abrams, "CBS Program Chief Picks Entertainment for 85 Million Viewers," *Wall Street Journal*, 28 September 1984, 1.
[46] Paula LaRocque, "Hooking the Reader," *Quill*, July/August 1995, 41.

22. Venture a little irreverence. Not too much, but a little. At the right time. Here is how Ellen Warren kicked off a *Chicago Tribune* article about how celebrities like Miss America face the same problems as everyone else:

There she is, all right. Miss America. Your ideal. She's been looking for a job. Her boyfriend broke her heart. And, after putting it off, she's getting the guts to start going to the gym again.

(Ellen Warren, *Chicago Tribune*)[47]

In the *Wall Street Journal,* Lee Berton traced the three-year process of getting desert tortoises classified as endangered, starting with this slow-but-sure lead:

Speaking of turtles, there is something slower: the U.S. Department of the Interior.

(Lee Berton, *Wall Street Journal*)[48]

And in a zoning story of all things, a *Palm Beach Post* reporter began a look at a local comprehensive plan this way:

Watch out, here come them double wides.
Right across the Royal Palm Bridge and down to South Ocean Boulevard, if the state has its way.
Shiny, new mobile homes. Pulled up and tied down right next to the Porsches and the Jaguars, the Guccis and the Vanderbilts.

(Matt Prichard, *Palm Beach Post*)[49]

23. Tell stories within stories. Well-placed inner stories can make points and also help entertain a loyal reader. The anecdote below, from *Preservation* magazine, draws a chuckle, and it also sets up the article's ending:

Fifty years ago, newspaper columnist Walter Winchell pushed the button to call an elevator at the Roney Plaza Hotel in Miami Beach and waited for it to arrive. He waited some more. Research tells us that New Yorkers typically become impatient after waiting for an elevator for 30 seconds, and Winchell,

---

[47] Ellen Warren, "The Long, Winding Runway," *Chicago Tribune,* 10 October 1993, section 2, 1.

[48] Lee Berton, "Turtles Are Swell, and Unlike Dogs, They Don't Drool," *Wall Street Journal,* 28 July 1989, A1.

[49] Matt Prichard, "No Mobile Homes in Palm Beach?" *Palm Beach Post,* 25 August 1989, "Local News," 1.

who grew up on West 116th Street, was a typical New Yorker. When the elevator finally arrived, Winchell turned to the young operator and asked, "Where were you?" The boy, perhaps a New Yorker himself, was nonplused. "Where can you go in an elevator?" he replied.

(Patrick Rogers, *Preservation*)

Several pages later, Rogers capitalizes on the Winchell anecdote by ending his piece this way: "Where can you go in an elevator? Why, to the top."[50]

In an intimate profile of pro football star Terrell Davis, Leigh Montville of *Sports Illustrated* incorporated an unforgettable story about Davis's father's drinking:

"He came home one night, and we had these puppies," Terrell remembers. "The puppies were making noise, whimpering and whining the way puppies do. He said he couldn't stand the noise. We had to give away the puppies. It was two o'clock in the morning. . . . We had to throw the puppies over fences into neighbors' yards. I remember hearing the puppies crying, lost, confused, on the other side of the fence. . . . We never saw the puppies again."

(Leigh Montville, *Sports Illustrated*)[51]

24. **Build up speed and momentum.** Sometimes a whirlwind of writing seems to sweep you up and send you soaring. In the following profile, strong words, vivid images, and rapid-fire delivery create a furious pace intended to portray a frantic personality:

The bulkiest talk-show hostess in the Twin Cities is gulping Diet Coke, tearing into a bag of crunchies from the vending machine and brandishing a wastebasket in case she throws up. She is distracted by a missing tooth. And she was late taking her Prozac, an anti-depressant. "Has it kicked in?" she screams.

It hasn't seemed to. . . .

(Ellen Tomson, *St. Paul Pioneer Press*)[52]

25. **Put it all together.** Words, images, insight, pace, tone, and a scintillating kicker are mixed in this galloping piece from the *Minneapolis Star-Tribune:*

By mid-week, they numbered perhaps a quarter of a million people in a place that never has seen so many and probably never will again: Hell's Angels

[50] Patrick Rogers, "Vertical Leap," *Preservation*, May/June 1998, 54.
[51] Leigh Montville, "Mama's Boy," *Sports Illustrated*, 28 September 1998, 60.
[52] Ellen Tomson, "Bad, Bad Barbara Carlson," *St. Paul Pioneer Press*, 20 September 1992, 1A.

and Banditos and leathered Christians "riding for the Son," lanky young men from Alabama and tattooed young women from Texas, and portly old bikers from nowhere with their graying hair bound in faded kerchiefs.

And happy to be among them at the Woodstock of biker rallies, the 50th anniversary Black Hills Motor Classic: doctors, lawyers and shoe clerks turned easy riders, partying and parading day and night on the hot, dusty prairie and up through the pine-covered hills to see the caverns and granite presidents. Born to be wild, if just for a week.

(Chuck Haga, *Minneapolis Star-Tribune*)[53]

SUMMARY

Dramatic writing seizes and holds the reader's interest. It comes from resourceful reporting, acute insight, and stellar composition, from both the overall angle and the particular words.

To apply these lessons, writers think big and think small. They begin with a strategic goal: the most interesting possible writing, story by story, sentence by sentence, word by word.

Then they concentrate on what makes writing interesting: arouse readers by surprising them with material that has impact, is presented with force, and has dramatic tension that makes them want to know more. The SIFT model adds solid shape to the general goal.

Then they apply specific techniques toward the goal. They familiarize themselves with all the tools, with the use of scenes, storylines, novelty, details, anecdotes, literary devices, quotes, wit, rhythm, tone, and pacing. They jettison the lackluster and dreary, unleash originality, and think of their phrases as spring-loaded instruments, straining with a reserve of pent-up energy awaiting release by an eager reader.

They put craft to work. Moving systematically through the steps of reporting, planning, and writing, they constantly look for ways to inject drama into their articles. They work hard to enhance color and meaning.

Then comes magic. Drama unfolds without respect for schedules, systems, and procedures. So writers immerse themselves in their material, keep careful notes of ideas and brainstorms, and stretch for inventive words, images, phrases, and combinations. They dig deep, living by the principle that they should push to make every story they write unique in some way. They know they must be ready when the masterstroke of inspiration comes within reach.

Have you ever watched a horse race? For most of the race, almost all the horses seem to run at similar speeds, loping along in a bunch. But the winners usually will execute at least one visible creative burst that separates

---

[53] Chuck Haga, "Black Hills, Biker Hills," *Minneapolis Star-Tribune,* 10 August 1990, 1A.

them from the crowded field. You can appreciate the surges as they happen—beautiful, graceful alignments of muscle and motion that seem to send the horse sailing, as if some personalized wind god had lifted it to a higher power.

That is the magic of horse racing: the steady run setting up the triumphant rush. To win, horses need both. And so do writers.

Practicing Craft and Magic

1. Go online, select your favorite search engine, and look up "Pulitzer Prizes." You will find a site listing the texts of prize winners for the past several years. Select any story (a good place to start is the "feature writing" category) and make a list of the techniques the writer used to achieve surprise, impact, force, and tension.

2. Create a SIFT checklist for yourself. As you prepare your next article, check off each item when you believe you have accomplished it. If you feel you have failed to achieve surprise, impact, force, or tension, re-report or rewrite as necessary.

3. Like the horse race described above, most stories benefit from a creative burst. Begin building into your work routines the expectation that such magical moments will occur. Prod your subconscious toward them. The next time one occurs, make careful notes about what seemed to prompt it: where you were, when it happened, what you had been doing, and so forth. Use that information to help create the conditions for further inspiration.

Chapter 10

Polishing
Your
Work

When you come to the end, your work is not finished.

A complete draft is a milestone, but it is not the destination. As writers we recognize that reality, but our language still betrays an ambivalence about re-examining work once it seems done. We resent "second guessing." We scoff at "20-20 hindsight." We dismiss criticism as "Monday-morning quarterback-ing." We urge one another to "get over it," "move on," and live with the "done deal." We embrace the Satchel Paige philosophy, "Don't look back." We oper-ate in a culture in continuous motion, leaning into the future. Forward spin is a journalist's mantra. Yesterday's story is ancient history.

So it should not come as a surprise that writers bridle at polishing and edit-ing. Reporting is glamorous and exciting. Writing is stimulating and creative. Both are forward looking. Revising is drudgery, and being edited is torture. Both look backward. Or so it seems.

Intellectually we know better. We recognize that first drafts are seldom pub-lishable, that work always profits from quality control and fine-tuning, and that we depend on the safety nets of editors and second readers.

Psychologically, though, writers seem programmed into a steep working curve. They move steadily up the front slope during reporting and planning, then come flying down the backside as they write. By the time they land at the bottom, article seemingly completed, they feel worn out. The last thing they want is to turn around and climb back up the hill. Too many new thrills lie ahead.

The consequence, simply enough, is that too many writers spend too little time revising and polishing their work and make only a minimal investment in healthy editing relationships. They turn in semicompleted copy and hurry on to the next project. You should avoid these mistakes. This chapter will show that creative revising, polishing, and editing often make the difference between the adequate and the outstanding and that your writing will benefit unfailingly from extra care in the final stages.

In large part, revision is craftwork. It means systematically reviewing work in a diagnostic mode, much like an internist conducts a step-by-step medical checkup. As always, magic plays its part. Just as doctors sometimes act on hunch or instinct, writers appreciate that the flash of inspiration often saves itself for later moments. Relaxed and unburdened, writers at the end stage are often most receptive to insightful inner promptings that lift work to new peaks.

Chapter 2 listed five objectives at the revision stage:

1. To critically review information, themes, and writing compared to goals and ideals
2. To adjust the overall shape, outline, and presentation for accuracy, clarity, drama, and maximum impact
3. To streamline syntax, sharpen focus, and power up language
4. To locate and correct the careless errors, omissions, and clutter that accompany most drafts
5. To fine-tune work to a professional level of excellence in content and structure

This chapter will take up revision and polishing separately, using "revision" as the broader term. Revision can entail anything from a full-scale overhaul to the selective rewriting of a paragraph. Most often, it involves a combination: some reorganizing, some redrafting, some significant additions or deletions. Of the objectives listed above, numbers one and two best describe revision. Polishing is the finishing coat, a final toning up of language and form—the kind of effort envisioned in objectives three through five.

REVISING COPY

Revision requires time. Writers seldom feel they have enough time, and they are anxious about how they ration it. Typically, they allot most of their time to reporting, some to writing, and a fraction to last-minute, looking-for-fatal-flaws editing. They tend to feel guilty about squeezing out of this tight budget the minutes or hours needed for revising.

Yet revision can be exceedingly satisfying. "What makes me happy is rewriting," columnist Ellen Goodman has said. "It's like cleaning house, getting rid of all the junk, getting things in the right order . . . I like the process of making writing neat."[1]

---

[1] Ellen Goodman, quoted in *Coaches' Corner*, December 1989, 5.

Recommendation one is simple: build time for revision into your schedule and discipline yourself to use it regularly and faithfully as intended. Make revision a habit, and you will become more and more comfortable doing it and reaping its rewards. Guard against considering an article finished at the point you produce a complete draft. By including revision in your routine and taking for granted that it will occur, you can break through the psychological barrier.

As you re-approach your copy in the revision stage, here are some guidelines for using the time effectively:

1. **Walk away.** Reporting and writing are intimate and immersive activities, leaving the writer too close to copy to view it with clarity. Remember the WRITE formula: *work* followed by *release* leads to *inspiration.* Whenever possible, set your work aside for a minute, an hour, or a day. If you can break the immediate bond, you will return better primed to analyze its strengths and weaknesses.

2. **Change format.** A good way to get critical intellectual distance from copy is to view it in multiple forms. You can do this in at least three ways: (1) read it on your computer screen; (2) print it out onto paper; (3) read it aloud. Each way produces a different experience, causing you to notice different things.

3. **Talk about the work.** Conversing with a friend or colleague about your copy is an indirect means of analyzing it. You yourself will call up important residual or suppressed ideas as you talk, and you will often get helpful feedback from others as you listen.

4. **Let ideas come to you.** Use the power of magic. Letting work submerge in the subconscious breeds new ideas and insights. They eventually make their way into clear view. Expect this to happen, and it most likely will.

5. **Circle back when necessary.** Keep an open mind about doing more reporting, revisiting your theme or outline, or experimenting with an alternative lead or approach. Try not to commit too rigidly or too early to anything from the overall idea to a particular phrase. If you are unhappy with a piece, the problem may lie not in your writing but in a reporting or focusing failure. There is nothing wrong with backing up a step or two and making adjustments.

6. **Spend time where it does the most good.** Occasionally you will need to start over, to rewrite a piece from top to bottom. Much more common, however, is the *selective revision,* the need to work on a section (such as the lead or the nut graf) or even a sentence. Concentrate your efforts for optimum payoff. If you lack the time or the will for a ground-up revision, then spend time revising the most sensitive portions of your copy.

7. **Experiment.** Retrace some early steps and rethink preliminary decisions. Write four or five alternative leads, even if you like the one you have. Try a new ending. Examine your leftover notes for quotes, details, or other material that may be superior to what you originally chose. Be sure you have not overlooked an obvious angle.

8. **Identify trouble spots.** Read your copy through and place a question mark beside any word, sentence, or section that seems fuzzy or pedestrian. Spend extra time massaging the passages you identify. Think about them as you work, drive, relax, or sleep, in hopes solutions will present themselves.

9. **Consider what is missing.** The word *revision* implies rewriting something that already exists. But another important aspect is to consider what is not present that should be. Look for holes and omissions in evidence, sourcing, or logic. Revise by addition when new material will improve the copy.

10. **Key on the big questions.** Here are two paramount questions that can produce tangible and profitable improvement:

   • What would make this a superlative article?
   • What can I still do to come closer to the ideal?

11. **Rethink each sentence and paragraph.** In his classic book *On Writing Well*, William Zinsser reports that he rewrites most pages four or five times:

   With each rewrite I try to make what I have written tighter, stronger and more precise, eliminating every element that is not doing useful work. Then I go over it once more, reading it aloud, and am always amazed at how much clutter can still be cut.[2]

He cites several examples from his own work:

BEFORE REVISION: "Thinking clearly is an entirely conscious act that the writer must keep forcing upon himself."
AFTER REVISION: "Thinking clearly is a conscious act that the writer must force upon himself."

BEFORE REVISION: "I can assure you that the difference is a bloody big one to the reader. . . ."
AFTER REVISION: "The difference is a bloody big one . . . ."

12. **Aim high.** The revision stage is often the place where good work kicks into the excellent category. Maybe you have all the physical ingredients

---

[2]   William Zinsser, *On Writing Well*, 5th ed. (New York: HarperPerennial, 1994), 10–11.

but have yet to recognize their metaphysical message. Maybe you have splendid specifics but need a great phrase or image to dramatize them. Maybe you have a powerful abstract point but lack the superb examples that make it unforgettable.

The bottom line for revision: Do not give up until you have raised your work at least a notch on your personal 1-to-10 scale of quality.

POLISHING COPY

Self-editing is a skill every writer should cultivate. For one reason, it improves copy. For another, it reduces conflict with editors. Writers who are apprehensive about working with editors should know that the cleaner they make their copy, the less most editors will change it.

Writers have changed their working habits over the years, and one trend stands out: because of the speed and convenience of using computers, more and more writers work by rapidly producing a first draft and then going back to rework it into final form. In the days of handwritten and typewritten copy, revising was so laborious that writers typically tried to perfect each sentence before moving to the next. That system had some advantages, but it tended to keep magic at bay, to discourage those flights of inspiration that set writers off in a rapturous blur. When you are worried about typos, it is hard to charge ahead at full throttle.

The modern system works better, with one stipulation: "write-fast/fix-later" succeeds as long as writers take seriously the fixing-later task. Speed drafting produces good ideas and overall content, but it also produces loose organization, imprecise wording, and excessive careless errors. Polishing is necessary to close the essential distance between a pretty good draft and a first-quality finished product.

While revising calls on both artist and artisan, polishing is more craft than magic. The microscopic inspection of final copy calls for a focused, linear approach. You cannot duck the discipline. Finishing touches are by necessity detail driven.

Even here, however, do not entirely cast away your artistic side. To the last comma, you should stay receptive to new ideas, last-second insights, sudden bursts of connection. An inspiration to change a key word or phrase in your lead can turn bland into blazing. Thomas Jefferson tapped immortality by streamlining "the enjoyment of life and liberty, with the means of acquiring and possessing property, and pursuing and obtaining happiness and safety" into the imperishable phrase "life, liberty, and the pursuit of happiness."[3]

---

[3]   Pauline Maier, *American Scripture: Making the Declaration of Independence* (New York: Knopf, 1997), 134.

So apply the systematic method, but stay tuned to your channels to the muses.

Polishing lends itself to a checklist. Here are some important actions to take in your final rundown.

- **Concentrate.** Even after several drafts and revisions, copy often contains excessive careless errors. They stem from things we do not notice rather than things we do not know. To combat carelessness, close your eyes, block out distractions, focus 100 percent attention on the copy at hand. Do not let your mind wander. Some people can get into such an intense editing zone that they will not hear the phone ring. The more you can concentrate exclusively on your copy, the more likely you are to notice errors both large and small.
- **Scrutinize Every Fact for Accuracy.** Triple-check every fact, especially names, identifications, numbers, attributions, and sensitive or controversial assertions. It is amazing how often important errors manage to survive into the final stages of writing. The more you read your copy, the less you tend to challenge each point. On your last trip through an article, recheck everything.
- **Emphasize the Lead.** Everything in an article is important, but the lead is all-important. Make sure the lead conveys your meaning, contains an active verb, and boasts at least one unusually colorful word, image, or description.
- **Check for Key Elements.** Focus on the top section of your article, looking for strong quotes, vivid details, human voices, compelling nut grafs. Use your best material to entice readers five or six paragraphs into an article, and by then you probably will have hooked them.
- **Inspect for Legal and Ethical Problems.** Guard against libel, invasion of privacy, or intellectual property violations. Consider matters of taste and ethics. Try for diversity in sourcing and viewpoint. Make sure your language is gender-neutral and inclusive.
- **Do a Verb Check.** Look at every verb and consider whether you can substitute a sharper one. If you can improve 10 to 20 percent of the verbs in your copy, the electricity level leaps.
- **Cut Wordiness.** Shorten sentences, tighten expressions, and weed out passives and *to be* constructions.
- **Vary Style.** Glance paragraph by paragraph, looking for variety of structure. Avoid starting successive paragraphs with articles *(a, an, the)*, attributions *(She said . . . She said . . . She added)*, or phrases and clauses. When you run your eye down the first word or two of each paragraph, you should see many different parts of speech.
- **Check the Basics.** Do a word-by-word inspection of spelling, grammar, punctuation, usage, and style. Slow yourself down; read one word at a time, "aloud" in your mind. A good tip: read to the bottom of the first page on

your computer screen, then bring copy onto the screen one line at a time. The bottom of your screen frames each line and helps your eye focus on it. Otherwise—for example, when you try to edit a line at the middle of your screen—your eye tends to wander, possibly overlooking obvious errors.

- **Read Backward.** This is an old copyeditor's trick. If you read a sentence backward, you are forced to go slower. You lose any sense of logic, of course, but you are more prone to notice typographical errors, misspellings, and stray punctuation marks.
- **Let It Sit One Last Time.** Go away, and come back. Ask yourself, what still bothers me the most about this article? Fix the problem if you can. If not, call for backup. You have done all you can. Bring on the editor.

COACHING: EDITORS AND WRITERS AS A TEAM

In a healthy system, of course, you should not have to "bring on the editor." The good editor is already there. Good editors involve themselves early and stay connected throughout the writing process.

Before looking at the art of editing copy, I want to discuss something equally important: editing people. Chapter 2 introduced the premise that publishing is a team effort and that both copy and morale improve when writers and editors work in harmony.

We have come to call the editor's role "coaching." Though coaches' styles differ widely, many of their basic strokes seem common:

- Participating at every step, from the idea through reporting through writing and rewriting
- Listening, as writers grapple with loosely formed ideas and inspirations
- Helping writers lock on to the most compelling aspect of their ideas
- Keeping the passion and energy levels high (Joel Rawson, a longtime *Providence Journal-Bulletin* editor, is remembered for once leaping across a desk to get closer to a writer)
- Encouraging writers to take risks with unusual topics or unconventional formats
- Offering friendly technical advice about reporting, focus, structure, organization, leads, transitions, and style
- Completing the editing process with authority, sensitivity, and professional competence

How do editors perfect these coaching techniques? Carole Rich, an author, former reporter, and journalism professor, stresses six actions: listening, lauding, limiting, reinforcing, reassuring, and rewarding.

How do writers find coaches who use such helpful methods? Unfortunately, not every editor is the paragon you seek. But writers need to look after their own interests. Your mission: find and use the best editor you can.

Writers have to take the initiative and create the affiliation. The luckiest writers are those already assigned to able editors. If you have a good editor, make the most of it. If you are assigned to a nonsupportive editor, work on the relationship. Be open and direct about what you need, encourage your editor to become a better coach, thank the editor for being helpful, and lobby your organization to train, develop, and reward good coaches.

Beyond those efforts, you may also need to find informal means of getting yourself coached: turn to helpful colleagues or cultivate the attention of other editors when you can. If you work as a freelancer or without a supervising editor, then you have to find someone you can trust to volunteer editing help.

Most writers have a strong independent streak, but in the long run few can succeed alone. Almost nothing is more powerful than the synergy generated by a good writer-editor team, and almost nothing is more toxic than a writer and editor in perpetual turmoil.

Coaching, like all else about writing, has an operational side that includes specific objectives and practices. Here are some ways writers can benefit from good coaching.

The Best Gift

The single most positive step is for coaches and writers to talk more before anything gets written. *Editing* connotes after-the-fact review, which is important. But as we have seen, writers make their pivotal decisions early, in selecting ideas, gathering information, mulling various themes and approaches. Coaches have the most impact when they push and prod writers from the beginning toward the best possible work.

The Six Conversations

Editors and writers should have brief conversations at six crucial points. Generally they need last only a minute or two, though they can and should sometimes take longer.

1. **The idea stage**—where the coach pushes hard for the best available story
2. **During the reporting**—where the coach serves as a resource person
3. **Before writing**—where the coach helps with focus and approach
4. **After the writing**—where the coach makes suggestions for revisions
5. **During the editing**—where coach and writer work together, negotiating the final version

6. **After publication**—where the coach debriefs the writer on what went well, what went wrong, and what could be done better the next time

The Specific Goals

Coaching conversations cannot accomplish everything. Priority setting is vital. So two precise goals apply during each coaching conversation: (1) to help writers focus on the single most important problem at the current stage; and (2) to set writers on the road to solving it themselves. Coaching does not mean that the editor jumps in to dictate solutions or to handle every problem. The coach's job is to help writers see and manage both problems and opportunities.

The Ground Rules

Granted, maintaining this relationship is not easy. Natural tension necessarily exists between writers, who tend to be high ego and insecure, and editors, who must judge their work. Jon Franklin, an author and two-time Pulitzer Prize–winning journalist, once put it this way: "It's sort of like with dentistry, I guess. I have much respect for dentistry, and I like many dentists, but I don't relish them drilling holes in my teeth."[4]

Good ground rules can lessen the friction. They begin with mutual respect. Editors and writers should treat each other more as professionals and colleagues than as bosses and underlings. Writers should level with editors and respect their ideas. Editors should hear writers out and always consult before making any substantial changes to copy.

Good coaching is the best possible predicate for the final step in the writing process: editing the copy.

EDITING COPY

It is an ineluctable law of publishing that editors edit. Sooner or later all writers must yield their copy, in a symbolic and actual surrender of control that leaves most of them anxious and some of them truculent. However, this crucial conclusive step is no time for the writer to preen or pout. Nor is it time to disappear. Even without their own hands on the copy, writers have tremendous leverage over the high-stakes end game.

Being edited is unavoidable, but both the quality and stressfulness of editing have almost as much to do with the writer's behavior as the editor's. As

---

[4] Carl Sessions Stepp, "Can This Relationship Be Saved?" *American Journalism Review,* April 1997, 34.

this book has repeatedly maintained, teamwork and positive, professional attitudes make a vital difference. Strong writers and editors, working respect-fully and cooperatively, raise the level of both quality and morale. Writers should consult with editors throughout the process, avoid surprises, respect deadlines, and turn in clean copy that meets the specifications.

Even then, despite the apparent transfer of responsibility, the weary writer's work has still not ended. Editing, like writing, is a team enterprise, and writers remain on assignment as it progresses.

Teamwork in Editing

The companion lists below help show how writers and editors should operate in parallel:

Writer's Role	Editor's Role
• Respect the editor	• Respect the writer
• Respect the copy	• Respect the copy
• Accept coaching	• Coach, don't boss
• Provide art, sidebars, caption material, multiple versions for online and print, and any other items editors need	• Keep writers posted about length, packaging, display, format, and any other information that affects their work
• Be available for consultation	• Consult often, if possible during editing with writer at your side
• Alert editor in advance to sensitive themes or wording you feel strongly about	• Deal with the biggest and toughest issues early before positions harden
• Defend your work without bullying	• Negotiate changes without defensiveness
• Do not fight every change—let editor win some changes	• Do not overwhelm writer with changes—let writer win some
• Stay open to editor's suggestions and creative input	• Offer constructive ideas but keep story in writer's voice
• Recognize editor's ultimate authority	• Make decisions confidently but not arbitrarily
• Ask for third-party mediation	• Agree to a referee of hotly disputed points unless principle makes you unwilling to yield
• Expect to see finished copy	• Don't make any significant change the writer doesn't see

The Editor's Technique

Good editors are not primarily writers or even rewriters. Their role is to help the writer achieve the best result. In the final copyediting stage, editors should apply a rigorous and systematic quality control standard but try to preserve as much as possible of a writer's intent, style, and language.

They should start with three cardinal rules:

1. Do not make changes that you cannot explain with precise reasoning (that is, avoid changes that simply reflect personal preference).
2. Do not change anything important without consulting the writer.
3. Never add an error.

Given that credo, editors proceed methodically through the copy. Though different editors will have their individualized systems, the following editing model is typical. It is also a model that writers can use on their own copy.

- Prepare to edit by reducing distraction and concentrating on the copy.
- Read the copy through at least once with little if any editing; you want to make a "cold read" to get a feel for the overall impact, just as a reader will do.
- Edit for *content,* the larger issues: accuracy, balance, fairness, focus, law and ethics, numbers, organization, quality of evidence, theme, thoroughness.
- Edit for *structure,* the fine-tuning: grammar, punctuation, spelling, style, usage, wordiness.
- Wherever possible, question the writer before making changes and give writers the first opportunity to fix problems or perform revisions.
- Read copy a final time looking for errors you have overlooked, mistakes you have added, or any other problems you have failed to notice.
- Ask yourself: am I ready to vouch for everything in this copy? Is it ready to go to the public?

SUMMARY

A first version is rarely finished work. Writing is a creative continuum that calls for several rounds of drafting. Though writers sometimes resist and even resent the time required for rewriting, they should see it as a compulsory, constructive step en route to excellence. Build revision time into your work schedule, and use it.

Rewriting can be full-scale or selective, an overhaul of everything or a tune-up of a troubled part. Use your limited time to work on areas that will benefit the most. Skillful revision should raise most articles by one or two points on a 1-to-10 scale of quality, often the margin between acceptable and outstanding.

Once revisions are complete, take time for final polish. Reexamine every theme and word. Remember that there is no such thing as a small error. Readers make large judgments about your work based on small things they notice. The careless mistake, the factual flub, the embarrassing typo can be suicidal to an otherwise exemplary project.

Both craft and magic can serve you. Revising and polishing is in large part linear, systematic craftwork, with the expected payoff that accompanies most attention to detail. But revision and polishing also benefit somewhat disproportionately from last-minute magical interventions. At this late stage, writers have lived with their work for so long that their minds often astonish them with climactic creative outbursts. Stretch toward those quantum leaps as you enter the ultimate stages of the process.

Exploit the editing system. A wholesome coaching relationship with an editor provides you with an ally and with extra technical muscle. Involve editors early and squeeze good ideas and suggestions from them. As you approach final copyediting, consider their needs, make yourself a partner in the editing operation, and both give and expect respect and assistance. On parallel tracks, defend your work yet stay open to suggestions; assert your own vision yet recognize the editor's ultimate authority.

Writers do not have to dread revising, polishing, and editing. Instead, these steps can be rallying points for enriching copy, a welcome chance to crown a good project with a near-faultless sendoff.

Practicing Craft and Magic

1. Examine your last published or graded article. In hindsight, what section would have benefited most from revision? Can you see parts that could have been substantially improved with 15 or 20 minutes of rewriting? On your next assignment, try to identify similar opportunities for improvement and complete the revisions before submitting your copy.
2. Conduct a verb check on your next writing assignment. Weigh all the verbs. Can any be perked up without loss of accuracy? Aim for strengthening 10 to 20 percent.
3. Think about your relationship with your instructor, editor, or coach. What helps you the most? What needs attention? Over your next several assignments, stress a positive coaching model: mutual respect, the six key conversations, teamwork throughout the process. Repeat these steps until they become an integral part of your routine.

Chapter 11

Packaging
and
Presentation

The editor was inspired. Zack Binkley, editor of the *Huntington (W. Va.) Herald-Dispatch*, envisioned an ambitious narrative to help his community come to grips with a high-order human drama, a love affair that had gone tragically wrong, leading to kidnapping and murder. His problem: who would report and write it? His creative solution: pair ace feature writer Jeanne Curry with street-savvy sports editor Mickey Johnson. Build a team of photographers, artists, and designers, and produce the finest package a small newspaper could muster.

The result, "A Day of Rage," was tautly written and arrestingly illustrated, a notable example of well-coordinated teamwork in writing, packaging, and presentation.[1]

Binkley's innovative attempt paid off. But if you have ever written for the media or observed how news operations work, another scenario may seem more typical to you. Someone (let's say the top editor) has an inspired idea. She passes it on to someone else (the managing editor, say), who mentions it to an assigning editor, who assigns it to you.

At some point the assigning editor also alerts the art director, the chief photographer, and the online producer. A graphic artist, a photographer, and an online journalist are assigned to the project, and they try to locate you, the writer, to briefly plan an approach. Hurried conversations take place on the run.

Everyone works diligently, and eventually you all turn in completed work. By this time, the original assigning and directing editors have moved on to other duties, so your text and images go to still another editor, who ultimately

---

[1] Jeanne Curry and Mickey Johnson, "A Day of Rage," *Huntington Herald-Dispatch*, 29 May 1988, 1.

routes them to the design desk, the copy desk, and the online center. The material passes along the elaborate chain until it is, ultimately, published and posted.

Throughout all this, at least a dozen people lay their hands on the copy. Most never talk to one another. They all consult whoever is just above or below them in the chain, but that's about it.

Now pose these questions:

1. How much do you suppose the finished product resembles the editor-in-chief's original vision?
2. How well-coordinated do you think the images and the words will be?
3. Whose story is this?

The likely answers: (1) probably not very much; (2) probably not very well; and (3) probably no one person's.

Sobering answers to writers, are they not?

The scenario may be a tad extreme, but the problem it illustrates remains frustratingly common. Writers may get star billing, but their supporting casts are large and loosely directed. Although magazines and online media outperform newspapers in coordinating their projects, few if any media outlets excel at this process.

In Zack Binkley's case in Huntington, he himself took the time to oversee the project from beginning to end. But such efforts by top editors are relatively rare, especially at bigger publications. Largely because of time pressures and production demands (but in part because journalists have simply neglected to update their systems), media people tend to ship their words and images along an assembly line, with no one person maintaining control from start to finish.

Journalists break the process down into its parts, dispersing responsibility for text, art, headlines, and design, and seldom giving any one person the time and authority to reassemble the parts in a coordinated fashion. Too often the result is similar to painting a room by having four crews come in and independently choose colors and patterns for each wall. If the overall result harmonizes, it is a rare and lucky accident.

These conventions may help journalists meet deadlines and maintain efficiency, but they do not serve readers and they put writers' work at risk. To readers, what matters are results and impact, not journalists' routines—the whole of the presentation, not isolated parts. To writers, what happens after copy leaves their hands can determine the success or failure of an entire project.

This chapter explores how writers can and should become fuller partners in packaging and presentation, whose unprecedented growth and prominence should lead writers to reevaluate their own traditional remoteness from the production operation. It also examines differences writers must recognize in preparing material for various forms of presentation: print, broadcast, and online media.

WRITERS AS PARTNERS IN PACKAGING

Packaging remains principally an editing responsibility, but writers cannot afford to ignore it. For most of the process, after all, a story clearly "belongs" to the writer. Readers and colleagues, not to mention writers themselves, will associate the published version with the writer, no matter how much editors and designers modify it.

Having labored through the many stages already described in this book, the writer understandably feels a profound proprietary interest in the work, an indissoluble parental connection. As the moment of publication nears, power may transfer to editors, designers, and production workers, but the writer, as primary creator, retains an indisputable ownership claim. And the writer's byline will top the story.

Smart writers, then, will act both defensively and proactively to contribute to quality and to defend their interests as a story winds toward publication. They can take many steps, both early on in a project and even at the eleventh hour, to sway the outcome.

A writer's most constructive course is to demonstrate friendly, professional, high-profile commitment to a project from its beginning to its end. The production phase can be bureaucratic, politicized, and time-devouring, but writers who overly insulate themselves lose leverage and risk the calamity of late-stage mismanagement. Modern publishing is demanding and competitive, a high-ante enterprise that rewards a writer's full involvement and understanding. Writers should not expect to control every decision, but they are entitled to be consulted and considered.

Writers, then, must do more than write. They must heed the realities of contemporary publishing

- By respecting audience members as increasingly interactive partners and by understanding how consumers use various media
- By appreciating differences among print, broadcast, and online media and by adapting material for multiple modes and channels
- By cooperating toward a blend of text, images, and design to give their project maximum effect

Some of these responsibilities may seem beyond the limits of traditional writing. However, writers who do not wish to be left behind in the rising information age should embrace rather than resist the expanded roles.

For many of us, changing times mean rethinking some of the received wisdom from generations past. First, we have to let go of the notions that those in the media can be divided neatly into *word people* and *image people* and that the wordsmiths should rule. For centuries, word people dominated newsrooms. They arrived first and took control. In the last half of the 20th century, the image people surged forward, boosted by rampaging technological change and spiffy new high-tech toys.

But the truth is that words and images are simply tools used to do a larger job, getting a message across as effectively as possible. No method—writing, photography, or computer imaging—works best for every message. What is demanded today is journalists who can think both verbally and visually and choose the best ways to get across various messages. There will always be specialists, those who are exclusively writers or designers or artists, but more and more the reigning model will be those who can successfully integrate words and images.

Many traditionalist writers, therefore, may have to learn to think visually and to disown their natural bias toward the hegemony of words. For their part many contemporary journalists may have to rededicate themselves to text and to renounce any superficial notion that form outranks substance. All writers have to think from the reader's perspective about how to coordinate every communication element to deliver points forcefully and attractively.

The linear world, the way people have thought and read and learned for centuries, is fading. We are now well beyond the first generation of people who have learned more by watching (mostly television) than by reading. The traditional notion was that a reader would start at the beginning and read to the end. A viewer, by contrast, might process images and ideas in a variety of patterns, quite often, for instance, beginning in the middle.

The traditional print media package features a photo or image above a headline above an article. This way of packaging assumes the traditional linear behavior of audiences, that people process material in the order in which it is presented, from start to finish, top to bottom, left to right. Audiences act that way less and less, however. The sequential system has not disappeared, but it has become less dominant. It is now the unnatural, rather than the natural, pattern of receiving information.

Instead of moving from one point to the next to the next in direct linear sequence, today's viewers jump and skip, sample and surf. They cut quickly from image to word, from article to information box, from headline to summary deck, from one online frame to the next. They prefer to take in information in shorter, multiple, layered segments rather than in a single lengthy unit.

We have entered the age of the nonlinear narrative, the story that takes multiple forms and offers the reader-viewer a variety of options. Writers and editors must now concede this landmark change and adapt to it. As Chapter

8 stressed, these developments do not require a "dumbing down" of content or an abandonment of serious communication. On the contrary, today's technology and expanding multimedia formats offer more ways to convey more messages with more impact to more audiences.

Used wisely and adroitly, the new tools empower writers to enlarge meaning and make complex topics more understandable than ever before.

READERS AS PARTNERS

On September 14, 1982, a group of editors convened to design the inaugural front page of the national newspaper *USA Today*. I was among them, serving as the infant paper's national editor. Despite months of planning and days of stockpiling special stories for our first issue, we faced an unexpected splurge of breaking news stories: a DC-10 crash in which 55 people died, an auto accident that killed Princess Grace of Monaco, and the assassination of president-elect Bashir Gemayel of Lebanon.

How should we rank these stories? We had no institutional memory to consult, no clear lineage of standards for front-page copy. And we operated, we felt, in a fishbowl: millions of readers would examine the first issue of *USA Today* and scrutinize our judgments.

Should we give readers what they *wanted* (presumably the latest developments in the death of the beloved Princess Grace) or what they *needed* (sober attention to the repercussions of the Gemayel assassination in the unstable Mideast)?

Not everyone agreed, and there was vigorous debate. Eventually, we led the page with Princess Grace's death. The page's centerpiece was a color photo from the DC-10 plane crash site. Gemayel's assassination was given one paragraph in the front-page news digest, with reference to more coverage on page 9A.

Critics seized on the decision as a turning point, a deliberate strategy to downplay the serious at the expense of celebrity. As someone who was there, I do not think we meant anything quite that precedent-smashing. We simply made an on-deadline decision about how to handle a big news day. But the decision colored people's evaluation of *USA Today* for months if not years. It underlined the enduring complexity of balancing readers' needs and desires.

Readers have more media choices today than ever before, a fact that gives them spiraling influence. Journalism has always been a transaction between supplier and consumer. News has long been treated as a commodity traded to audiences to satisfy their demands. Definitions of news have always been dynamic, changing over time, subject to negotiation between writers and readers.

Until now, however, the news producers have enjoyed the upper hand because most markets were monopolized by relatively few information outlets. It is crucial to recognize that changing times have shifted influence in the direction of news receivers. For today's consumers, choices have burgeoned. Cable channels, specialized publications, and online information sites give audiences infinite information options. Computerization lets aggressive consumers select, retrieve, and bundle information however they wish. In addition, the increasing interactivity can amplify exponentially the audience's voice, allowing direct and immediate feedback straight into the heart of media institutions.

All these developments give readers more muscle. Collectively they have perceptibly changed most mass media. On the positive side, the changes tend to make media more responsive, competitive, open to change, attentive to detail, and dedicated to improvement. On the negative side, they tend to promote homogenization, reduced risk taking, fear of controversy, and a myopic keep-them-happy mind-set that rewards bottom-line marketing values over long-range public service. These may seem like stratospheric matters of management, but they have direct bearing on writers and their work.

STRATEGIES FOR WRITERS

How does this new interactive age affect writers?

The short answer is that more than ever, today's writers have to consider reader needs, desires, and demands and to deliberate over how best to engage busy audiences. Media consumers have outgrown the role of passive recipients. They are increasingly assertive and empowered affiliates in a two-way information flow. Writers feel the consequences in every aspect of their work, from the opening discussions of which ideas will be assigned to the final decisions on how stories get presented.

At a conceptual level, writers can respond in several ways:

1. **Respect the audience and its role.** As this book has repeatedly emphasized, writing is like holding hands: it is no fun alone. Successful communication requires a capable sender and a satisfied receiver. Readers are writers' legitimate partners.

    Which should prevail, their needs or their desires? In good journalism, the principle of parallel tracks should apply. Writers should transform this either-or question into a both-and opportunity. Both readers' needs and their desires are important, and writers should try to fulfill both sets of demands.

    Mitchell Stephens, in his excellent book *A History of News,* reminds us that news coverage has always blended the solemn and the entertaining into "a spicy, hastily prepared mix of the portentous and the anomalous."[2] Evidence strongly suggests that most audiences appreciate a varied menu of reliable hard news, spirited storytelling, and a good dash of entertainment.

2. **Exercise leadership.** Readers should share influence but not dominate. Ultimately they must trust writers to serve their needs. In the same way that we entrust our bodies to doctors, our vehicles to mechanics, and our children to teachers, we must entrust our media to those with talent and training. Writers venture out into the unknown on our behalf and return with important information and exciting stories that they alone can convey.

So writers owe readers the benefit of expertise and experience. The news media, for example, know it is important to monitor government and business operations even when they seem boring. Society's long-term civic prospects depend on oversight and information. To take another example, writers, like artists, recognize their responsibility to introduce audiences to unsettling new ideas and to challenge complacency. Progress depends on this warming-up process.

The ethics of writing and journalism compel writers to serve the public trust, even at the occasional expense of popularity or profitability. On a parallel track with satisfying reader desires, writers also bear the leadership responsibility of reporting the unpleasant, the unpopular, and the unappreciated.

3. **Be helpful.** Packaging and presentation exist not merely to prettify pages and postings but to attract readers, hold their interest, and lubricate communication. Good design makes reading easy, enjoyable, and edifying. It aims to maximize both readership and comprehension.

In a nutshell, the goal of both designers and writers should be to offer readers a path of least resistance. Clarity and drama count, as do theme and focus. Images and art, and in some cases audio and video, matter. Headlines, subheadlines, sidebars, and breakout materials play a part. How copy strikes the eye is important. Length and format considerations (such as whether one long story or several shorter ones are more effective) apply.

The writer's obligation is to join in forging decisions about what elements and approaches will work best.

4. **Keep presentation in mind during reporting and writing.** Like most decisions, those about packaging should not be left until the final hour. Writers should consult early and often with editors and designers.

Ideally, a team should form very early in a writing project. Assignment editors, copyeditors, illustrators, and designers, for print and online media (and sometimes broadcast too), should join writers in mapping and executing a plan. These plans often affect how writers proceed.

---

[2] Mitchell Stephens, *A History of News* (New York: Penguin Books, 1988), 301.

For example, suppose you are assigned to cover this year's high-school graduations in your city. Maybe designers want to feature excerpts from student speakers, broken out in boxes. Maybe your online report will include references to the online home pages of individual schools or students. In your reporting you would need to collect the excerpts and references, but from the beginning you would know they were going outside, not within, your main article.

Making these kinds of decisions early saves time and aggravation for everyone. The last thing you need as a writer is to craft a full article based on student speeches and then have it determined that those quotes will be pulled out of your copy, or to have online producers entreating you for references after you thought your reporting was complete.

By factoring in presentation issues from the beginning, writers can increase their influence, save time, and better serve readers.

THE PRINT FORMAT

Writing for newspapers, magazines, newsletters, 'zines, wire services, and some electronic publications still seems largely linear. A mainbar—one overall and comprehensive article—often dominates coverage. Readers start at the beginning, and at least some of them proceed through toward the end. But contemporary design also recognizes that there is more to the story than the story. An entire package usually includes images, graphics, and an assortment of reader service material, some produced by writers, some by artists and editors. The total presentation looks more like a tree with many branches than a straight-line linear report.

To some degree, writers are servants of the process, supplying not only articles but additional information needed by artists, designers, webmasters, and other colleagues. But writers can influence and sometimes control the process, by understanding it fully, involving themselves thoroughly, initiating presentation ideas, and supporting or challenging packagers' plans.

Here are three key areas where writers should both weigh in and listen to the advice of others.

1. **Story length and structure.** No single story format always works best. Let's say you have space available for 1,000 words of copy. The most traditional approach would be to write one 1,000-word article. That approach serves best for some assignments, for instance, a dramatic narrative that recounts a heroic mountaintop rescue. But other configurations might work better for other stories:

   • A 200-word wrap-up of a medical breakthrough atop an 800-word backgrounder on how it came about

- A 600-word main story and two 200-word reaction sidebars on a key court decision
- A 200-word introduction and four 200-word breakouts on contenders for elective office
- A twin set of 500-word pieces on two musicians playing in town

One-size-fits-all journalism is outdated. We need to discard the reflexive tendency to think of packages as one longish story plus art. The configuration of every assignment needs to be tailored to achieve its special purpose and serve its various audiences.

2. **Art and illustration.** An enduring adage of journalism once cautioned against including any material in a package that was not also in the main story. This adage, too, is outdated. Writers and designers should look for ways of telling stories visually and graphically above and beyond the main article.

A simple map of a plane crash site or a chart showing line items in next year's school budget, for example, conveys information far more understandably than words and relieves writers of wrestling with information that does not fit into story form. To describe how cloning works, a graphic that combines text and drawings performs better than words alone.

Writers should imagine and suggest photos, illustrations, and graphics for their work, contribute information that makes them more effective, and help ensure that all packaging elements are compatible. By cultivating their visual-thinking abilities, writers will not only increase their clout in the newsroom but also exercise the mental muscles associated with inspiration and magic.

3. **Layered design.** Layering involves presenting images and words in ways that appeal to varying audiences, using a variety of often overlapping visual and verbal techniques. Layering recognizes that some consumers are "skimmers," desiring quick summaries, while others are "readers," seeking depth and detail. Effective presentation takes into account these and other ways people use media.

Suppose you write a magazine article about how online communication is creating new kinds of communities among young people. A layered package might include your main article plus several other elements: an impressionistic headline to catch reader attention; a subhead in sentence form that summarizes the theme; an illustration to capture the mood of the piece; photos of computer users; breakout boxes on the demographic characteristics of computer usage and on how one computer community works; a sidebar transcript of a chat session; a list of tips on computer safety and etiquette; a reader-service box on how to connect to key online sites.

"Skimmers" can easily get the gist of the package by reading the headlines and sampling the breakouts. "Readers" can munch on every word.

Layering also increases the chances of enticing a reluctant or at first uninterested consumer. The presence of several different elements provides what designers call extra "points of entry," additional opportunities to catch the eye of a busy page turner.

Writers, not just editors and designers, should share the duty of imagining and creating layered presentations. Your initial budget proposal for an article or project should include recommended illustrations, graphics, sidebars, breakouts, and reader-service devices. Your approach to writing the main article should take into account what other material readers will be viewing. And revising and polishing should be guided in part by emerging design plans, such as what the main headline is likely to emphasize.

THE BROADCAST FORMAT

Writing for broadcast has long been considered a specialized art, but more and more often the multimedia news environment demands writers proficient in both print and broadcast styles.

Broadcast copy differs from print in several important ways:

- It is meant to be spoken (by the broadcaster) and heard (by the audience), rather than read. So broadcast copy must be *conversational*.
- Its audience is usually more passive than the print audience. Reading requires an active mental engagement, but many if not most people listen to broadcast with a distracted half-attention. They may use radio as "background noise," or glance occasionally at the television while cooking dinner, or crank up a car engine and catch a report in mid-sentence. So broadcast copy must be *compelling*.
- It is ephemeral. The audience has only one chance to grasp the message. You cannot go back and reread a broadcast paragraph. So broadcast copy must be *crystal clear*.
- It features audio and video, sometimes intertwined with the script, under tight time constraints. So broadcast copy must be *concise* and *coordinated*.

For writers, these conditions require a style that is simple, direct, and dramatic.

Conceptually, broadcast copy must be well-focused and pointed. Where a print report may have four or five themes and subthemes, a broadcast story will zero in on one. In broadcast, personalized words and images are preferred over abstractions. If you are covering a story on new treatments for cancer, for instance, it is better to build it around one person's experience than to be overly clinical. A broadcast item about government action will focus more on the substance and less on the process.

Structurally, broadcast uses clear and concrete language, simple sentences with few phrases and clauses, subject-verb-object construction, and present tense. It has the informal cadences of conversation. Beware of words that sound alike (such as *brakes* and *breaks, AIDS* and *aides, a* and *eight)* or that may be hard to pronounce ("specializing in super-sensitive systems for the security conscious").

Here is how a writer might cover the same event for print and broadcast:

> **PRINT:** Maryville School Board members voted 6 to 3 last night to spend $250,000 next year on the city's first sex-education classes. Supporters said the classes will provide vital personal health information for a changing world. Opponents countered that such private matters should be left to parents.
> **BROADCAST:** Maryville schoolchildren will receive sex education for the first time next year. . . . Sixth and seventh graders will study about reproduction, contraception, and sexually transmitted diseases. . . . Last night, school board members set aside a quarter million dollars for the controversial classes.

Good broadcast copy makes information conversational, personal, and palpable to busy but news-hungry consumers.

THE ONLINE FORMAT

Is online journalism more like print or more like broadcast? It resembles print in that it requires consumers to actively read text and navigate pages. It resembles broadcast in that it incorporates audio and video and is transmitted electronically. Yet in other ways it resembles neither: online's immediate interactivity and unlimited multidimensionality are unmatched by traditional media.

As an evolving format, online journalism has borrowed from both print and broadcast, but it has developed its own signature style different from any predecessor. Rather than considering the online style as a modification of traditional print or broadcast, writers should appreciate it as its own unique and powerful form of expression.

Almost all writers need to feel comfortable planning, gathering, and producing material for online distribution. We discussed earlier how important it is to build format considerations into the earliest planning stages. You will report, organize, write, and design materials differently for online distribution than for traditional print. The earlier you know which media format or formats you are writing for, the more efficiently and effectively you can complete an assignment.

In preparing online reports, writers and their online producers are responsible for the customary overview articles and sidebars but also for many other potential elements: key audio and video clips, photos and illustrations, background material (such as chronologies or glossaries), full texts of speeches and documents, links to earlier archival information, links to other relevant sites, and ideas for interactive sessions with the audience, just to name a few.

Editors and producers handle many of these duties, but writers, as always, should be partners in producing a package whose elements are credible, compatible, and compelling.

A specific example, online coverage by the *Chicago Tribune* and the Cable News Network of an historic and controversial visit to China by a U.S. president, can illustrate several characteristics of the online format.[3]

- **Online is infinite.** Newspapers run out of space and broadcast runs out of time, but cyberspace runs forever, allowing for both depth and breadth. The *Chicago Tribune*'s online coverage of the presidential trip to China, for instance, featured a 37-paragraph main article, 12 additional stories, a time line of Chinese history, an interactive discussion forum, several photographs, links to innumerable sites about Chinese business and culture, and an informal question-and-answer discussion with a *Tribune* reporter on the scene. CNN's Web site offered a similar batch of materials plus a transcript of the president's major speech, a video showing delivery of the speech in China, and several audio clips.
- **Online is multilayered.** Early on, online pioneered in "tunneling," or routing readers through several levels of information on a topic. Both the *Chicago Tribune* and CNN, on their main opening pages, covered the presidential trip with a small photo, a brief headline, and a link to the next level. At its second level, the *Chicago Tribune* displayed its main story and art, along with a framed "package index" that included links to 12 other stories, the time line, the interactive forum, and links to government and private sites. A viewer could follow coverage through eight more levels before running out of current and pertinent material.
- **Online is multimedia.** Both the *Tribune* and CNN offered color photo galleries and interactive opportunities, and CNN also delivered audio and video coverage. Today's reporters may well find themselves on assignment armed with notebook, pens, laptop, tape recorder, digital camera, and video camera. While most writers do not produce full-scale multimedia coverage, more and more do. And all writers should at least play a coordinating role and adjust their own copy to the presence of other elements in a package. If you know, for example, that the audience can see and hear for itself the president's speech, then you may add helpful cues to your copy ("early in his talk, the president said . . . "). And, of course, knowing

---

[3] "A Historic Visit," *Chicago Tribune* online, 29 June 1998; available from http://www.chicagotribune.com; Internet; accessed 29 June 1998; "Clinton to China," CNN online, 29 June 1998; available from http://www.cnn.com; Internet; accessed 29 June 1998.

that full text and video are available will make every reporter extra conscious of getting the quotes and descriptions exactly right.

- **Online still features good writing.** For all its techno-bells and cyberwhistles, online journalism still depends on strong writing. Both the *Chicago Tribune*'s 37-paragraph main article and CNN's 33-paragraph report on the China trip read like traditional print media stories, with standard leads and theme development. Here is the *Tribune*'s lead, by Roger Simon:

> BEIJING—Telling Chinese college students that civil liberties are the "birthright of people everywhere," President Clinton made a stirring defense of democracy Monday but did not directly rebuke China's Communist leadership with whom he had sparred two days earlier.

Stylistically, online writing resembles print more than broadcast. It tends to be somewhat simpler and more conversational than conventional print, and it requires stressing the main point early, at least by the end of the first screen. Links are typically built into the article itself, sometimes as inset boxes, sometimes in subheadlines, sometimes simply in hyperlinked words and phrases that are part of the copy.

Writing original online material does not call for special technical expertise, nor does adapting print material for online use. As always, writers should stay true to their audience and purpose, adjust their planning and performance to the needs of whichever formats they are using, and make themselves involved and informed members of the overall presentation team.

SUMMARY

In the mid 1990s, the *Orlando Sentinel* created what it called a "bridge," a large computerized area in the center of the newsroom where print, broadcast, and online editors worked side by side. From this command post editors and producers channeled copy into television broadcasts, Web reports, and newspaper pages. Writers and artists were expected to "feed the beast," as journalists like to say, with material suitable for a variety of formats and audiences.

Traditionally, writers have probably operated too much as individuals and not enough as teammates. Effective media packages need coordination, and writers should gamely participate for several reasons: to influence how "their" stories ultimately appear, to champion their approach and values, and to represent their understanding of reader interests.

Today's media writers must respect the growing influence of readers, appreciate differences among various media, adapt material for a variety of formats, and cooperate toward a master plan for distributing copy to audiences. They will respect both reader desires and needs, following audience tastes at times and challenging them on other occasions. Helpfulness is the watchword. In a ferociously competitive marketplace, writers should use every legitimate technique to get and hold audience attention.

Through craft, writers work alongside editors, producers, and designers through each step of the packaging process. Good presentation calls for the staples of artisanship: planning and meetings, checklists and systems, attention to detail and application of standards.

But presentation owes much to magic. Attracting readers is an art, a contest of imagination. Who better than writers—saturated with and consumed by their material—can visualize winning designs? Participation in packaging allows, even forces, writers to consider their work from new angles and with new goals, a shift of vantage point that often triggers fresh inspirations and insights. A creative burst at this crucial stage can pump up energy and appeal.

Many writers will continue to specialize, but most should master the differing requirements of print, broadcast, and online styles. Excellent reporting and writing remain at the core of all good journalism, but they will be wasted if the audience never stops to read.

Everyone has heard the old saying If a tree falls in the forest and no one is around, does it make a sound? Writers can put their own spin on this expression. If a great story is published and no one notices it, does it matter?

Presentation is the art of engaging readers, without whom writers are lonesome creatures indeed. Given the stakes, writers should mobilize maximum enthusiasm and vigor to collaborate toward reaching every potential reader.

Practicing Craft and Magic

1. As part of your next writing assignment, attach a list of three suggested visual accompaniments (for example, photos, charts, or computer illustrations) that will enhance reader understanding of your material. Stress substance, not simply decoration.
2. For your next assignment, write both a print lead and a broadcast lead. Compare their similarities and differences. Think about how writing for different media should affect your approach.
3. Create an online presentation plan for your next story. Map out the first three screens. Decide what headlines, copy, and images should appear on the main page. What stories, sidebars, photos, and images should follow? Include at least three outside links. Suggest a place for an audio or video link. Add at least one interactive opportunity. Think about how this exercise forces thinking and writing different from a traditional linear article.

Part 3

Achieving Excellence

Chapter 12

Models
and Common
Story Types

Do *not* take this chapter too seriously.

It will offer some models and examples showing how various story types are often handled. But the last thing writers need is to yoke themselves to rigid formulas. Originality and innovation are hallmarks of good writing. Every assignment should be approached with imagination and treated as a one-of-a-kind opportunity.

Still, so many kinds of stories recur that there is value in examining some commonplaces of coverage. The models and approaches described in this chapter can help acquaint writers with the standards for some typical assignments. Try to regard them as starting points, not the final word. Use them as a baseline, but also critique them and consider alternatives. Most editors expect writers to master the basic story forms, but they also welcome freshness and new approaches.

Assimilate the standard forms, but dare to tweak them when you have good reason.

The sections that follow focus on several common types of news articles: the news event, the nonevent news story, the meeting-speech story, the human interest story, the police-fire-disaster story, the court story, the government story, the specialty story, and the obituary.

For each type, writers are typically expected to assemble the cardinal elements of a news story—to answer the *who, what, where, when, why,* and *how* questions. They need evidence and examples, authoritative sourcing, good quotes, details, and anecdotes, all triple-checked for accuracy.

Beyond the basics, they aim in every story for something special, for material that shocks or surprises, providing a depth or heft that separates extraordinary stories from the run-of-the-media.

Given good material, writers must select from various potential structures and leads. Bearing in mind that each assignment should be treated individually, you can gain insight into how writers solve the repeating problems of each genre by analyzing how various types of stories are commonly presented.

Prior chapters have described many components of a well-written article:

- An *idea* that attracts readers
- A *lead* that informs, underlines, and stimulates
- An *amplification paragraph,* usually paragraph two, that builds on the lead
- A *focused structure,* often including a *nut graf* to summarize the main theme
- An attention to *clarity* and *drama* throughout the body
- A *satisfying ending*

This chapter considers how writers weave these elements into stories of several common types.

THE NEWS MODEL

If you study enough examples of how writers combine the various elements of a story, you will discern a template that tends to describe the generic news article. Once again, remember the disclaimer: we are not talking about inflexible commandments but about an archetype that has evolved to meet the needs and desires of audiences.

For news articles, the model typically looks something like this:

1. **Lead.** The readers' gateway, a beginning that both expresses the main message and entices the reader to continue
2. **Amplification Paragraph(s).** One or two paragraphs that build on the most compelling point of the lead, often adding "how" and "why" elements to a lead that communicates "who-did-what"
3. **Best Quote on the Main Point.** Adding passion, color, or insight plus a human voice
4. **Nut Graf (If Needed).** For complex or multiple-point stories, a brisk summary of the main theme, making clear why the reader should care enought to proceed
5. **Documentation Section.** A short section adding vital details, evidence, sourcing, or background on the main point
6. **Refocusing Paragraph.** For longer articles, a transition from the lead section to the body of the story, cataloging the subthemes in the order they will be discussed

7. **Additional Details on Main Point.** If needed, a section continuing to develop the central point
8. **Subsection One.** The first subtheme mentioned in the refocusing paragraph
9. **Subsection Two**
10. **Subsection Three**
11. **Ending.** A strong sign-off, punctuating the story with a rewarding little jolt for the reader who has persevered

This news model serves as a point of departure for the writer's creativity. In some cases, it can work as is, functioning as a frame or outline to guide the writing. More often, you will adapt the model to suit the particulars of an assignment. You start with it but avoid dependency on it. Familiarity with the model increases your discipline on matters of focus and order.

The model also operates as a kind of safety net or fallback position when you are struggling. If you do not yet have a better approach in mind, then the model offers a workable starting place. If you do have a preferred alternative, then you can set aside the model or simply use it as a tickler, a reminder of elements that need to be covered.

A key step is to move from *understanding* to *applying* the model. Models are by nature abstractions, while articles must be concrete. How can you use models to produce better stories? Perhaps the most fruitful and direct way is to complete your reporting, outline your story, and then compare your outline to the models and structures discussed in this chapter. Check whether your outline includes all the needed elements. Consider whether your proposed structure will achieve the desired goals of its story type. Do not feel you must conform to models in a rigid fashion, but use them to help test the strengths and weaknesses of your planned approach.

The following sections look at several types of news writing. They assume you have done sufficient brainstorming, reporting, and planning. The focus now will be on identifying the defining qualities of each story type, listing its special problems, and understanding how writers can successfully complete the assignment.

THE NEWS EVENT

News events happen every day, and journalists write about them. As events, they are discrete, observable, anchored in time and place. Their finite qualities facilitate coverage. Somebody does something important. Something happens that is interesting. Writers learn about it and write about it.

Newspapers, broadcasters, and online news providers probably concentrate on events more than any other category of article. For example, on the day this chapter was written, I turned to a typical heartland newspaper, the

Kansas City Star; an online news source, MSNBC; and a broadcast network, ABC News. Here is what they were covering:

- *Kansas City Star*—Its front page contained five news articles, including four event stories and one trend story. The local news section front held seven stories, all tied to events.
- *MSNBC*—Home cover page contained seven news items, all involving events.
- *ABC News*—Transcript for previous evening's "World News Tonight" broadcast contained nine items, comprising six news events, one nonevent news item, and two features.

These findings are probably typical. Events tend to dominate the news. In fact, major media often draw criticism for their preoccupation with events. Events, while convenient to cover, often have less long-range importance than issues, trends, and values. It is easy enough to cover the mayor's press conference, which seldom produces news of lasting consequence but has a predictability and accessibility that attract journalists. It is far harder to cover the mayor's character, influence, or overall effectiveness. These are subtle, intangible matters that have great moment for the audience but ooze and develop in ways that make coverage difficult.

Writers should learn to look beyond daily episodes and incidents to find deeper kinds of news. Trolling for better ideas is an imperative discussed often in this book.

Nonetheless, writers must also produce the basic event story. It is a starting point, and few media writers can survive without mastering it.

What are examples of basic news events? The president appoints a Supreme Court justice. Firefighters rescue three children from a burning house. Banks raise interest rates. The hometown soccer team wins the state championship. Scientists announce a new treatment for breast cancer. A hot rock group cancels a concert in town. The biggest church in the area fires its minister. A new airport opens. The oldest hardware store in the city closes.

How do writers commonly approach the basic news story?

Special Qualities

We will stipulate that you have reported thoroughly and amassed strong information. For the basic news event, you need adequate detail about the event itself—the time, place, setting, and attendance, for example—plus relevant descriptions.

Vitally important, though, is *meaning.* Meaning is the special element that a good basic event story needs. It must quickly answer the reader's question, "so what?"

Too many routine events will seem boring and lacking in impact: the mayor makes a speech; the police arrest a suspect; a thunderstorm moves through town; a theater production opens. You must stress substance over process, what matters to the audience over what happened at some venue. Your goal here: *find the element that makes this event different from every other one and deserving of a reader's immediate attention.*

Here are two examples that fail to answer the so-what question. They have been adapted slightly to keep from embarrassing anyone.

> County Commissioners Rita Smith and Joe Sanchez drew lines in the sand yesterday over the scheduling of a meeting to give people the chance to draw lines on a map.

> City Council on Tuesday night took a step toward installing a sewer system on Market Street by reallocating about $70,000 in state funds for the project.

Perhaps you disagree, but both leads could be criticized as remote and confusing. They lack urgency. They need meaning.

Here is a lead that tells the news and pinpoints its impact:

> DAYTONA BEACH—A wave of fire swept across North Florida on Wednesday, touching off a mandatory evacuation for the 30,000 residents of Ormond Beach and closing I-95, the state's main north-south route, for more than 30 miles.
>
> (Lori Rozsa and Gary Long, *Miami Herald*)[1]

Even when you find yourself stuck covering something ordinary, you want to make it novel in some way. For example, one event that makes news regularly is the weather. Writers can use good information or clever wordplay to make each day's weather story a little distinct from all the others:

> A floppy sun hat and SPF 30 sunscreen just aren't going to cut it this week as triple-digit temperatures roll into Southern California and stay—like unwelcome guests—for at least 10 days.
>
> (David Haldane, *Los Angeles Times*)[2]

---

[1] Lori Rozsa and Gary Long, "30,000 Evacuate Homes in Ormond Beach," *Miami Herald,* 2 July 1998; available from http://www.herald.com/docs/062645.htm; Internet; accessed 2 July 1998.

[2] David Haldane, "Hot Spell Expected for Next 10 Days," *Los Angeles Times,* 15 July 1998, 3B.

Structure

Chapter 6 distinguished between the news and news-plus leads: a news lead tells the news directly to audiences who presumably do not yet know about it, while a news-plus lead conveys the news but builds on it in some significant way for audiences presumed to have already heard about the main development. If you are providing the initial report about a compelling news event, then the news lead applies. A strong news lead uses subject-verb-object form to describe what happened and what twist made it worthy of attention.

More often in print media, the news-plus lead is needed because audiences already know something about the event. You need to report the event but add value to your lead in some way, perhaps through an exclusive piece of reporting, a preview of what comes next, a new window into the "why" or "how" questions, or significant detail that increases insight.

THE NONEVENT NEWS STORY

> The golden years lost their luster for many senior citizens when they opened their mail last month and saw how much their homes had increased in value.
>
> (Al J. Laukaitis, *Lincoln Journal Star*)[3]

News sometimes breaks and at other times evolves. When it breaks, you cover the pieces. When it evolves, you try to put pieces together into a meaningful whole.

Nonevent stories tend to focus on trends, connections, and patterns that represent important changes in our way of life. They can be harder to come by than event stories, for they are seldom as obvious. Event stories, by and large, are called to your attention. A tornado, an election, or a rock musician's death creates an obvious news event. Finding nonevent news requires more initiative.

In the example cited above, writer Al J. Laukaitis finds several examples of elderly couples upset by steep increases in their property assessments and, therefore, in their taxes. His story exemplifies a common type of nonevent news: the government policy change that affects numerous people.

Nonevent news surfaces in many ways. Even if these stories do not arise from specific events, they often have a peg, or a connection to something that is currently going on. In the Laukaitis example, the peg is the government's

---

[3] Al J. Laukaitis, "Valuation Hikes: Too Much, Too Often," *Lincoln Journal Star,* 2 July 1998; available from www.nebweb.com/news/monday/local2.htm; Internet; accessed 2 July 1998.

recent mailing of property reassessment notices. Good reporters and writers troll constantly for such pegs.

Another common source of nonevent news is enterprise or investigation. Acting on hunches, tips, or other leads, writers develop news stories by conducting interviews and following document trails. A similar nonevent category stems from observations made over a longer term. These stories typically document a trend or pattern of change. The *Wall Street Journal* is famous for its stories presenting overview insights into changing business, lifestyles, and culture:

> HOUSTON—Every year, about three million children are hospitalized for problems ranging from leukemia to a nasty bump on the head. On average, they stay 5.3 days before being discharged. That is way too long, says Robert Yetman, a pediatrician who has compiled a 400-page book of guidelines that could significantly change medical care for many children. . . .
>
> Such guidelines are wriggling into every corner of American medicine. . . . Hospitals and health plans are setting up detailed checklists ahead of time, telling doctors how to accelerate treatment of almost any serious illness.
>
> (George Anders, Laurie McGinley, *Wall Street Journal*)[4]

Special Qualities

Nonevent news stories need to quickly show readers their *impact*. Because they do not involve events and happenings, they tend to lack action. The writer must stress instead their effect on people and their importance to a threshold level of readers.

Structure

Nonevent coverage lends itself to news and narrative leads. News leads work best when the writer has identified meaningful nonevent news that is not already known. For example, an investigative discovery might begin with a hard-news, here-is-what-we-have-found lead.

Narrative leads serve when the writer prefers to drive home the point by first illustrating its significance. For example, a trend story about middle-class families losing out on scholarships might lead with a family whose first child gained scholarships and loans but whose next child, because of eligibility changes, had to work and save for a year before entering college. When you use the narrative lead, consider it almost compulsory to include a nut graf within the first three to five paragraphs. Otherwise, readers who do not immediately catch the relevance of your lead will be confused.

---

[4]   George Anders and Laurie McGinley, "Actuarial Firm Helps Decide Just How Long You Spend in Hospital," *Wall Street Journal,* 15 June 1998, 1.

SPEECHES AND MEETINGS

A primal part of human life, an open fire on the family hearth, may soon go up in smoke in new homes in Berkeley.

(Charles Burress, *San Francisco Chronicle*)[5]

Speeches and meetings, in themselves, are not news. What people say and do during speeches and meetings, however, often makes news. The above lead grew out of a meeting, but the writer properly placed the focus on an *issue of interest* rather than the meeting setting.

Speeches and meetings make up a special category of event stories because they are so common. Reporters gravitate toward them like yellow jackets to a cookout. Speeches and meetings are convenient and accessible, with an official predictability that almost guarantees some kind of story.

However, few writers yelp with glee when assigned to cover these gatherings. Too often they produce lackluster copy. A special odor of unimaginativeness often clings to stories about press conferences, commencement addresses, government meetings, conventions, and the like. Writers sometimes jokingly refer to them as "spinach journalism," stories that are good for you though not very interesting.

But good writers can resist this defeatist outlook. Even on assignment to their hundredth meeting, writers should never take them for granted. Excellent stories can originate in speech or meeting settings, if resourcefulness and creativity are applied.

Special Qualities

One secret is to turn the event coverage into an issue story. A meeting or speech itself is almost never a story, but what you learn during a meeting or speech can generate a story of great interest. In the example at the beginning of this section, the writer turns a preview of the next day's City Council meeting into an issue story about banning wood-burning stoves and fireplaces.

To take another example, when a controversial religious leader made a brief stop for a speech in my area recently, a local reporter arranged to drive him to and from the airport. Her story included comments from his speech, but it was not just a speech story. It had the fuller flavor of a profile, a behind-the-scenes visit with a colorful character.

Do not limit your coverage to the parameters of the event itself. Gather background information before the speech or meeting so that you can provide

---

[5] Charles Burress, "Berkeley's Mayor Wants Fireplace Ban," *San Francisco Chronicle,* 11 January 1999, A13.

context for what is said or done there. Afterward, follow up with additional reporting. For instance, maybe the state school board decides to experiment with year-round schooling. That is news. But you can deepen your coverage by pursuing the story outside the meeting. Dig for what-next details (When will the change begin? How will it work? Who will make the key decisions?), context (How do other jurisdictions handle this?), and reaction (What do parents think? students? people who have already tried this idea?).

The worst speech and meeting coverage can bring out a writer's laziness, but exercising a little creativity can add value to these staples of the news trade.

Special Problems

Poor note taking may be the biggest snare here. For speech stories, writers need plenty of full, direct quotes, especially on the main points. If you are not a fast note taker, you may find yourself with a notebook full of partial quotes but no full sentences or completed thoughts. For meeting stories, you also need lively quotes plus exact details on actions and changes.

Tape-recording or videotaping the event is advisable, and taking thorough notes is imperative. Immediately after the event, go over your notes and clean them up, for example, by writing out more legibly something that you hurriedly scribbled the first time. Remember a basic writer's rule: notes are worthless if you cannot read them.

Also collect any available documents (speech texts, explanatory handouts), and get contact phone numbers or online addresses from sources in case you develop questions later.

Structure

The most challenging problem in writing about speeches and meetings may be how to organize a complicated meeting story. News, news-plus, and narrative leads can all serve, depending as always on your purpose. A central principle is to avoid roundup leads. That is, do not overload your lead by trying to summarize everything that happened. Instead, focus on the most interesting or most meaningful action, not on an overview of the entire proceedings. Specifics engage readers more surely than generalities.

A common format is to start with a compelling specific, amplify it with more detail in the second paragraph, add your best quote, and then write a roundup graph listing other topics or actions.

> **AVOID:** The local airport authority decided last night to repave two runways, ban flights after 11 p.m., upgrade equipment in the air control tower, and renew the contracts of three food and beverage franchises.

TRY INSTEAD: Noisy late-night flights to Happyville Airport will end Nov. 1, signaling a victory for nearby residents whose own roar was heard clearly last night.

HUMAN INTEREST STORIES

MAITLAND—A tiny bald eagle chick given up for dead may be beating the odds. Scientists have detected a faint heartbeat and scratching sounds from its quarter-pound egg, which fell 50 feet from a tree toppled by vandals.

(Carlos Moncada, *Tampa Tribune*)[6]

Why is this story news? It is news not because it affects many people, or because it will change anyone's life, or because it represents substantial action. It is news because it will interest people. Stories about the human condition (or sometimes even more about the animal condition) touch a high percentage of the audience. Popular themes include children and animals, underdogs and long shots, heroism and villainy, triumph and tragedy, love and loss.

Special Qualities

Human interest writing features the *universal motif represented by the individual case.* Writers can often settle on this motif by asking themselves, what is this story really about? In the above case, for instance, the story is not really about one chick inside one egg. It is about the human family's irresistible urge to pull for an underdog trying to beat the odds and survive.

Structure

At first glance, the chick story seems to have a standard news lead. But human interest writing often involves creating an appropriate *tone* of concern or sympathy. The words "tiny," "given up for dead," "beating the odds," "faint heartbeat," and "scratching sounds" all underscore the fragility that makes this story poignant. They establish a mood that differs from the detached and clinical perspective of most harder news articles. Human interest writing tends to follow the basic news model, but the writer will use tone, pace, and detail to swiftly show readers that the story's power is emotional as well as informational.

---

[6]   Carlos Moncada, "Unhatched Eagle Survives Vandals' Attack on Nest," *Tampa Tribune,* 31 December 1992, 1.

POLICE, FIRE, AND DISASTER STORIES

> Dena McMillin never made it to her surprise 16th birthday party on Saturday. A two-hour drive with a friend was meant to divert her attention while her parents decorated. Minutes after the two left her father's house, they were in a car wreck that killed Dena.
>
> (Barbara Hollingsworth, *Kansas City Star*)[7]

Police, fire, and accident news never takes a holiday. From the 1830s, when James Gordon Bennett and other editors discovered a bottomless public thirst for such coverage, the mass media have brimmed—and perhaps overflowed—with tales from the police beat. Few writers make it through a career without their share of police, fire, accident, and disaster stories.

Special Qualities

Accenting the twist is the key to most police-type stories. Writers must isolate what makes each story singularly interesting and must spotlight that drama in the lead. Over a lifetime readers are exposed to so many episodes of mayhem, misadventure, and even murder that they often become desensitized and stop paying attention. Headlines that announce "Local man shot" or "Robbers hit Third National Bank" or "Fire sweeps through apartment complex" are seldom enough to overcome this built-up reader resistance.

Writers, through diligent reporting, must uncover enough unique specifics of each case to make it distinctive and dramatic. What makes this murder different from every previous one readers have heard about? What makes this fire particularly interesting? Why should anyone read about the tenth bank robbery in town this year?

To answer questions like these, stories need strong human interest properties: unusualness (perhaps the tenth bank robbery was committed by a teenager using a water pistol); impact (forest fires force the evacuation of an entire county); irony (a couple loses their new house to fire just weeks after a tornado destroyed their first home).

Frequently, these stories have a horrific side (the *Challenger* spacecraft explodes and plunges into the sea). They can be gruesome (a mass murder, a plane crash) or perverse (parents held for sexually abusing children). But readers do not want to wallow in the grotesque, and writers do not want to succumb to the sensational, so balance is also indicated. Some stories should

---

[7] Barbara Hollingsworth, "From Dena to Many," *Kansas City Star,* 2 July 1998, C1.

focus on heroism (passing motorist rescues driver from burning semi), humor (armored truck spills money onto freeway), and good deeds (teenager rows elderly neighbors to safety during flood).

Special Problems

Ensuring accuracy is always the writer's first responsibility, but in police and disaster reporting it is especially obligatory. These stories occur unpredictably, often late at night in out-of-the-way locations. Early reports, even from authorities, often contain errors. Sources, including victims, witnesses, and officials, may be uncooperative or indiscreet when operating under great stress. Stories typically involve death, pain, and loss, making them especially sensitive. Writers should always

- Conduct themselves professionally while covering police news
- Triple-check and triangulate every piece of information
- Attribute stories precisely
- Avoid libel and other legal problems
- Present material in a sensitive and tasteful way

This does not mean that you should refrain from persistence and digging. Often your job is to ask difficult questions at tough times. The best reporters and writers proceed both politely and professionally, navigating the slippery slope between dramatic, public-interest reporting and sensation seeking. For example, most editors consider it appropriate for a reporter to approach friends and family members of someone killed in an accident and to courteously ask if they would be willing to talk about their loved one. Many relatives appreciate the chance to share their memories, and touching interviews often result. Others prefer to be left alone, and good reporters will not pressure them. Seeking an interview in a sensitive way is considered proper behavior; harassing the grief-stricken is not.

Structure

Writers have ample latitude in choosing a style for police and disaster news. News or news-plus leads work well by emphasizing the twist, the one element that singles out a story for notice. Because so much police coverage involves dramatic storytelling, writers often prefer a narrative approach, featuring a main character in a suspenseful situation. Make your decision based on the specifics of each situation and on consultation with your editors.

Here are three different approaches to the same incident:

News Lead

A Greyhound bus driver on his last scheduled run was killed early Saturday along with his wife, his 8-year-old son and four other passengers, when their bus crashed into a tractor-trailer parked on the Pennsylvania Turnpike.

(Sacramento Bee, from news services)[8]

News-Plus Lead

It was supposed to be Scott Wisner's final ride as a Greyhound bus driver. Instead, it was the last ride of his life.

(USA Today, from staff and wire reports)[9]

Narrative Lead

Scott Wisner Jr. stood on the porch at the Boothwyn, Pa., firehouse last week and talked about the leisurely days he planned after he retired as a Greyhound driver.

He'd spend more time at the firehouse, where he had volunteered for 20 years. He'd play with his 8-year-old ward, Christian Jorgenson, and his soon-to-be-arriving grandchild. And he'd stay at home more, rewarding his wife for all that time on the road.

But Wisner, 61, died four hours from retirement. . . .

(Newsday, from the Associated Press)[10]

COURT STORIES

For religious reasons, Barry Davis of Salem wants to close his three Oregon gas stations from sundown Friday to sundown Saturday each week.

For business reasons, Texaco wants him to stay open and sell its gasoline.

And for legal reasons, they're now battling in federal court.

(Dave Hogan, Portland Oregonian)[11]

A court case pits one party against another in a struggle over cherished values. Courtrooms beget powerful stories of an almost literary quality, showing real-life people (the characters) in tangled conflicts (the plot) that produce verified winners and losers (the action, with a convenient climax).

Special Qualities

Court stories spotlight what lawyers call "the facts of the case," those nitty-gritty, ordinary-life details that certify realism. Great quotes, examples, and

---

[8] "Bus Runs into Parked Truck: Seven Killed," *Sacramento Bee,* 21 June 1998, A7.

[9] "Driver in Bus Crash on Eve of Retirement," *USA Today,* 22 June 1998, 4A.

[10] "Bus Driver's Last Day," *Newsday,* 22 June 1998, A30.

[11] Dave Hogan, "Render unto God, or unto Texaco?" *Portland Oregonian,* 28 April 1993, A1.

anecdotes abound. Drama is supplied almost by definition. Disputes wind up in court precisely because they are so knotty and impassioned that no other remedy works. And court stories often have a big-picture angle as well. They may reinforce social mores (for example, by showing that malpractice gets punished), define cultural values (such as the limits, if any, on free speech), or profoundly affect public policy (for example, through Supreme Court rulings on abortion or capital punishment).

The formula is a winner: dramatic specifics + a social message = irresistible reading.

> Stretching their necks to reach a microphone, two 8-year-old children testified in court Wednesday in Savannah about how their substitute teacher grabbed, slapped and shook them.
>
> (Ben Schmitt, *Savannah Morning News*)[12]

Special Problems

Above all, accuracy! You especially want to avoid errors in stories that nearly always feature lawyers. Beyond accuracy, fidelity. The judiciary works in complex, technical ways and speaks in its own Latin-laden language. Nuance means almost everything in court cases. Entire decisions often turn on the interpretation of a word or phrase. Writers must be meticulous in their simplifying and translating, so that they stay faithful to both the letter and spirit of legal holdings. When the least in doubt, it is best to double-check facts and phrasings with cooperative legal sources.

Structure

Like police coverage, court stories can be told as news or narrative. A good test is to ask yourself, What is the main reason for writing this story? If you are writing because a case sets important precedents or changes major policy, then look toward a newsy lead. With judicial decisions or jury verdicts, pay special attention to answering the "why" question, usually in the amplification paragraph. When jurors exonerate or convict, readers wonder what they were thinking. When the local court throws out a popular case, readers want to know the rationale.

Sometimes the drama lies more inside the human conflict than in its consequences to society. In those cases, consider a narrative approach, a case study probing the interior of a compelling slice of life.

---

[12] Ben Schmitt, "Judge Finds Probable Cause Against Teacher," *Savannah Morning News*, 2 July 1998; available from http://www.savannahmorningnews.com/smn/stories/070298; Internet; accessed 2 July 1998.

GOVERNMENT STORIES

> The city of Atlanta will sue gun makers this year, in an attempt to hold them accountable for the havoc and expense created by shooting injuries and deaths, Mayor Bill Campbell said Monday.
>
> (Carlos Campos, *Atlanta Journal-Constitution*)[13]

Ask a hundred citizens to describe government coverage in the news media, and they immediately haul out the word "boring." I once asked journalists to critique their own monitoring of government, and they disdained it with pejoratives like "an awful lot of minutiae," "the turn-of-the-wheel kind of thing," and "the kind of things that get gnashed around in city council meetings week after week." Even though we know that government affects our lives every hour of every day, Americans project a love-hate ambivalence toward its institutions and inner workings.

Perhaps we have tumbled into a cycle where readers expect boring stories and reporters reflexively oblige. Luckily, writers and editors are fully empowered to write better stories. If government actions truly touch lives universally, then compelling stories lie waiting, and writers should pounce on them.

Special Qualities

The watchword for government copy is *substance over process*. The good stories stress the impact of government action or inaction on real people in real life. In the example at the top of this section, for instance, notice how the Atlanta reporter led with the action (a plan to sue gun makers) rather than the setting (a speech by the mayor).

Often, government's impact is formidable. Here is a starter list of things government does or decides: Whose streets get plowed during a snowstorm? How fast do police respond to emergencies? How thoroughly are meat plants inspected? How safe are your savings? Who can own a gun, control air traffic, perform heart surgery, manufacture drugs, use lasers on your eyes? What standards are enforced for child-safety seats, airplane engines, home electrical wiring, natural gas pipelines, heart pacemakers, school-bus brakes? Who oversees car dealers, nursing homes, nuclear power plants, street food vendors, foster parents? If a hurricane hits your town, who arrives to help? If you are marooned at sea, who rescues you? If you get imprisoned in a foreign

---

[13] Carlos Campos, "Atlanta Plans to Sue Gun Makers," *Atlanta Journal-Constitution*, 5 January 1999, 1B.

country, who visits? If you work in a coal mine, clash with a harassing supervisor, or work with toxic chemicals, who enforces the rules? If you lose your job, who supplies benefits?

Government news coverage may be boring, but government is not. The challenge: show the impact in your copy.

Special Problems

Even if we agree that government itself is demonstrably important, it does not follow that every government activity is newsworthy. Covering every official meeting makes no more sense than staffing every high school teachers' meeting or every panel at the annual barbers' convention. Selectivity and news judgment should be applied. One strategy for reenergizing government coverage—and presumably for reengaging the audience—is to target government stories that weigh heavily in readers' lives and to construct stories to stress their impact.

To narrow the search for relevant government copy, writers can look for several characteristics:

- **Imminence of change.** Focus on what government is doing or is on the verge of doing to change constituents' lives. The further from taking effect a matter is, the lower priority it usually deserves. For example, if a House Transportation Committee subcommittee takes a preliminary vote to update highway laws, it probably means little. Numerous rounds of action are still needed before any change will occur. But if the vote is a turning point signaling that legislative sentiment now favors raising the driving age to 17, then a key change has taken place and should be reported.
- **Intersection with people's lives.** Frame stories according to their connection to the public, not their connection to insiders or processes. It is usually better to focus on what happened rather than *how* it happened (although there are exceptions, if the process is especially controversial, colorful, or unexpected). In general, avoid leads like "The School Board voted 5–2 at its monthly meeting Thursday to raise limits on class size next year." Connect the story directly to real life: "Class sizes at Hooperville Elementary will grow by 10 percent next year because of budget cuts and teacher resignations."
- **Delivery of services.** Monitor what government does well and does poorly. What services have been added recently and which ones reduced or eliminated? Are Social Security checks on time, potholes filled, school textbooks updated, local restaurants inspected? Are library hours convenient, license renewal offices efficient, parks maintained? Is water pure, air clean, seafood safe to eat?

Structure

The news-plus lead often wins out in government stories, summarizing the action and connecting it with readers' reality. Here are some other tools for writing government stories:

- *Translate* jargon and bureaucratic lingo into English. It is a "tax increase," not "revenue enhancement."
- *Find the winners and losers,* the victims and beneficiaries present in almost any government endeavor. You usually find both by (1) following the money, and (2) following the power.
- *Speed up* the routine aspects of meetings, hearings, press conferences, and the like by summarizing the routine so you can devote the most space to the action.
- *Look ahead* as best you can, answering readers' questions such as "What next?" and "How will this affect me?"

SPECIALTY STORIES

> A University of Hawaii researcher has created live mice using dead sperm, and now he's going to try it on other animals.
>
> Ryuzo Yanagimachi has shown that mouse sperm can be freeze-dried—just as coffee or other foods—and used to fertilize eggs.
>
> (Helen Altonn, *Honolulu Star-Bulletin*)[14]

More and more, writers specialize, covering beats ranging far beyond traditional government structures. Sports has long been a popular beat. Business coverage has boomed in the past generation. Science, health, religion, the environment, agriculture, technology, education, commerce, and the arts draw increasing attention. Topics once dismissed as "soft" and relegated to back sections now win regular front-page, cover-page, or home-page display: parenting, aging, shopping, leisure, commuting, pop music, dating.

Special Qualities

What distinguishes specialty stories, of course, is a narrowness of focus. They have the lure of the exotic ("mouse sperm?" a reader might ask about the above story). They offer *depth* and *surprise*. But they must remain *accessible*

---

[14] Helen Altonn, "UH Research Breeds Mice from Dead Sperm," *Honolulu Star Bulletin,* 1 July 1998; available from http://starbulletin.com/today/news/story6.html; Internet; accessed 2 July 1998.

and *understandable* to broad media audiences. A prime challenge for writers is to master the material well enough to translate specialized information into lay language, quickly show the impact, and balance detail and explanation.

Special Problems

Two key questions arise.

1. **Should specialty stories be aimed mainly at the general readership or at those people already versed in a topic?** Suppose the subject is an exhibition of modern art by young sculptors. Presumably some readers will be attracted to such an article because of their love of art. Others may know little about art but be open to a compelling story. What strategy best serves both camps? Many editors suggest *beginning* the story with the lay reader in mind, keeping the language simple and reducing technicality so almost anyone can understand and appreciate the main themes. Then add depth and complexity as you go, so that by the *middle* you are offering significant detail that will enthrall even the experts.

2. **How do you know when to omit or explain technical terms?** As always, err on the side of clarity. When you can, omit technical terms and use their common translations. Write about "allergies" rather than "rhinitis." At times, however, insider language may be in such widespread use that it cannot be avoided. In those cases, use the terminology but define it. If competitive figure skaters are attempting "triple axels," you can explain that they are jumps in which skaters start facing one direction, spin three and a half times in the air, and land facing the place they started.

Structure

Specialty stories are, pretty much by definition, about topics that are somewhat unfamiliar to most people, so the writing should stress the topic's meaning and impact. Bright writing, human interest examples, and everyday detail can raise these stories' appeal. Here are two leads from the same issue of *Forbes*, showing how a business magazine works at producing readable articles:

> In the overcrowded, cut-throat restaurant business, you need a gimmick. Chris Sullivan's gimmick is Australia—you know, Crocodile Dundee stuff. Sullivan's Outback Steakhouse serves slabs of high-grade beef in dining rooms festooned with surfboards, stuffed kangaroos and boomerangs. Average check: $17 per diner. Annual gross: $1.3 billion.
>
> (Erika Brown, *Forbes*)

> On a recent *Late Night with Conan O'Brien*, actress Sarah Jessica Parker spent most of her time raving about a pair of frilly cotton pajamas she had just

bought at Target for $12.99. The next morning it was high-fives all around at the . . . Minneapolis-based Dayton Hudson Corp.

Besides giving Target millions in free publicity, the incident showed the executives that their message was getting through: Target is a cool place to shop.

(Michelle Conlin, *Forbes*)[15]

OBITUARIES

Roy Rogers, the "King of the Cowboys" who sang, smiled and occasionally shot his way into the hearts of multitudes of Little Buckaroos, died Monday. He was 86.

(*Los Angeles Times*)[16]

I wrote my first obituary when I was 14 and working at my hometown weekly. More soon followed, the sequence of events generally going like this: We would hear through the community grapevine that someone had died. "Call the family," my editor would order. I would comply, in terror. Within minutes, I would be having a warm and tender discussion about what a great storyteller Grandpa had been or how inspirationally Sister had fought the cancer.

Soon I understood: an obituary is the story of someone's life, not just the death. Once the initial stab of grief subsides, people often want the world to know what a loved one was really like. Reporters regularly encounter relatives who say, "We've been waiting for you to call," or who prepare special reminiscences to share with the news media.

Not that obituary assignments are easy. You do encounter people who are overcome or inconsolable, some who consider writers as intruders and even vultures. It can be tricky blending sensitivity and professionalism, deciding when is the right time to approach a mourner, what are the right words to say. In general, approach gently, then let yourself be guided by the reaction.

People die every day, and few news writers escape the duty of reporting on this biggest of all stories.

Special Qualities

Obituaries, or "obits" as they are widely known among journalists, are news stories with a biographical twist. Their definitive ingredient is material showing the unique character of the person who has died. In illuminating what

---

[15] Erika Brown, "Beef and Boomerangs," *Forbes*, 11 January 1999, 172; Michelle Conlin, "Mass with Class," *Forbes*, 11 January 1999, 50.

[16] "Roy Rogers, 'King of the Cowboys,' Dies," *Los Angeles Times*, 7 July 1998, 1A.

made this individual special, obits resemble mini-profiles. Fond quotes, telling anecdotes, illustrative details from the past all contribute to an overall portrayal of an individual's impact and personality. Almost every obit contains a centerpiece "who clause," summing up the deceased person's legacy, and many obituaries continue for several paragraphs of biographical detail.

Here's a typical example:

> Francis Bernhard Libbe, 72, of Flossmoor, a trial attorney of 36 years with a colorful sense of humor, died Sunday. "He made life fun," said his son Francis G. Libbe. "Even in difficult times, he made people laugh. . . ."
>
> *(Chicago Tribune)*[17]

Special Problems

A writer's accuracy is seldom more scrutinized than in obituaries. Supersensitive relatives read them warily and treat them as semihistorical documents, to be framed, encased in the family Bible, passed on to subsequent generations. Errors are hurtful, and always noticed.

A second problem arises in treating delicate and controversial episodes in a deceased person's background. Our culture frowns on besmirching the dignity of the dead. Sensationalizing the negative aspects of someone's life will seem offensive. But glossing over important issues can be untruthful and a disservice to the audience, which expects balance and thoroughness.

How, then, do you handle unpleasant material in an obituary? The best course is to present unflattering information in the obit in proportion to its weight in the individual's life. If you cover the death of a serial murderer, the fact that he killed a dozen people should go into the lead. But, in an obit for an elderly good citizen, you would likely omit the night spent in jail for rowdiness a half century ago.

I once handled an obituary for a prominent businessperson who early in her career had been convicted of running a bawdy house. The incident was mentioned briefly midway through the obit but was overshadowed by reports of her later accomplishments. The key: think *proportionality.*

Structure

For all the earlier warnings against formulaic writing, you cannot help noticing that obits follow a remarkably standardized format:

* *The lead*—Name of the deceased, age, "who clause," fact of death, and cause of death

---

[17] "Francis Bernhard Libbe," *Chicago Tribune,* 15 July 1998, Metro Chicago, 9.

- *Bio section*—One paragraph for most people, expanding to an entire section for the prominent. Summarizes key biographical information and the individual's contribution to society. Often includes quotes and remembrances from colleagues and relatives
- *Survivors*—Names and current cities of immediate family members
- *Funeral arrangements*

Overall, obituaries are a quasi-literary form that inspires some of the media's most stirring writing. They deal with the ultimate in human interest drama: life and death and the meaning of the individual. They invite the telling of cherished anecdotes, the revelation of deep feelings. They present writers with a lifetime's worth of material to draw from and with an audience aware of its own mortality and ready to contemplate the life's journey of a fellow traveler.

You can even employ some humor in an obituary. Consider this example:

> Marion Donovan, a onetime Connecticut housewife who had to change one damp diaper too many, died on Nov. 4. . . . She was 81 and had helped spearhead an industrial and domestic revolution by inventing the forerunner of the disposable diaper.
>
> (Robert McG. Thomas Jr., *New York Times*)[18]

SUMMARY

Writers should approach every story as distinct and special, but they are also expected to master the basic forms of news presentation. By understanding that many stories share certain structures and qualities, they assimilate the standards and models of their craft, the baseline specifications. Fuller appreciation of these inner workings helps you gain the confidence and earn the competence to adapt and extend story forms in original ways. For most artists and craftspeople, mastering the routine is a first step toward improvisation and innovation.

For a writer, nothing is more urgent than finding what is distinct and compelling about every assignment and highlighting that unique quality for the audience. The basic news model can be a starting point, a sort of default setting to be used or adapted as a given assignment dictates. Its typical components are a lead, amplification paragraph, best quote, nut graf, documentation section, refocusing paragraph, blocks for each subtheme, and ending.

Through craft, writers can systematically use this model to help guide their reporting, focusing and writing toward a finite goal. If they can visualize the

---

[18] Robert McG. Thomas Jr., "Marion Donovan, 81, Solver of the Damp-Diaper Problem," *New York Times*, 18 November 1998, C25.

format, they will be prompted to collect the needed ingredients. If they understand the interior architecture of stories in general, they can arrange and rearrange their elements into the most fitting pattern for their particular story.

If this process sounds too mechanistic, then remember the preeminent role of magic. Models have limitations. A dressmaker can follow a pattern and produce a passable garment, but the ruffles and flourishes of the truly resplendent gown require the inspired imaginative touch of artistry.

In the same way, a great story has soul, a singular and defining spirit, a meaning and import transcending its parts and patterns. The creative churning of magic breeds the breakthrough idea, the deft phrase or grand stoke that pushes writing beyond the mundane.

Court stories, government coverage, even obituaries benefit from the winning detail or the inspired line. Never settle for the routine. Push yourself to find ways to turn seemingly ordinary assignments into stories with some special quality.

Without models and structures, we flail, but models alone leave work incomplete. Even the simplest-seeming, most routinized-looking assignments deserve both the discipline of craft and the marvels of magic.

Practicing Craft and Magic

1. Examine the front page and the local news page of your daily newspaper. First consider the range of topics: how many fit into the types discussed in this chapter and how many do not? Then look at the writing: how many follow the basic models discussed here and how many do not? Think about why the writers applied the standard types and models in some cases and why they chose to depart from them in others.

2. For your next assignment, use one of the models here as a beginning point for your writing. Gather the needed information, heed the special qualities of the story type, and prepare an outline that you can check against the model. In what ways does the model help? In what ways does it interfere with originality and creativity? Try to use the model as a baseline standard without adopting it inflexibly.

3. Before you complete the assignment, call on magic. Besides comparing your outline to the model, ask yourself whether you have a breakthrough idea, a special artistic touch that makes your story truly distinctive. Reach beyond types and models until you are satisfied that your story has your unique imaginative imprint.

Chapter 13

Mastering
the
Feature

Journalist Rick Bragg experienced a feature writer's epiphany while interviewing 87-year-old Oseola McCarty, a Mississippi laundry woman who had
amassed $150,000 and then given it away. As McCarty cradled an ancient
Bible, Bragg felt magic strike.

"I was seeing the pages of her dilapidated, falling-apart Bible stretching
up over her old hands," Bragg recalled in an interview. "I thought, she's so
frugal she won't even replace her Bible. The most important part of her was
her God, and she didn't even replace his words."[1]

Bragg, a Pulitzer Prize winner for the *New York Times*, had located the two
most important qualities of a successful feature: a *compelling theme* and the
specifics to authenticate it. The third paragraph of his page-one article read:

> She spent almost nothing, living in her old family home, cutting the toes
> out of shoes if they did not fit right and binding her ragged Bible with Scotch
> tape to keep Corinthians from falling out.
>
> (Rick Bragg, *New York Times*)[2]

Feature articles probe behind, underneath, and around the news. Where
the primary purpose of news is to reveal important developments, features
typically aim to put issues in larger perspective, to offer a special slant, to
engage the reader with a good story or a backstage view.

However, absolute distinctions between news and features can be hard to
articulate. News is often written in innovative and nontraditional styles.

---

[1] Rick Bragg, interview by the author, 16 April 1998.
[2] Rick Bragg, "All She Has, $150,000, Is Going to a University," *New York Times*, 13 August
     1995, 1.

Features often carry serious information. We even speak of the *news-feature*, an especially blurry category in which the writer builds on some matter directly in the news.

In his book *Writing for the Mass Media,* James Glen Stovall makes this perceptive point:

> Dividing feature stories from news stories is misleading. The two actually have a great deal in common. The difference is in emphasis. . . . Feature stories generally contain more detail and description. They go beyond most news stories by trying to discover the interesting or important side of an event that may not be covered by the six basic news values.[3]

It is a mistake, then, to believe that features are not timely or informative or that they mainly show off fancy writing. Feature articles almost always have currency and impart new information and insight. Their chief goal may not be to break news, but most features strive to be meaty and substantial, generally requiring even more reporting than news stories.

Features are sometimes characterized as "entertaining," although this description too can mislead. With few exceptions (such as a humor column), features need significance and heft to capture and hold the attention of harried readers. They function as entertainment in that they are by nature supplementary and sometimes less serious than breaking news. They trade less on the reader's need to know something immediately than on the desire to know more about interesting or important subjects.

Perhaps the biggest challenge in defining and crafting features is to recognize that reading them is an elective activity. Features are like the rich dessert following a full-course meal, tempting but easy to skip if you are feeling stuffed or in a hurry. News stories are entrees, more or less compulsory. If a development is new enough, important enough, relevant enough, then the consumer immediately understands the need to pay attention. There is less imperative to pause for a feature story. Thus, writers face the extra challenge of convincing readers that features are worthy of their discretionary reading time.

This chapter is devoted to the special challenges of feature writing, techniques for organizing and structuring feature articles, and ways to capitalize on both craft and magic in raising their quality.

SPECIAL CHALLENGES

Like all excellent writing, good features display the three qualities discussed throughout this book: great storyline, surprise, and stylishness. Beyond that,

---

[3] James Glen Stovall, *Writing for the Mass Media,* 4th ed. (Boston: Allyn and Bacon, 1998), 187–188.

it is risky to generalize. As already mentioned, features come in limitless varieties. Many textbooks offer classifications: the profile, the how-to, the trend, the seasonal, and so forth. Features can be about both the unusual (sudden riches, heroic rescues) or the usual (the story behind an old statue in the park). They can be first-person essays or third-person narratives. They can be long or super short (newspaper "brights," for example).

Rather than worrying about classifications, it may be more helpful to concentrate on some common qualities of features, particularly the in-depth type:

- Emphasis on strong human interest topics
- Ambition to provide depth or insight beyond breaking news
- Complexity of theme, material, and structure

When these elements are present, the genre provides several distinctive challenges. These challenges include winning reader commitment, establishing a compelling theme, unifying complex material, and sustaining appropriate voice and tone.

Winning Reader Commitment

A news article announces its point more or less by definition. If a story reports on a plane crash that killed 38 people, the point is obvious. Potential readers are oriented instantly to the substance and essence of the message, and their cognitive processes move seamlessly from topic to headline to text. Efficient communication takes place quickly and directly.

Features, on the other hand, tend to have points that are more subtle, indirect, or intricate. They may have thematic rather than action headlines, narrative rather than hard-news leads, complicated rather than straightforward structures. Casual readers scanning the text may not immediately grasp the purpose and point. They may find it easier to simply move on to the next item.

A vital obligation for the writer (along with the editor and designer) is to swiftly convince readers that a feature story will repay their commitment. As Chapter 5 stressed, writers must be desperate for every moment of a busy reader's time, and they have only a few seconds to break the hurry-up pattern of the typical news skimmer.

Features first, then, must grab and hold the reader's attention.

Establishing a Compelling Theme

Christopher Scanlan, a wonderful writer and teacher, likes to prod writers with the question, "What is your story really about?" Once, for example, he asked a group of journalists to write about their favorite soups. People selected a huge range, soups their grandmothers used to make, soups they associated with memorable vacations, soups that recalled special times or places. One person even chose the pea-soupy fog he drove through to get to work. But when Scanlan asked the writers what their essays were *really* about, the answer was not soup. The stories were really about close-to-heart topics like family, tradition, loneliness, and well-being. Writing about soup was the writer's means, not the end.

Every feature needs to be *really about something,* and that theme needs to be quickly evident to the reader. The headline, the art, and the first few paragraphs of a feature package need to stamp a meaningful and recognizable theme into the reader's consciousness. This is the storyline, one of the three qualities of excellence. Especially in features, writers need to articulate the theme, or storyline, to themselves and then dramatize it clearly and logically for readers.

Unifying Complex Material

Features need narrative drive and organizational unity. Too many features meander through various points without a discernible guiding vision. Readers may not consciously diagnose the problem, but their response is too often to stop reading, abandoning a piece in confusion.

Every article—but a feature above all—needs an outline, a game plan, a road map, an organizational logic. Call it whatever you wish, but make sure your article has it. Like construction workers erecting a skyscraper, you need a scaffolding to support and connect each tier of the story you are raising. Maintaining strong inner unity is one of the most powerful ways to keep readers from dropping out of a feature.

To see how writers unify their material, you might start by imagining a ladder of abstraction. At the top of the ladder is the theme expressed in its most universal way. Maybe it is "love" or "redemption" or "homecoming." Let's try an example, "the bonds of family." The next rung down is your immediate storyline, which illustrates the abstract theme through a specific case or story; for example, "how a child switched at birth discovers the many true meanings of family." On the next level, you rough out an outline: introduction (the main point and a listing of secondary points), body (points discussed in logical order), and ending. Another rung downward, and you map out a lead, a nut graf, a refocusing paragraph, a plan for proceeding through each point, to the ending, using the specific details and materials of your story.

Now you have a plan. By moving down the ladder, from the most abstract theme to the immediate specifics, you have solidified a logical relationship between your storyline and your material. That cohesion will make your story easier to understand and more enjoyable.

Sustaining Voice and Tone

Feature stories should sound right. They should broadcast the writer's voice, hitting the proper tones like an operatic soprano.

Voice probably comes more naturally than most writers believe. Many writers describe the struggle to "find" their voice, but most writers' voices will emerge spontaneously if they just clear away some the obstructing professional underbrush: the artificial constraints, expectations, and hobgoblins that haunt many newsrooms, writing studios, and writer-editor collaborations. Writers who are steeped in good material, relaxed and enthusiastic about their assignment, comfortable in their surroundings, and encouraged to be original and inventive do not have to find a voice—it rings out instinctively. Have you ever listened to yourself on a tape recording? Often we do not recognize our own voices. But everyone else does. The voice is there for others to hear.

Tone, on the other hand, is chosen sound. Writers must work at it. Stories can be sad, funny, tragic, wry, whimsical, fanciful, pathetic, heroic, arousing, playful, empowering, frustrating, inspiring. An obituary needs one tone, a joke another. A visit to a war zone calls for a different tone than a visit to a nudist beach. Like music arrangers selecting notes for calculated effect, feature writers should analyze their stories and select phrasings, rhythms, inflections, stress points, and punch lines that echo the natural pitch of the subject. Complementary form reinforces good content.

The rest of this chapter will elaborate on how writers can apply craft and magic to meet these special challenges.

REPORTING FOR FEATURE STORIES

Features, like other assignments, activate the basic writing model: launching, reporting, focusing, limbering, writing, rewriting, copyediting. In particular, features require a magnitude of reporting that surprises some novice writers.

Information, not flashy style, drives a good feature. The article can be only as good as the material it contains—the material you gather. Because of their heightened aspirations, most features require far more work than news stories, more sources, more angles, more in-depth interviews, more details.

Features often aim to show *cause and effect* (for example, why is air pollution increasing or decreasing?), *motivation* (what energizes a controversial rap musician?), or *impact* (how are children affected by changing welfare rules?). They seek to *explain* (how do scientists approach AIDS research?) and *show patterns* (are certain groups discriminated against in bank loans?). Achieving these goals, plus adding the necessary *perspective*, can require extraordinary levels of detail and evidence.

Features typically make use of extensive human and documentary sources. More than most news stories, they also draw heavily on the writer's personal observations, which contribute descriptions and insights that provide vital texture.

Several kinds of information and literary devices turn up regularly in good features. Knowing in advance that they may be needed, writers can build in specialized reporting techniques to get them.

- **Anecdotes and examples.** It is axiomatic to say that features should show as well as tell. Nothing works better than illustrative, insightful vignettes. In an article showing the horrors of war in Zaire, Jack Kelley of *USA Today* vividly conveyed his point: "You try to close your eyes. But do that and you'll slip on human feces and land atop a corpse. You try to pretend a crying child isn't holding on to your leg begging for help. But she is."[4]
- **Details.** In his splendid book *Intimate Journalism,* writer and teacher Walt Harrington talks about "gathering a full range of sensory details—trying to report through all five of our senses" to establish "documentary detail" that accumulates to verify reality.[5] Sometimes the details can be whimsical or amusing. In a story about a cat who somehow dialed for help while choking on his collar, the *Tampa Tribune* reported: "One button lower and he could have called pay-per-view. One button to the right and he would have called Orlando. But police say a 9-week-old gray and white cat hit just the right speed-dial button to call 911."[6]
- **Description.** You are profiling a titan of industry. What is on her office walls? How messy is her desk? Does she lord it over visitors, elevated behind a big walnut desk, or sit beside them on a soft couch? How fast does she walk? What kind of calendar does she carry? What sites are bookmarked on her computer? Who has her private phone number? What look crosses her face when someone interrupts her? Does she know the name of her receptionist? In a crisis, what do her eyes look like? How does her voice sound? Does she lean forward, pace, sit tensely, withdraw, yell, shut her eyes, turn on soothing music? If a movie director was filming her, what would viewers see, hear, and feel in the opening shot?
- **Dialogue.** Like most stories, features need good quotes. More than that, they often reproduce entire dialogues, which adds action and realism. These quotes must be accurate: take extensive notes, and use tape recorders when you can.

---

[4] Jack Kelley, "I Thought I'd Seen It All," *USA Today,* 4 August 1994, 6A.
[5] Walt Harrington, *Intimate Journalism* (Thousand Oaks, CA: Sage, 1997), xx.
[6] Brian Cooper, "Keep the Reader with Interesting Perspective," *The American Editor,* November 1996, 25.

- **Time lines.** As we will discuss shortly, many features eventually turn into chronologies, the narrative flowing from earlier to later in time. In reporting, you need to collect detailed step-by-step information of how events and situations develop over time.
- **Scenes.** A feature is often cinematic in the way it plunges readers into the middle of a situation, as if they were viewing it live. Re-creating these scenes requires an abundance of quotes, observations, descriptions, and corroborative detail. Reread the scenes in the story that opens Chapter 9. Imagine the reporting necessary to present these specific moments.

In almost every case, you want to assemble far more information than you will actually include in a story, so that you have a profusion from which to select. Your goal is to have, say, 10 quotes, from which you select the one great one, not one or two quotes that may be merely adequate.

Many writers speak of "saturation reporting" or "immersion reporting" to characterize the level of effort required. Writing will be infinitely easier if you confront the terminal feeling secure you have mastered your subject.

SHAPING THE FEATURE

As you approach the writing stage, the artisan and artist should both be busy. The artisan has been dutifully laboring to provide abundant, authoritative, and interesting information and to identify potential themes and approaches. The artist has begun to noodle, to rummage around in the mass of material, to tease and stimulate the intellectual electrical system in hopes of striking a spark. In short, the artist is incubating the breakthrough idea.

Try not to become confused as we interchange terms like "breakthrough idea," "high concept," "theme," and "storyline." The artisan lobbies for strictly distinguishing among them, but the artist holds out. The artist likes varying the phrases. Each one hits you slightly sidelong, triggering subtle shadings and new reactions. It is like having several windows in the same room. Each provides a fresh angle. One may serve you better, another may appeal to someone else.

Whatever term you prefer, the point is that outstanding feature writing relies on answering the essential question, What is this really about? Finding that breakthrough idea turns an assortment of data into a story that connects to human experience and identity. True stories are hard to resist.

To shape the feature, then, you go channeling for themes and storylines, consumed by your material, exercising every lightning rod of inspiration, alert for the muse's visit at any moment day or night.

Sometimes the breakthrough idea articulates itself abstractly. For example, you may suddenly realize that your profile of a local minister is really about managing the tension between spiritual ideals and secular realities. Other times, the breakthrough may come from a jarring specific. For instance, the newspaper reporter, author, and screenwriter David Simon once told about an encounter in an alleyway. He was researching his book *Homicide: A Year on the Killing Streets* (later converted into a network television series), following detectives who were frustrated by a child's murder case. In a dingy Baltimore alley, Simon stumbled onto a perverse scene: "This huge, huge rat was walking down the alley and came across a cat, and the cat actually backed away from the rat." To Simon, the symbolism was immediate and obvious: evil taunting good; murder thwarting justice. The scene embodied the storyline.[7]

Related to storyline is the concept of a *spine*. The spine is a literary thread that carries the theme through an entire article—it is the "line" that carries the "story." For instance, it can be a single person's story that illustrates a wider issue (how one unemployed family copes with the pressures of poverty). It can be a recurring problem common to many people in many situations (the tricks students use to get the attention of college admissions officers). It can be a chronology (how scientists found and explored the sunken *Titanic*). The spine can even grow out of a sense of place (David Simon also wrote a book about the drug transactions and other activities surrounding one street corner in Baltimore).

To summarize, then, the feature writer needs

- A compelling starting topic
- A wealth of material
- An inspired breakthrough idea that turns the general topic into a specific and unique story with broad and universal appeal
- A literary device, outline, road map, or plan for ordering the piece

Finally, the writer needs to select an organizational structure or form, a shape that holds together all the themes and material for top impact on readers. The next section discusses several specific methods of organization that feature writers can consider.

STRUCTURES FOR FEATURE ARTICLES

Golfers carry several different clubs, salespeople vary their pitches depending on the client, and percussionists can perform swing, jazz, rock, or classical. Feature writers, too, need a variety of available modes. Once you have

---

[7] David Simon, interview by the author, 6 May 1998.

ample information, a breakthrough idea, and a general sense of how you want to advance the story, more hard work looms. You have to map a plan and carry it out. The more you understand about structure and technique, and the more models you have from which to choose, the easier this task will be.

In their emphasis on storytelling, features borrow from the world of creative literature. It must be emphasized that we are discussing *nonfiction writing* here. Everything is factual and accurate; nothing can be made up. Still, nonfiction writers can and should draw on techniques also used by authors and dramatists. Good features often use, among others, a *strong plot, character development, dramatic tension, rising action, climactic moments,* and *resolution*—all grounded in fact.

One reason feature writers must report so thoroughly is to accumulate the abundance of fact and evidence necessary to support these literary devices. Before you can incorporate a plot into a feature, for instance, you must learn as much as possible about how the plot, or real-life situation, evolved in reality. Before you can describe your characters or subjects, you must know enough about them to substantiate your observations or insights.

If you survey the literature on creative and journalistic writing, you will probably conclude that there is an infinity of potential structures for features. And you should feel free, perhaps even obligated, to invent your own. Here, we will summarize several of the most common and useful structures, and then describe in more detail a relatively new format that may be especially suitable for modern audiences and media.

The Classic Narrative

The classic narrative is a storytelling form used by writers from Homer to Shakespeare to Anne Rice. It begins in the middle of things, at or near a dramatic turning point or climax. It sucks the reader into the action, then builds in exposition and background, and often, once the dramatic tension hooks readers, reverts to a straightforward chronology for the bulk of the story. This form works well for stories involving a lot of action that builds over time to a climax.

The elements of the classic narrative include

- A dramatic hook that draws readers into the action and cues them to the storyline
- A nut graf or section that summarizes the theme and provides needed background or explanation
- A block-by-block development of the story, often but not necessarily in chronological order
- An ending that completes the action, circles back to the lead, or revisits the main character

Here is how Jerry Bledsoe, writing in the *Greensboro News & Record,* launched his eight-part true-crime series on a mysterious murder case:

> Dr. Tom Lynch was about to leave his dental clinic late on a Tuesday afternoon in July when the Albuquerque police chaplain came in and introduced himself.
> "I've got some real bad news," the chaplain said.
> Tom felt fear surge through him.
>
> (Jerry Bledsoe, *Greensboro News & Record*)

Bledsoe ended the series, thousands of words later, with another scene featuring Tom Lynch, this time standing in a graveyard contemplating all that had happened. The final words of the package: "And he began to cry."[8]

The Terrapin

Hard on the outside, softer inside, that is a terrapin. It also describes one of the most common feature structures. It is especially effective for trend stories, investigations, and newsier features because it combines the directness of news with the depth and power of narrative. This structure is named after the mascot of the University of Maryland.

Like the terrapin's outer shell, the lead tends to be fairly hard, a revelation or disclosure that readers need to know about early. After an introductory section announcing and documenting the disclosure, the terrapin-structured story typically drops back to a more narrative form. In a trend story about college students with unusual summer jobs, for example, the writer might write vignettes about several interesting cases. In an investigation, the narrative might read like a detective story as the writer recounts how the probe unfolded.

For a trend story on the proliferation of gated living communities, Alan Scher Zagier began this way:

> Debbie Leonard grew up behind a white picket fence. It wrapped itself around her family's house [with] its manicured lawn and all the other trappings of a secure suburban life in the '50s.
> Four decades later, Leonard still enjoys suburbia—from behind a wrought-iron gate, guarded by a security camera and a brick wall.
> She is one of about 8 million Americans who live in gated communities.
>
> (Alan Scher Zagier, *Raleigh News & Observer*)[9]

---

8 Jerry Bledsoe, "Bitter Blood," *Greensboro News & Record,* 21 August and 1 September 1985; special reprint section, 1–19.

9 Alan Scher Zagier, "'Gated' Living Inspires Debate," *Raleigh News & Observer,* 7 June 1998, 1A.

The Chronology

Few features are organized as a sheer chronology. Many use a modified chronology, with a dramatic beginning that soon drops back into a chronological telling. Occasionally, however, a writer finds a story worth telling strictly from beginning to end, when the very heart of the story is the evolution, over time, of some person or situation. When Bonnie Harris followed a class through the local police academy, she started literally at the beginning:

Day 1
Three days after Labor Day, 31 cop wannabes take their seats at the Spokane Police Academy and listen to a string of strangers tell them how their lives will never be the same.

(Bonnie Harris, *Spokane Spokesman-Review*)[10]

The *Wall Street Journal* Story

Not many newspapers or magazines find themselves identified with a particular writing approach, but the *Wall Street Journal* does. For years the *Journal* has produced a signature trend feature, one that uses a person or company's individual story to illustrate a more universal point. For instance, it may frame a broad look at some social or economic issue by examining its effect on a specific family. Or it may isolate one small business coping with changes or pressures common to others.

Typically, the *Wall Street Journal* story begins with an interesting individual or institution in some dilemma or exotic situation. Then comes a transitional paragraph that broadens the lens, and the story proceeds to look at the larger picture or theme. The stories feature a wealth of detail and a breezy writing style.

In *The Art and Craft of Feature Writing*, the *Journal*'s respected writer and editor William E. Blundell describes the four stages of a typical *Journal* feature as follows: (1) "Tease me, you devil," the seductive lead; (2) "Tell me what you're up to," the direct theme statement; (3) "Oh yeah?" the section that proves the theme with logic and evidence; and (4) "I'll buy it. Help me remember it," the ending that seals it in memory.[11]

For its report on the lucrative and combative "Elvis industry," the *Journal* began its story this way:

MEMPHIS—In the United States District Court for the Western District of Tennessee, on the ninth floor of the Clifford Davis Federal Building, in the

---

[10] Bonnie Harris, "The Thin Blue Line," *Spokane Spokesman-Review*, 11 December 1994, H2.
[11] William E. Blundell, *The Art and Craft of Feature Writing* (New York: Plume, 1988), 95.

federal court clerk's file folder, there are three pairs of panties of questionable legality.

The panties would be uncontroversial—ordinary cotton, one pair pink, one white, one blue—but for what Sid Shaw has done to them. Mr. Shaw, an entrepreneur who lives in London, has decorated them with a picture of Elvis Presley's face.

(Timothy K. Smith, *Wall Street Journal*)[12]

The Cinematic

The cinematic story spotlights an individual person, place, or situation and tells the story through episodic, scene-by-scene construction. It takes the reader somewhere, turns on the camera, and shows the story through close-ups, overview shots, and you-are-there reality. This technique lends itself to stories where the place, the setting, or the situations are colorful and meaningful.

The lead usually zooms in on a scene that quickly establishes the mood and theme. There is usually a nut graf within the first five or six paragraphs, to orient the reader, and then the rest of the story alternates scenes (usually presented in the present tense to simulate "real time") and connective sections (usually shorter segments summarizing key points, offering needed explanation, and providing transition between scenes).

To introduce readers to how schools now teach sex education, writer Kathy Holub used her lead to propel the audience directly into a classroom:

It is Tuesday afternoon at Campbell Middle School and the seventh grade is learning to Recognize a Risky Situation. This is a euphemism. What they're really learning is How to Avoid Having Sex. But here in Family Life class (formerly known as sex education), it's not called sex any more. It's called Risk Behavior.

(Kathy Holub, *West* magazine, *San Jose Mercury News*)[13]

The Map

Canadian journalist David Hedley coined the term "mapping" for an article format that helps readers navigate complex material. A mapped article is not so much a fluid and unified narrative as a body of information organized so readers can efficiently use it.

---

[12] Timothy K. Smith, "Elvis Merchandisers Are All Shook Up," *Wall Street Journal*, 30 June 1988, 1.

[13] Kathy Holub, "They're Not Afraid to Ask," *West* magazine, *San Jose Mercury News*, 4 September 1988, 6.

Typically, a mapped article opens with a standard inverted-pyramid lead. However, where the inverted-pyramid story would continue with information in descending order of importance, mapping follows a different route. A mapped story clusters information into sections of related material. Each section is labeled with a clear subhead, providing readers with a "map" to find the information they need. According to Hedley, the subheads "usually give a description of the type of information to follow. For example: The Conflict; The Case; What Happened; What Next. This gives readers a familiar reference point."[14]

USA Today used the mapping format for a report on developments in the slaying of basketball star Michael Jordan's father. After a brief introduction, the report was divided into sections headed "The charges," "How Jordan was killed," "What happened after the shooting," "The cremation controversy," and "Others arraigned Monday."[15] Readers could identify the sections at a glance and quickly locate information of interest.

As you can see, mapped articles usually are not stories at all. They are reports. Readers are not expected to read them from beginning to end but can skip around to select the segments that most interest them.

The First-Person Essay

If any writing style can be called controversial, it is the first-person approach. Tradition-minded editors cringe at the prospect of writers who litter their copy with the pronoun *I*. The style can be self-indulgent, narcissistic, a departure from expected journalistic detachment. It seems to exalt opinion over information and writer over subject.

Yet first-person writing has flourished in recent years, a comeback driven in part by its popularity in online media. Pioneering electronic magazines such as *Salon* and *Slate* depended heavily on first-person essays, and the personalized, conversational nature of the Internet quickly seemed especially hospitable to the style.

For example, in a feature on whether public rest rooms are safe for children, *Salon*'s writer began this way:

> In a low growl, I threatened my 4-year-old, Ian, that he would not see [the end of the movie] if he continued to talk loudly, throw candy wrappers and run up and down the rows. . . . He needed to go potty. . . . Temporarily free of his mother's wrath, he gleefully swung open the door while I waited. But as I stood outside the door, another mother towing two children . . . purposefully

---

[14] David Hedley, "Mapping: A New Way to Consider Readability," *Coaches' Corner,* December 1991, 3.

[15] "Death Penalty Might Be Sought for Pair," *USA Today,* 17 August 1993, 2C.

walked over to me. "What are you doing?" she said. . . . "How could you possibly let your little boy go in there alone. . . ."

(Diane Lore, Salon)[16]

In limited amounts first-person writing can be uniquely powerful and moving. But overindulge and readers quickly feel bloated. Think of first-person stories as a commodity that every writer must ration over a lifetime. Pretend you have a modest number of first-person chits in some imaginary account, and you must space them over a career. Use them too soon, and they are gone. Space them out, and they remain available for just the right assignment.

In short, first person should seldom be a first resort, especially for print media. It should be strategically applied to certain topics after consulting with your editor and agreeing that no other approach would be as effective. Online, the first-person approach feels more natural and conversational, but even here writers should be wary of focusing too much on themselves.

When is first person appropriate?

Its most obvious use comes in opinion writing, such as personal columns, a form that lies beyond the bounds of this book. Within conventional news and feature writing, the first-person approach most commonly applies to articles recounting dramatic or amusing personal experience: a reporter who survives a plane crash, witnesses an execution, keeps a journal during an extended illness, participates in a scientific experiment, trades places for a day with a rock musician, gets a fashion and beauty makeover, umpires a kids-league ball game.

When the *Milwaukee Journal* undertook an investigation of child mortality around the world, it sent two reporters into Haiti, Brazil, India, Nepal, and Bangladesh in an effort to "explain why 40,000 children die in the world each day." The resulting series, "Empty Cradles," jettisoned the standard reporter's detachment and let the writers, themselves parents of small children, produce what were called "personal accounts." Their reports were heart-breaking and riveting:

> Today I held a dying boy in my arms. He looked like a rag doll as he lay waiting with his father to see the doctor. . . . I felt the boy's bony arms. They were not much thicker than broom handles. . . . A tuberculosis vaccine could have spared Ernso, but like 73% of Haiti's children he was not immunized.

(Meg Kissinger, Milwaukee Journal)[17]

---

[16] Diane Lore, "The Men's Room," *Salon,* 1 December 1998; available from http://www.salonmagazine.com/mwt/feature/1998/12/01feature.html; Internet; accessed 8 December 1998.

[17] Meg Kissinger, "Politics Stops Health Advances," *Milwaukee Journal,* "Empty Cradles" special reprint, 1987, 7.

Tears welled in my eyes as I watched this small boy and his brother, the sons of a leper, so innocently and respectfully ask about my sons who were probably just waking on the other side of the earth in their warm home and flannel pajamas to a big breakfast in front of "Sesame Street."

(Richard Kenyon, *Milwaukee Journal*)[18]

The Hourglass

One of the first people to describe the hourglass format was Roy Peter Clark, the acclaimed writer, coach, and teacher associated with the Poynter Institute in St. Petersburg, Florida.

The hourglass structure features a wide opening at the top (the lead), a narrowing toward the center (the transition or, in Clark's terminology, "the turn"), and another widening at the base (the body of the story, usually a chronology).

The lead summarizes the story so that readers receive the key information immediately. After a few opening paragraphs, a transition then takes readers back to the beginning of the episode. The transition, or turn, can be as simple as "Here's how police described the incident" or "Based on interviews with surviving passengers, here is what happened during the crash." The story then takes the form of a chronological narrative.

The hourglass is recommended for the retelling of dramatic action yarns, such as crime or court stories, tales of heroism and adventure, or recapitulations of suspenseful incidents. Clark offers as an example a story about how a gunman held a five-year-old boy hostage for several hours before surrendering. The first few paragraphs summarize the story and its happy outcome. Then the writer offers the turn, a sentence saying "police and neighbors gave this account of what happened," and the remainder of the story is a chronological narrative of the event.

"Stories written in the hourglass structure," Clark writes, "are richer in detail than stories written in the traditional pyramid. The form seems to inspire reporters to work a little harder to gather those details that bring the narrative to life."[19]

Next, we will move to a first cousin of the hourglass, a story form that can help further reconcile the need to appeal to both skimming readers and those looking for detail and drama.

The Swinging Gate

Not long ago, I was interviewed on a public radio call-in program, and I was struck again by a familiar polarity in the listeners' comments. Some people

---

[18] Richard Kenyon, "Hope Amid the Horror," *Milwaukee Journal,* "Empty Cradles" special reprint, 1987, 5.
[19] Roy Peter Clark, "A New Shape for the News," *Washington Journalism Review,* March 1984, 46–47.

rejected media stories as too long and boring. Others complained they were too short and superficial.

Too long or too short? This is an old and haunting issue. Skimmers want a quick executive summary. Depth readers crave detail. Most newspapers, newsletters, magazines, and online sites attract many readers and viewers from both camps.

The challenge for writers is that obviously no single story can satisfy both groups. Or can it? Consider the following story form, which we will call the "swinging gate," and whether it can help writers speak to contrasting audiences.

Imagine a large field, bounded by a fence, with a gate at the north end and a large meadow inside the fence. This visual image represents an overview of the swinging-gate story form.

To put this concept into words, a story using the swinging-gate form begins with an entranceway section (the gate) that clearly summarizes all the main points. The story then merges, via a transition (the hinge), into a longer, narrative version (the great meadow).

Here is more on each major part:

- **The Gate.** This is the passage into the story. It is a concise overview of the main points, presented directly and in crystal-clear prose. The gate is a full section, not simply a lead. It closely relates to the kind of 400-word summary that the Associated Press often produces after a newspaper or magazine has published a lengthy investigative or enterprise article. The gate, of course, is designed for the skimmer, and it is written with the explicit understanding that many people may read no further. At the same time, the gate also serves the depth reader, because it provides an orientation that situates readers comfortably at the outset of a complex undertaking, tantalizing and preparing them for the adventure to come.
- **The Hinge.** This is a transition in several ways. First, it is a physical bridge from gate to narrative, designed to hold the reader's attention and to keep the entire article unified. It also serves as a transition from the newsy tone of the gate to what may be an entirely different writing style in the narrative. The hinge may be a standard short transition of a few words; it may be a section of several paragraphs. Most often, it will be about one full paragraph. But it needs to physically connect the gate to the narrative so that the overall effect is of one seamless structure.
- **The Great Meadow.** This is the narrative, as long, complex, and innovative as seems suitable. All forms, tones, and styles can be accommodated. Because the readers have come through the gate together, everyone is oriented, no one should be confused, and the writer now has a relaxed, committed, well-grounded audience eager for the full story. The meadow can consist of one large story, or it can be subdivided into several components.

Then it becomes the great fairgrounds, with booths (stories, sidebars, graphics, breakout vehicles of various kinds) catering to many different audiences and interests. The great meadow can—in fact probably *should*—take on an entirely different voice and style from the newsier gate.

What benefits flow from this form?

First, it puts responsibility on the writer, from the beginning, for attracting both skimmers and depth readers. As discussed in Chapter 11, editors and designers contribute immeasurably to packaging writers' work. But too often their efforts come late in the process. The swinging gate both challenges and liberates the writer to think of various audiences from word one.

Second, the swinging gate represents an effort to blend tones and functions into one manageable whole in a way that serves the modern reader, whose reading style is no longer strictly linear and who is receptive to a variety of formats within an overall package. It recognizes that people read and use media packages in different ways.

Finally, the swinging gate offers both structure and artistic freedom. The gate offers focus and boundary, but on reaching the great meadow the writer is freed almost entirely from format restrictions.

When would the swinging gate be appropriate? It could apply both to breaking news and to features, when there are both key news developments and important perspective.

For example, suppose a company in your community announces that it will build a multimillion-dollar plant creating hundreds of new jobs. This is a big story, one that will play heavily in word-of-mouth and over broadcast stations long before most people see it in the newspaper or online. Using the swinging gate, you might begin with a gate that announces the news but also incorporates your behind-the-scenes look into how local officials attracted the industry. The great meadow could be a dramatic, step-by-step playback of how a local task force wooed and won the new firm.

Even obituaries can be presented in the swinging-gate form. Let's say a minister dies after serving a neighborhood for 30 years. The gate is a standard news obit. The great meadow homes in on the lives the minister touched.

With feature projects like trend stories, investigations, and explainers, the form seems even more appropriate. The gate summarizes the findings; the great meadow tells the story.

As you can see, this form is close kin to Roy Peter Clark's hourglass form. The swinging gate differs by putting less stress on chronology, expanding the introductory section, and offering more options for style, tone, and display within the great meadow. But both forms have the similar goal of integrating both newsiness and readability.

BEGINNINGS

Feature leads range from the matter-of-fact to the luxuriantly descriptive. In all their various incarnations, they have two goals in common:

1. To reveal or illustrate the main theme
2. To make the reader want to know more

As you think through potential leads, a good exercise is to buttonhole a friend or spouse, begin telling your story, and notice what approach you naturally select. If the story is surprising enough, you probably will tend to disclose it immediately: "You'll never believe it. I've won the lottery!" For stories of that magnitude, such as investigations or trend features, a direct news-style lead may work best.

Here is an example from a newspaper's investigation of hazardous dams:

> Dam owners in Cambria and Somerset counties have disregarded crucial dam safety laws, possibly dooming Johnstown to another deadly flood, a *Tribune-Democrat* investigation has found.
>
> (Robert Long and Debra S. Moffitt,
> *Johnstown (Pa.) Tribune-Democrat*)[20]

Many features benefit from the basic news approach, but even more common is the narrative. The narrative style is indicated when you find yourself telling your friends a little story that signals the bigger storyline and sucks in the audience: "My cousin was home alone the other night when she started hearing funny noises in her garage. She hadn't picked up the baseball bat in her closet for years, but she grabbed it and headed for the door." If you find yourself relating the story in dramatic fashion, then a narrative lead is probably most appropriate.

What you must remember, however, is that immediacy is essential. When you tell stories to friends, you enjoy many advantages that writers lack: you have a respectful, captive audience; you can use voice, volume, and body language to supplement words; and you can speed up or change pace based on instant feedback. Writers have no such blessings. They must halt harried readers in their tracks, seize their attention within seconds, and deliver the goods quickly before the audience can wander away. The kind of elaborate windups that can work well when telling a story in person become wasteful

---

[20] Robert Long and Debra S. Moffitt, "Dam Owners Ignore Safety Measures," *Johnstown Tribune-Democrat*, 20 March 1995, A1.

and counterproductive when a writer is trying to entice a disembodied cast of edgy media customers.

In short, the first sentence has to catch them, or all is lost.

Here is an instance where the writer began with a scene but wasted no time whatever in signaling its significance:

> On the morning her world was turned on end, Jean Brinegar lay in a hospital bed, overwhelmed with pride. Katie was the daughter she'd always wanted.
>
> (G. Wayne Miller, *Providence Journal*)[21]

If you choose the narrative approach, do not underestimate the immensity of the challenge. Forget the leisurely and laid-back. Resist complacency. Demand of yourself a lead that pulsates with power and urgency, with dynamic words and images mighty enough to bulldoze through every layer of reader resistance.

Magazine editor Art Carey offers a splendid three-part test for narrative leads, in a passage quoted in Melvin Mencher's *News Reporting and Writing*. Carey recommends that the lead (1) *introduce the main character* (2) *in a colorful setting* that (3) *epitomizes the main theme, personality trait, trend, or adventure at the center of the story.*[22]

In a *Sports Illustrated* profile of an effervescent college football star, Tim Layden used a scene-setting lead to achieve all three of Carey's goals:

> The children were lined up against a fence at one end of the school playground, a ribbon of billowy T-shirts, ponytails and fourth-grade innocence, awaiting their teacher's command to begin the footrace. Moments earlier they had sat spellbound in their classroom . . . as Texas running back Ricky Williams answered their many questions. (*Who was the biggest influence in your life?* My mom. *What was your favorite subject in fourth grade?* Social studies. *Do you have a son?* Huh? No.) Finally they would ask how fast could he run. "I'll race you guys," Williams had said, beaming, and at the back of the room, two teachers nearly fainted, because it's not often that a guest speaker proposes recess.
>
> (Tim Layden, *Sports Illustrated*)[23]

ENDINGS

Feature stories need well-thought-out endings almost as much as jokes need clever punch lines. If you think of most feature writing as storytelling, then it follows that features, like stories, should have meaningful endings. They

---

[21] G. Wayne Miller, "The Very Best," *Providence Journal,* 17 November 1991, 1.

[22] Melvin Mencher, *News Reporting and Writing,* 7th ed. (Madison, WI: Brown & Benchmark, 1997), 206.

[23] Tim Layden, "Long-Running Longhorn," *Sports Illustrated,* 18 May 1998, 73.

should not merely drift off. Endings provide resolution for the enduring reader, a sense of shared completion.

An exceptional feature is one that makes you read to the end even if you had not originally intended to do so. When you run across such a story, turn back and analyze what the writer did that proved so magnetizing. It can be especially revealing to examine how the writer chose the beginning and the ending. Often they seem specifically conceived to work together, providing literary bookends for the story they enclose.

Several kinds of endings occur often:

- **The Perspective Ending.** An overview quote or observation that helps bring the entire theme into focus. This device probably serves as the most common ending, and it usually relies on a powerful panoramic quote. Below are two examples. A word of caution, however: writers should beware of overreliance on quote endings, which can seem clichéd or pat. Before automatically ending with a quote, consider all the other options and make sure you are persuaded that none would work better.

  On its Pulitzer Prize–winning investigation of medical malpractice, the *Indianapolis Star* ended its main piece with this patient's quote about a doctor:

  "How do you get away with killing somebody?" he asks. "He didn't even get disciplined."
  (Joseph T. Hallinan and Susan M. Headden, *Indianapolis Star*)[24]

  On a feature about street violence, Deborah Barfield ended with this quote from a teenage shooting victim:

  "I never thought it would happen to me," said Jordan, who expects to return to school in a few weeks. "After it happened, I realized it could happen to anyone. You don't have to go to violence, violence can come to you."
  (Deborah Barfield, *Albuquerque Journal*)[25]

- **The "Circle Back."** An ending that returns to the theme or situation introduced in the lead, effectively completing a circle for the reader.

  A *Los Angeles Times* feature on homeless illegal immigrant children opened with a scene of children dodging customs officials in a park. The ending returns to the same children, in a similar episode that shows the

---

[24] Joseph T. Hallinan and Susan M. Headden, "A Case of Neglect," *Indianapolis Star,* 24 June 1990, A17.

[25] Deborah Barfield, "America's Culture of Violence," *Albuquerque Journal,* 6 February 1994, B4.

circular pattern of their lives. Notice the evocative power of the last five words:

> . . . one boy spotted what he thought was an approaching Border Patrol vehicle. The children of the border bolted upright, snatched up the bags of food and drink and sprinted away into the trees, on the run again, silhouettes fading in the dusk.
>
> (Sebastian Rotella, *Los Angeles Times*)[26]

- **The summation.** An expository ending that wraps up the story's status. When Nicole Johnson, Miss America 1999, undertook a national tour to educate the public about diabetes, *USA Today* produced a feature with an typical summation ending:

> Johnson says it's very important for her to help find some of the millions of Americans who don't know they have diabetes. "They could be inching toward a diabetic coma," she says. She is challenging all Americans to get a blood test for diabetes.
>
> (Kathleen Fackelmann, *USA Today*)[27]

- **The kicker.** A punchy tagline that leaves the reader with a jolt. In this story about marathon swimmers, the writer ends with the scene of a competitor launching a 28-mile swim:

> "Goodbye. Maybe, I'll see you next year—maybe," she called out. Then Ms. Hersey walked down the gangway and disappeared into the Hudson River.
>
> (Winnie Hu, *New York Times*)[28]

- **The look ahead.** A "future spin" ending that propels the reader's thinking to what will happen next.

  In the article quoted at the beginning of this chapter, Rick Bragg begins by focusing on Oseola McCarty's philanthropy. He then turns to the people her good deed will help, closing with a look at its ongoing impact on Stephanie Bullock, "the first young person whose life was changed by her gift":

> She feels a little pressure, she concedes, not to fail the woman who helped her. . . . She counts on Miss McCarty's being there four years from now, when she graduates.
>
> (Rick Bragg, *New York Times*)[29]

---

[26] Sebastian Rotella, "Children of the Border," *Los Angeles Times*, 3 April 1993, A23.

[27] Kathleen Fackelmann, "Search Is On for 'Missing Millions,'" *USA Today*, 14 December 1998, 6D.

[28] Winnie Hu, "Getting Around Manhattan the Wet Way," *New York Times*, 12 July 1998, 25.

[29] Bragg, 22.

One kind of ending to avoid is the *editorial commentary*, a puffy, preachy, or chatty conclusion that forsakes the writer's professionalism: "After all her hard work, it's clear that Nguyen has a bright future on the stage of her choice." Resist this kind of ending. Stick to material facts or observations, or use a scene strong enough that readers can predict for themselves the prospects awaiting your protagonist.

SUMMARY

Features delve into the deeper regions of news and culture. They are distinguished by high journalistic ambition: intense human interest themes, in-depth research, and complexity of content and structure. For the audience, features are discretionary reading. They challenge writers to quickly gain reader commitment through compelling storylines, organized and approachable writing, and originality of tone and voice.

The feature writer's checklist runs something like this:

- Start with an interesting assignment.
- Amass a wealth of material through immersive reporting.
- Alight on an inspired breakthrough idea that articulates your special angle and approach.
- Select a storyline to carry the breakthrough idea throughout the piece.
- Develop a detailed outline or plan for ordering the material.

Through craft, feature writers break down a large assignment into manageable parts. They know that feature reporting demands an unusual quantity and quality of information: a search for causes, motivations, impacts, patterns, and perspective. They know that the writing will require certain kinds of information: dialogue, descriptions, examples, and scenes. They know that features need structure, and they are familiar with various traditional choices (narratives, chronologies) and less-conventional approaches (the hourglass, the swinging gate). They recognize the special attention necessary for feature beginnings and endings. They apply themselves assiduously to each step.

But craft alone is insufficient. Feature writing is intense and absorbing. Nowhere in writing does magic serve more vitally. Finding the breakthrough idea launches a feature beyond the ordinary and mundane, and the quest calls on every power of imagination and vision. Whether by evolution or eruption, application or alchemy, the arrival of the what-this-is-really-about insight is pivotal. Apply all resources in pursuit of the inspired storyline: brainstorming, prewriting, exercising, visualizing, and stretching ideas, images, and words toward higher and higher art.

In features as in other writing, craft lays the foundation for the fulfillment of magic.

Practicing Craft and Magic

1. Pick up a newspaper or magazine or visit an online news site. Find an example of a feature that seems appealingly organized and a second example you consider unsuccessful. Compare their structures. What techniques make one more effective than the other? What lessons does this comparison offer for your own writing?

2. For your next feature article, consider at least two of the story forms described in this chapter. Develop outlines based on each form. Which seems more suitable, and why?

3. Once you have selected a story form for your feature, use it as a stimulus for your artistic side. Following the WRITE model, release yourself to think about the elements needed to succeed. Prod your imagination toward stronger and stronger material, whether it is a narrative hook, a nut graf, a striking scene, or an eye-catching lead. Keep mulling your assignment both directly and indirectly with the expectation that breakthrough ideas will occur.

Chapter 14

Reaching Higher Levels

My son Jeff played kids' baseball for years, always wanting to pitch but hardly ever getting the chance. Then one season a new coach took him aside, said he was counting on Jeff to become the team's leading pitcher, and taught him a grip to make the baseball curve.

Jeff came home that day with a new state of mind. He actually believed he was a pitcher. He began thinking and acting like a pitcher. And he had learned something about pitching. He had a new technique and skill to apply. He went on to an all-star season.

Reaching higher levels, in sports or art or writing, hinges on two qualities: competence and confidence. Competence corresponds to craft; as a rule, the more you learn about something, the better you perform. Confidence parallels magic; the more you believe in yourself, the higher your aspirations and achievements can sail.

In aiming higher, writers build on the virtues of *creative balance.* The goal is to progress simultaneously toward more sophisticated craft and more trustworthy magic. The result should be twofold:

1. Steady headway toward greater ideas, material, and words, the properties that lead to superior stories
2. Occasional quantum leaps in the direction of artistic virtuosity, the magic that enkindles excellence

Steady headway and quantum leaps can drive work forward in an ever improving spiral. This chapter lists some examples and characteristics associated with advanced craft and advanced magic. They can prove instructive and inspirational in helping writers surge ahead as both artisans and artists.

ADVANCED CRAFT

Study with the sages. Learn from the maestros. Deconstruct the masterpieces. Advancing in the craft of writing should be a lifelong educational adventure. It is not a passive process. Active observation, attention to detail, scrutiny of technique all matter. Every writer's guide to survival and prosperity should include an action plan for analyzing top writers and writing.

What you seek is specific and tangible: methods for developing better ideas, better material, better words, and better ways of presenting it all.

The following sections present some methods and techniques that characterize the work of leading writers.

Better Ideas: Raising the Degree of Difficulty

One summer when I was a teenager, I decided to read as many great novels as I could. I started with Steinbeck's *Grapes of Wrath* and Mitchell's *Gone with the Wind,* two enthralling page-turners. Then I dipped into Faulkner's *The Sound and the Fury,* and found myself bewildered from the first page. The lesson was soon clear: you need a lot more reading experience before taking on the likes of Faulkner.

This lesson carries over into writing. You start with simple assignments and grow into tougher ones. Unfortunately, however, most writers tend to level off after a while. We arrive at a comfortable niche—perhaps a certain genre, perhaps a satisfying specialty—and begin cruising.

Just as Olympic divers know that success involves raising the degree of difficulty of their attempts, Olympic-caliber writers need to feel the same prodding. Growth in writing requires constantly raising the bar for story ideas.

Here are some suggestions:

- **Never stop setting goals.** Whether you are a first-time writer or an accomplished pro, you should set short-term, mid-term, and long-term writing goals. Short-term goals get you through the typical workday. Mid-term goals look ahead a few days or weeks. For many writers, especially those on constant deadline, short- and mid-term demands can be consuming. They can eat up all your time. But never neglect long-term goals, those extending out several weeks or months. Every writer needs to establish an aggressive long-range work plan, including a steady steepening of the kinds of stories to attempt.

- **Always work toward one great story, no matter how busy or frantic your life may otherwise be.** Devote a little time each day and week toward developing a story you consider truly special. Aim high, work steadily, and you will be surprised how revitalizing—and achievable—the effort will be. The writers who burn out soonest are often those who let short-range subsistence demands overwhelm them. The most satisfied writers always seem to be working toward a special story, a long-range ambition. Even if it takes six months or a year to do, even if you can devote only minutes a day or a few hours each week, commission for yourself an exceptional, challenging project and move with discipline to accomplish it.
- **Brainstorm regularly with others, including but not limited to your editors.** Earlier chapters discussed the need to confer regularly with editors and to bounce ideas off a variety of other creative people. Separately, perhaps two or three times a year, you should make time for brainstorming higher-altitude ideas. One specific goal: at least once a year you should focus on selecting the best article you can produce over the next year. Then produce it.
- **Try the unusual.** Once when I was a city editor, my managing editor had an inspired idea for a special project, a difficult story that required delicate reporting and a deft touch. One day we stood gazing across the newsroom, wondering what reporter could possibly handle such a sophisticated assignment. Eventually our eyes settled on the paper's human interest columnist, a person who wrote wonderful columns day in and day out but was rarely called on to handle regular assignments. We offered him the idea, he jumped to accept it, and, outside his regular groove, he produced a brilliant story. The moral: don't get complacent in your comfort zone. Try new kinds of stories, assignments that scare you, challenges that may seem unlikely. How else will you grow?

Better Material: Perfecting Information Gathering

The better your information, the better your writing. Repeat this often enough, and maybe we will all appreciate its profundity.

To raise the level of information gathering, start with improved interviewing. Where possible, *conduct more interviews per assignment* and *spend more time per interview*. Depth is to some degree a function of time invested. One reporter, for instance, insists that you cannot fully know a source until you have spent a night in the source's home. Writer-teacher Walt Harrington talks of "immersing ourselves temporarily in the lives of our subjects so that they become relaxed in our presence and so that we can see real events unfold, develop and be resolved."[1]

---

[1] Walt Harrington, *Intimate Journalism* (Thousand Oaks, CA: Sage, 1998), xxi.

If you cannot spend additional time, then use your time more wisely. Depth is also to some degree a property of good planning, good questions, good observations, and good thinking. The magazine and book author Ken Auletta says that a writer is like an anthropologist. Auletta describes the process this way:

> Your mien is that of a visitor to another planet. You ask questions because you wish to understand the customs, the habits, the culture of the natives. Implicitly, this conveys an impression that you seek understanding, not quick deadlines. This encourages people to help you.[2]

Do not overlook the value of returning to sources several times to build on interviews and answers. Rosemary Armao, a former executive director of Investigative Reporters and Editors, advises reporters to "always call back or revisit. After an interview, people think about what they should have said. Give them a chance to tell you."[3]

Finally, hold fast to the age-old principle: *never give up.* Chris Ison, whose work helped win the *Minneapolis Star Tribune* a Pulitzer Prize for investigating arson, tells this illustrative story:

> When we knocked on one fireman's door, he promptly told us to get lost. He knew what we were up to, he said, and there was no way he was going to answer any questions. He wouldn't even open the door so we could slip a business card to him. We didn't argue, but we asked him a question about his work. He answered. We asked him another, and he answered that. An hour later, we were still standing on his doorstep, reading from our long list of questions. He stood behind his closed screen door and answered almost every one.[4]

Better Storylines: Applying the Complication-Resolution Model

Chapter 13 outlined several approaches writers can take to features and other in-depth assignments. The writer-teacher Jon Franklin has spelled out a complication-resolution model that underlies many of these approaches. Franklin's thinking, presented in his book *Writing for Story,* is detailed and demanding, but studying it will reward most writers. It usefully and incisively breaks down "dramatic nonfiction" into what Franklin calls "a step-by-step cookbook approach."

Franklin commands writers to think seriously about storylines and structure before launching into a major project. His well-defined system helps writers turn huge undertakings into a series of components, each of which can

---

[2]   Ken Auletta, "Writing In-Depth Profiles," *IRE Journal,* January-February 1998, 6.
[3]   Rosemary Armao, "Interviewing Insights," *IRE Journal,* November-December 1996, 3.
[4]   Chris Ison, "The Art of the Confrontational Interview," *Coaches' Corner,* September 1990, 4.

be identified and labeled prior to writing. Some writers find it too rigid, and it may not apply to every complex article, but the system provides a specifically articulated model that can help force discipline and structural order.

Franklin begins by defining a story as "a sequence of actions that occur when a sympathetic character encounters a complicating situation that he confronts and solves."

To make a mnemonic, call this the SCAR model:

Sympathetic character
Complication
Action
Resolution

Putting this model into operation makes major demands at the reporting stage. Writers must locate a sympathetic character and collect sufficient information and insights to identify and fully draw out the complication, action, and resolution.

Franklin then calls for a five-part outline, beginning with the most vital element: a simple but precise definition of the complication. He suggests a three-word, noun-verb-noun format. One example he offers is "Cancer strikes Joe." Part five is the resolution: "Joe overcomes cancer." In between are three action phases taking the main character from complication to resolution.[5]

In literary terms, the five-part outline amounts to a plot. It moves the story, through action, from complication to resolution. Franklin also offers specific suggestions for ordering each section of the narrative.

Not every assignment lends itself to the Franklin model, but it can often serve as an excellent guide to making the transitions from broad idea to functional storyline to effective outline.

Beyond its immediate application to individual stories, Franklin's thinking also pushes writers deeper into studying the infrastructure and architecture of language and storytelling. As much as possible, the aspiring great writer strives to become a super-technician, an authority on story contour and form.

Better Writing: Stocking Up on Technique

Writing can and should be studied, as the work of Franklin and others shows, and writers can and should apply themselves to methodically improving craft. Another surefire course is to observe the techniques other writers use and to constantly build up your own arsenal. To some extent, writing is a never-ending round of problem solving. Your goal is to identify various obstacles and

---

[5] Jon Franklin, *Writing for Story* (New York: Plume, 1994), xvii, 71, 84.

prescribe for yourself ways to surmount them. In writing as in medicine, a professional needs diagnostic skill and broad knowledge of available remedies.

Jack Hart, longtime editor and writing coach at the *Portland Oregonian*, has spoken and written extensively on what he sometimes calls "the tools of storytelling":

> Great cooks have great kitchens. Expensive cookware hangs near the range. Gadgets for every culinary purpose fill the drawers. Recipes jam file boxes. . . . The best writers have their own collections of utensils, garnishes and recipes. They, too, know what each is called and how to call it into play.[6]

From Hart and many others, we can draw examples of advanced techniques that both rookie and established writers can call on:

- **Summary narrative versus dramatic narrative.** Summary narrative, according to Hart, is the kind of description, common to everyday reporting, that reconstructs or compresses a series of actions. His example: "They moved to three states in three years." By contrast, dramatic narrative, "the soul of true storytelling," lets writers slow down to describe specific activities in something simulating real time: "He rose from the chair, strolled to the door, turned the knob and pulled."[7] Many good stories alternate dramatic narrative (the scenes) and summary narrative (the connections). In feature stories, lead writers often have to choose between summary narrative, which gets to the point quicker, and dramatic narrative, with its stronger storytelling power.
- **Flashby paragraphs.** Also identified by Hart, the flashby is a quick umbrella-type paragraph that repeats phrases to drive home a point: "It's happening in California. It's happening in New York. And it's happening here."[8]
- **Jab paragraphs.** Bob Baker of the *Los Angeles Times* defines the jab as a small paragraph that gives "a sense of personality and energy" to a story and catches readers' attention with a "bam effect." An example from a story where the writer wants to quickly show that a popular restaurant has abruptly closed: "The 'foodski, funski and brewski' are gone-ski. Gorky's is kaput."[9]
- **"The secret garden."** Tom French, master writer for the *St. Petersburg Times*, exhorts writers to "take us into the secret garden" by supplying "the

[6] Jack Hart, "The Tools of Storytelling," *Second Takes, Portland Oregonian* newsroom newsletter, July 1997, 1.
[7] Hart, 1.
[8] Carl Sessions Stepp, "Coaches' New Testament," *Washington Journalism Review,* October 1990, 29.
[9] Bob Baker, ed., *Nuts & Bolts, Los Angeles Times* newsroom newsletter, June 1998, 3.

unofficial version, the real story," which he calls "more interesting and more complicated than the official version."[10]

Better Writing: Exploiting the Tiniest Opportunity

"I obsess over everything," confesses Sara Rimer, whose lyrical articles have appeared in the *New York Times* and elsewhere. Rimer specializes, among other things, in the telltale small touches that bespeak elegance. With talent and experience, writers come to know the value of these perfectly timed subtle strokes, perhaps like artists who intuit when to add the unexpected splash of color or designers who instinctively apply the enchanting finishing flourishes.

In the following lead, notice the comma near the end:

> CAVENDISH, Vt.—At age 75, after 20 years in exile, nearly all of it spent in solitude in this mountain town, Aleksandr Solzhenitsyn today began the long journey home, to Russia.
>
> (Sara Rimer, *New York Times*)[11]

Grammar does not require the comma after "home," but here its use is masterful. It makes the reader pause and meditate briefly on the mightiness of the idea of "home," especially for someone in exile 20 years.

In a small but mind-opening way, one tiny punctuation mark spotlights a universal theme, the exquisite emotion we invest in sundering and restoring ties with home.

Asked about the comma, Rimer replied, "I read the story aloud, and it just seemed to sound better" with the comma. Rimer said she always reads copy aloud, trusting her ear for guidance.

Like many so-called small touches, this one did not come in isolation but from Rimer's larger effort to "have an emotional response" to the story. "Obsessing" as writers do, she studied Solzhenitsyn, read articles about him, and reflected on his feelings, "trying to imagine what it was like for him." Her overall effort led not only to a strong storyline but to a final dash of craft that drove it home.[12]

ADVANCED MAGIC

Craft is the cake, magic the icing. Craft is the functional infrastructure, magic the gleaming exterior. Craft is the foundation, magic the palace atop it. Craft

---

[10] Tom French, "Tips from the 1998 National Writers' Workshop," *Second Takes, Portland Oregonian* newsroom newsletter, July 1998, 8.

[11] Sara Rimer, "Solzhenitsyn Looks Home, to Russia," *New York Times,* 26 May 1994, A14.

[12] Sara Rimer, interview by the author, 22 January 1999.

is the capable, magic the virtuoso. Craft is competence, magic excellence. Craft is the satisfactory, magic the sublime.

We could parade around these metaphors indefinitely, but the point is probably planted: magic inspires the all-important creative leap, but magic almost always builds on craft.

One study of creative artists and scientists concluded that "creation is not merely inexplicable unconscious inspiration . . . it involves lengthy elaboration and working out by a skilled craftsman."[13]

In other words, a writer cannot skip straight to the magic. Magic is less spontaneous than induced. Craft and hard work first must fertilize the brain cells. So let us assume that the first step toward reaching the inspirational stage is an advanced level of craft. What else can writers do to jog the creative spirits?

Here is where confidence joins competence. Thinking of themselves as artists, writers should live and work in such a way that they fortify their self-trust and fine-tune their receptivity to inspiration. Three especially productive concepts involve *desire, setting,* and *stimulation.* In examining them, we can call on testimony from artistic masters both contemporary and classical.

Desire

Qualities like determination, tenacity, and persistence are often associated with successful reporters, but they also apply to superior writers. The irresistible desire to write well breeds intensity, and intensity often transports writers deeper into a creative zone. Once writers access this zone, they can seem unreachable. Say hello, and they ignore you. Look into their eyes, and they seem entranced.

The composer Richard Strauss once said

> I can tell you from my own experience that an ardent desire and fixed purpose combined with intense inner resolve brings results. Determined concentrated thought is a tremendous force.[14]

Discussing the composition of *Madame Butterfly,* Giacomo Puccini described this sensation with a spiritual conviction:

> I feel the burning desire and the intense resolve to create something worthwhile. This desire, this longing, implies in itself the knowledge that I can attain my goal. Then I make a fervent demand for and from the Power that created

---

13 P.E. Vernon, ed., *Creativity* (Middlesex, Eng.: Penguin, 1970), 53.
14 Willis Harman and Howard Rheingold, *Higher Creativity* (Los Angeles: Jeremy P. Tarcher, 1984), 25.

me. This demand, or prayer, must be coupled with full expectation that this higher aid will be granted me.[15]

"Laborious study" and "technical mastery of his craft" are vital to the artist, Puccini added, but without the higher aid one "will never write anything of lasting value."[16]

You may recall an earlier discussion in this book of how writers' grand aspirations can make them nervous and tense. How do we reconcile this disabling potential with the intensity and desire that characterize giants such as Strauss and Puccini? The answer has several parts. First, remember that hard work must precede the fervent writing stage; writers cannot reach it until they are ready. Second, consider experience: the neophyte should not expect to vault straightaway into the exalted realms but should progress toward them in a graduated manner.

Third, remember relaxation. In another example of creative balance, writers must find ways to both relax and intensify simultaneously, to make themselves physically and mentally comfortable enough to exert the effort required to excel. That thought leads directly to the next two sections.

Setting

Writer Alice Steinbach relaxes by reading. "Reading good writing is a great tonic for me. It reminds me of how great good writing can be. It helps me form in my head an idea for what I want the voice to be, the tone," says Steinbach, an award-winning *Baltimore Sun* reporter and author.[17]

She prefers to write in the morning, in a comfortable place. Like Steinbach, most writers need a comfort zone. It matters to them when and where they write. A propitious setting helps move them into both a physical and psychological state of readiness.

Essayist and author Joyce Maynard writes while facing a wall decorated with 24 brightly colored masks. "Maynard has always felt these masks to be a benevolent presence while she writes," Larissa MacFarquhar wrote in profiling Maynard, "and she recently realized that they represent her readers to her."[18]

Lots of writers enjoy the luxury of working at home in a cozy study or a writing room arranged just so. Others must work more or less in public, in

---

[15] Arthur M. Abell, *Talks with Great Composers* (Eschwege, Ger.: Schroeder-Verlag, 1964), 156.

[16] Abell, 157.

[17] Alice Steinbach, interview by the author, 26 March 1998.

[18] Larissa MacFarquhar, "The Cult of Joyce Maynard," *New York Times* Magazine, 6 September 1998, 34.

newsrooms or business offices. If they have earned enough seniority or clout, perhaps they have private offices decorated and arranged to taste. But many if not most media writers toil in newsrooms, which are typically cluttered, noisy, and frantic, far less snug than the private hideaways most would prefer. Still, even those who perform in public have some influence over their physical surroundings. Making the most of the setting—without falling into laziness or undue self-indulgence—can help all writers relax and open themselves to inspiration.

As a simple beginning, you should try to write regularly in the same place. Soon you come to associate that place with writing. It is where you go to write. You know, and your subconscious knows, that when you arrive there, you are supposed to write. Even in a busy newsroom, you can carve yourself a small haven and condition yourself to consider it your special writing nook.

Select a comfortable but not too comfortable chair; you are working, not resting. Choose tools that vitalize you: a certain style of notebook or brand of pen; a special computer keyboard or a mouse pad with your family's picture embossed on it; a welcoming background for your computer screen or a favorite saying on the wall. Consider the direction in which you look. Do you prefer your face or your back to the wall? Do you want maximum privacy, or do you like to talk to others as you write? Are you spooked if anyone creeps up behind you and looks at your screen? Is there special artwork you like to stare at while writing? Is a window view distracting or stimulating?

Be open about your preferences. When he was a writer at the *Charlotte Observer*, journalist Frank Barrows was famous for strapping himself into a chair, sliding on earmuffs, and lining up bottles of his favorite soft drink; inside a bustling newsroom, Barrows made himself a safe harbor for writing. If you need quiet, post a sign that says "Danger—Writer at Work!" If you need music, wear earphones. If you prefer to write standing up, order an extra-tall computer stand.

There are, of course, limits. Writers work on deadline and cannot afford excessive indulgence. But too many media writers err in the other direction. They meekly acquiesce to manifestly uncreative, rote working conditions. They do not even allow themselves the treat of a modest comfort zone that will raise both productivity and creativity.

Your setting for writing is your intellectual and professional home, the nerve center for some of your most important moments. Put it to work for you.

Stimulation

The setting is just one sample of the full regime of superstitions, mannerisms, quirks, routines, habits, compulsions, and eccentricities that writers bank on to stimulate their creative juices.

It may seem weird that Edgar Allan Poe liked to write with a cat on his shoulder, or that Edith Sitwell lay in an open coffin before writing, or that the poet Schiller warmed up by sniffing the scent of rotten apples.[19]

But think how readily we accept similar practices in the physical sphere. Pitchers, ballerinas, roller bladers, and even middle-aged power walkers repeat spectacularly idiosyncratic regimens before performing. If unused muscles can atrophy, why not unused creative cells? If we sit in one position too long and a leg goes to sleep, we rub and shake it to restore vitality. Muscles, tendons, and other body parts regularly need to be flexed, stretched, and prodded into healthy motion. They require everything from tender stroking to wholesale resuscitation. Why treat our creative side differently? Like a smart slap of cold water to the face in the morning or a bracing whiff of garlic to cleanse the sinuses, a dose of stimulation before writing can fire up our confidence and competence.

Diane Ackerman, in *A Natural History of the Senses*, uses the word *synesthesia* to describe how "the stimulation of one sense stimulates another." She explains:

> While synesthesia drives some people to distraction, it drives distractions away from others. . . . Either writers have been especially graced with synesthesia, or they've been keener to describe it. . . . Artists are notorious for stampeding their senses into duty, and they've sometimes used remarkable tricks of synesthesia.[20]

Ackerman offers a lengthy list of writers' sensory-stimulating ploys. Katherine Mansfield used "terrific hard gardening." Amy Lowell smoked cigars (once buying 10,000 to make sure she did not run out). Colette picked fleas from her cat. Robert Louis Stevenson wrote lying down; Ernest Hemingway and Virginia Woolf standing up. Benjamin Franklin composed in the bathtub. Aldous Huxley wrote with his nose.

Quoting Malcolm Cowley, Ackerman writes that Hart Crane

> craved boisterous parties, in the middle of which he would disappear, rush to a typewriter, put on a record of a Cuban rumba, then Ravel's Bolero, then a torch song, after which he would return "his face brick-red, his eyes burning, his already iron-gray hair straight up from his skull. . . . In his hands would be two or three sheets of typewritten manuscript. . . . 'Read that,' he would say, 'isn't that the grrreatest poem ever written!'"[21]

---

[19] Diane Ackerman, *A Natural History of the Senses* (New York: Random House, 1990), 293–295.

[20] Ackerman, 289–295.

[21] Ackerman, 294.

Other writers need the soothing of solitude. Thomas Hardy took walks through the countryside, often scrawling ideas on large leaves, pieces of slate, or wood chips if no paper was handy.[22] Mozart once wrote to a friend:

> When I am, as it were, completely myself, entirely alone, and of good cheer—say, travelling in a carriage, or walking after a good meal, or during the night when I cannot sleep; it is on such occasions that my ideas flow best and most abundantly.[23]

Ultimately, whatever the stimulation of choice, writers find themselves alone with their thoughts in all-consuming creative rapture. As Charles Dickens once told a friend:

> How I work, how I walk, how I shut myself up, how I roll down hills and climb up cliffs; how the new story is everywhere—heaving in the sea, flying with the clouds, billowing in the wind. . . . [24]

Perhaps this all seems quaintly exotic for the humble media writer slogging toward deadline, but do not ignore the lessons from the most creative of our predecessors or assume that they cannot be applied to everyday situations. One writer recently got her dream job as a feature writer for a major publication. She came to its attention largely because of a single article she had freelanced elsewhere. Where did she get the idea for this career-changing article? While reading *People* magazine on a beach in Thailand during her honeymoon.

Great ideas and artistic leaps can happen to everyone. Stimulation stokes creativity and opens us to magical visitations. The typical online journalist or newspaper reporter may not spend time in a coffin like Sitwell or rolling down hills like Dickens, but many of the masters' customs are practicable within reason. Ideas come as you nuzzle a pet, sniff an apple, stroll through the woods, laze in the bath, or honeymoon at the beach. Writing improves if you find a comfortable setting, prepare yourself physically and mentally, and work, like Mozart, into a state of "good cheer."

Try for the perfect alignment of creative forces. Then accept that the ideal state will not always present itself, and make the most of every moment. "I am at my best," said Richard Strauss, "in the spring, above all in May when the apple trees are in bloom, when the sun is shining and the birds are

---

[22] Clive Holland, *Thomas Hardy, O.M.* (London: Herbert Jenkins, 1933), 79.

[23] Wolfgang Amadeus Mozart, "A Letter," in *Creativity*, P.E. Vernon, ed. (Middlesex, Eng.: Penguin, 1970), 55.

[24] Charles Dickens, "Letter to Mrs. Watson," *Letters of Charles Dickens* (New York: Scribner's, 1879), vol. 1, 472.

singing." But, he added significantly, "Ideas may come at any time and under almost any conditions."[25]

SUMMARY

For writers to reach higher and higher levels, they must cultivate both tangible and intangible attributes. They need a creative balance of both craft and magic, competence and confidence.

To the extent that writing is a process, writers can chart a linear progression toward fuller mastery of craft. Analyze the work of top colleagues and apply the lessons you learn. Undertake more challenging assignments. Improve interviewing and research skills. Study writing and story forms. Collect tools, tricks, and techniques and use them. Steadily move up a notch or two in performance level at every stage in the writing process.

If the pace of progress seems slow, why fret? Media writers tend to produce an abundance of words and articles in a short period. Many assignments are routine and predictable, service journalism churned out under deadline, and not every piece will be dazzling. Some writers stagnate under this smothering relentlessness, but ascending professionals can use the very routines of journalism for motivation and advancement. The more you write, the more you can learn, the more you can experiment, the more you can develop. If today's assignment disappoints, a new chance quickly follows. Learn from every assignment. Look ahead and set high goals.

Recognize, too, that steady progress often gives rise to the occasional sudden vault. Always keep your eye on at least one great story and work toward making it special. Not every story will sizzle, but some stories should. Use routine assignments to sharpen basic skills. Then seek out exceptional assignments to catapult yourself to new plateaus of excellence. One great story can mean as much to a writer as one great invention to a scientist or one world championship to an athlete.

Always pursue the magic. Magic is linked to craft but is less linear, less predictable, less tamed by step-by-step rigor. Inspiration is mysterious and elusive, but we have too much testimony from too many artists to doubt its powers. Silent tributaries of creativity flow within every writer, and locating them is a lifelong quest. Desire and determination seem to help. A comfortable setting and a positive mind-set relax the body and release the imagination. Stimulating the senses, through physical activity or some other meaningful personal regimen, sparks the creative nerve centers. Great artistic leaps come to writers who are most ready for them.

---

[25] Abell, 139.

Reaching for higher levels calls for supreme commitment of the artisan and artist within you. As Terence Smith once said of his father, the immortal sports writer Red Smith: "The actual writing of a column might take only a few hours, but it was a 24-hour-a-day occupation. . . . Writing the column was my father's life, his livelihood and his therapy."[26]

Practicing Craft and Magic

1. Spend half an hour with a teacher, editor, or colleague, brainstorming ideas until you settle on one exceptional assignment that challenges you in some new way. Set a reasonable timetable (the end of a semester, perhaps, or the end of a calendar year, or before your next vacation) and work steadily to complete the story.
2. Interview a writer you respect, by phone, in person, or by e-mail. Ask the writer what techniques most distinguish excellent articles from the ordinary. Does the writer have any personal "trade secrets" to share? Compile a list, and look for examples of stories where they are used.
3. Take inventory of your work habits in light of this chapter's advice on setting and stimulation. Are there practical improvements you can make in where, when, and how you write? Have you been neglecting small rituals that, if pursued, could stoke your creativity? Treat your artistic side to some reasonable indulgences and monitor their impact on your writing.

---

[26] Terence Smith, "Foreword," in *The Red Smith Reader,* ed. Dave Anderson (New York: Vintage, 1983), v–vi.

Chapter 15

Learning
from
Others

Shortly before starting this chapter, I received electronic mail from Rex Bowman, a former student who shares my fondness for writers and writing. A reporter for the *Richmond Times-Dispatch*, Bowman wanted to contribute an idea:

> Talking with other reporters, I've discovered the shared opinion that sometimes turning a reporting assignment into a narrowly defined writing exercise is the best way to improve copy. That is, sometimes you have to say, "I'm going to work on improving my syntax in this story," or "I'm going to try some offbeat diction," or "I'm going to work to vary sentence lengths." I and others find that, if you stop and consciously try to master a particular technique in a story, you end up paying more attention to the other techniques in the writer's bag of tricks.

A splendid suggestion. Even more gratifying were the generous collegial words that ended Bowman's note: "Hope this helps the next time you write to help writers."

Learning about writing never ends, and nothing buoys us more than writers writing to help other writers. Almost everything we know about writing is, in some way or other, derivative. We learn from every teacher, every student, every editor, every colleague, every book.

To write and to study writing is to become part of a huge continuing conversation. We have identified many power paradoxes in this book, and here is one more: writing is simultaneously a lonely pilgrimage and a communal adventure. To succeed, each of us must draw on the whole community of writers for suggestions, solace, and the support that springs from collective memory. And each writer also must turn within, for nowhere else can we find and sustain our unique voices and visions.

This final chapter, then, cites a sampling of the innumerable superb books about writing that have influenced and inspired writers for generations. It does so both in tribute and in order to further spread the gospel. These are only highlights, of course, so you are encouraged to add as many as possible of these volumes to your own (always-growing) writer's library.

Newsthinking: The Secret of Great Newswriting
Bob Baker
(Writer's Digest Books, 1981)

Several earlier examples have mentioned the work of Bob Baker, a *Los Angeles Times* editor and writing coach with an unusually thoughtful outlook.

Baker's book *Newsthinking*—hard to find but worth reading—promises "a new way to look at the chaotic world of newswriting," concentrating on what he calls "the pre-writing process." As one of the first authors to seriously relate left-brain and right-brain theories to media writing, Baker walks through numerous useful strategies for conceiving, organizing, and presenting information. The heart of his message is that what we call "magic" is actually a special way of thinking that can be understood and modeled:

> To succeed as a newswriter, you have to create a newswriting attitude that consciously models your skills after the brain's ability to confront huge amounts of information (sensory data), select what's necessary and put it in the proper perspective. (21)

Newswriting is both conceptually challenging and technically down-to-earth, covering topics ranging from right-brain outlining to crafting perspective paragraphs.

You may especially like a test Baker offers to help writers predict whether the right conditions exist for a creative burst: Do you have enough material to produce "a clever or inspired angle"? Have you wisely sorted out the many elements fed to you by your memory? Do some elements start to "suddenly leap out at you"? Do you feel an essential unity among the story elements, a sense that "the elements truly fit together"?

If these conditions apply, Baker writes, you have the makings of "a unique, creative combination of ideas." Otherwise, "you are probably kidding yourself" (165–166).

The Art and Craft of Feature Writing
William E. Blundell
(Plume, 1988)

The back cover fittingly describes this book as "filled with expert instruction on a complex art." William Blundell, a highly regarded writer, editor, and coach for the *Wall Street Journal,* unpacks many of the strategies and techniques associated with the *Journal's* supersuccessful front page features (described earlier in Chapter 13).

Blundell appreciates the creative process and understands writers:

> Writers are crazy people when they write, engaging in strange rituals that would earn anyone else a trip to the Rubber Room at the nearest mental hospital. They are obsessive about the paper and notepads they use, about pens (I take notes with one kind, draft copy with another, write letters with still a third), about the placement of items on their desks. (69)

Blundell also knows his craft. The bulk of his book presents sound, specific advice on finding ideas, developing themes, organizing complex material, and plotting stories section by section. Here is his take on focusing a theme:

> Carve out a piece of the story map you've drawn and express it in a couple of simple, tightly written sentences. Concentrate on action—the main development, one or two of its likely effects and the logical major reaction to them, if any. Ignore all else. Tack this main theme statement up where you can see it. Let it guide your work. . . . I consider the *main theme statement* the single most important bit of writing I do on any story. (27)

Becoming a Writer

Dorothea Brande

(J. P. Tarcher, 1981)

First published in 1934, this witty and companionable book was written by a fiction author and teacher, and it is aimed at fiction writers. But its insights can help and motivate media writers as well.

Like Bob Baker, Dorothea Brande sees writing as, in large part, a process of overcoming your own obstacles and insecurities. Brande also applies the word *magic* to writing, and she too believes it can be learned:

> There is a sort of writer's magic. There is a procedure which many an author has come upon by happy accident or has worked out for himself which can, in part, be taught. To be ready to learn it you will have to go by a rather roundabout way, first considering the main difficulties which you will meet, then embarking on simple, but stringently self-enforced, exercises to overcome those difficulties. (25)

Brande's discussion is almost entirely right-brain–oriented, and some of her exercises may strike news writers as artificial. Her most practical single suggestion is to force yourself to write each morning, "when the unconscious is in the ascendant":

> The best way to do this is to rise half an hour, or a full hour, earlier than
> you customarily rise. Just as soon as you can—and without talking, without
> reading the morning's paper, without picking up the book you laid aside the
> night before—begin to write. (72)

She believes that while genius cannot be taught, whatever inner gifts each
person possesses can be "released." Brande offers a specific and rather elaborate system for inducing what she calls "the artistic coma," or the higher
imagination that connects you with your genius. The final step is to enter a
dim room, lie flat, stay completely still, quiet the mind, and remain "not quite
asleep, not quite awake" for up two hours. At some point, she says, "you will
feel a definite impulse to rise, a kind of surge of energy. Obey it at once. . . .
The state you are in at that moment is the state an artist works in" (169).

Words' Worth: A Handbook on Writing and Selling Nonfiction

Terri Brooks
(St. Martin's Press, 1989)

This book is not only helpful and encouraging but, as a bonus, a pleasure
to read. A veteran writer and teacher, Terri Brooks shares hundreds of tips,
and she offers relevant examples for almost every point.

She spans the process, from finding ideas to selling stories to editors. But
her concentration is on writing itself. Her first six chapters cover leads, transitions, verbs, description, quotes, and voice. *Words' Worth* is a textbook,
incorporating the basics and filled with exercises, but the voice is more personal than that of most textbooks, and almost all writers will encounter some
new technique or insight.

A favorite quote is from the chapter on voice, and it illustrates Brooks' pen-
chant for the pithy: "Aim to write one sentence you love in every story" (117).

The Word: An Associated Press Guide to Good News Writing

Rene J. Cappon
(Associated Press, 1982)

Plain prose delights readers, and bloated, pedantic language torments
them. That is the no-nonsense message of this trim classic, written by an AP
editor with wit, wisdom, and the occasional wicked jab.

Rene Cappon opens with three keystone questions for every story:

- Have I said what I meant to say?
- Have I put it as concisely as possible?
- Have I put things as simply as possible? (6–7)

He abhors "the anemia of abstractions" ("Give concrete examples: The *tight housing market* is also an old lady evicted with her four cats"), leads that "mumble," and "pseudo-color" (which he describes as using "grand generalizations" instead of "particulars"):

> Writing is the art of the second thought. What first springs to mind is seldom good enough; the skill lies not in a ready gush of words, but in sifting them. (6)

Writing with Power: Techniques for Mastering the Writing Process

Peter Elbow
(Oxford University Press, 1988)

Peter Elbow is an influential figure in the movement toward teaching writing as a process, and this book often gets cited as a major contribution.

Elbow calls special attention to the early stages of writing: thinking about the material, experiencing it, totally absorbing it. He advocates freewriting ("the easiest way to get words on paper . . . write without stopping for 10 minutes") (13), and something he calls "raw writing," or "first stage writing" subject to later revision (11).

Revision is another cornerstone of Elbow's approach. He recommends that writers spend half their time doing raw writing and leave half for revising:

> Revising requires wisdom, judgment, and maturity. There is no way to get these qualities except through practice and experience. The most inexperienced writer can sometimes produce brilliantly but only scarred old pros revise brilliantly. (121)

Along the way, Elbow scatters innumerable genial asides and suggestions on everything from hard-core technique to writing mysticism. Here is an engaging example:

> Role playing as you write is one of the best ways to breathe experience into words. If you are writing about someone else's ideas or explaining information you don't care about, pretending to be someone else will help you get more involved. (352)

The Art of Readable Writing

Rudolf Flesch
(Macmillan, 1977)

The name Rudolf Flesch is commemorated in the Flesch readability formula, a cryptic calculation using sentence length, word complexity, and other measures to derive "reading ease" and "human interest" scores for writing. Don't let that technocratic legacy deter you from rummaging around in this amiable and avuncular book, originally published in 1949 and now, perhaps, underappreciated.

The Flesch formula appears here, but so does much more, all geared toward plain and simple expression. The book contains an unusually interesting chapter, for example, on ways that writers confuse readers. Flesch's inventory of examples includes "strange words," "legalistic jargon," "illogical negatives," and "allergic words" (184–190). He also cites a problem called "overpotency," where some words "may have so much meaning for a reader that they blot out the meaning of other words around them." For instance, a story about a town named Franklin confused a group of school children who thought the passage referred to Benjamin Franklin.

It may surprise you, in this book by the famous formula maker, to run across the chapter, "All Writing Is Creative." Flesch, too, it turns out, was an early convert to the power of inspiration:

> Bright new ideas are always combinations of old ones; they come to us usually after our mind has had a rest after a concentrated effort; and if we do it right, we can sometimes coax them to the surface. . . . The conscious mind, of course, is always more orderly than the unconscious. That's why the unconscious is so much better at combining ideas in a novel way. It puts things together that we never would put together "in our right mind." (58–59)

Writing for Story: Craft Secrets of Dramatic Nonfiction by a Two-Time Pulitzer Prize Winner

Jon Franklin
(Plume, 1994)

Chapter 14 quoted from *Writing for Story* in some detail, so we will try to avoid repetition here. Jon Franklin's book is a staple of hard-headed technique for feature and in-depth writers. It proposes a blueprint, albeit a complex one, that helps turn the broad art of feature writing into a set of discrete, followable steps.

The effect is to light up the interior structure of a story like a museum exhibit in a shadow box: you can see the patterns and connections as they flow together into a narrative.

Franklin's approach fits stories into a complication-resolution model, requiring a sympathetic character who faces a complicating situation and moves through several action stages to resolving it. A five-part outline guides the writing. Franklin labels each step as a "focus": the complicating focus, three developing action focuses, and the resolving focus.

Within each focus, he discusses what he calls the outline level (the conceptual relationships between character and action), the structural level (the organization and composition of each section), and the polish level (the grammar, word usage, imagery, and so forth). The goal is to create "a dramatic story . . . a world unto itself . . . a world which the reader can enter and become absorbed in" (138).

This is invaluable advice: a manageable system for recognizing a storyline, dividing and ordering it into logical sections, and composing each section to reinforce and advance the whole.

Writing Down the Bones: Freeing the Writer Within

Natalie Goldberg
(Shambhala, 1998)

Writer, poet, and teacher Natalie Goldberg approaches writing from the magical side:

> Learning to write is not a linear process. There is no logical A-to-B-to-C way to become a good writer. One neat truth about writing cannot answer it all. There are many truths. To do writing practice means to deal ultimately with your whole life. (6)

Not surprisingly, then, her book has a nonlinear feel and will serve more as an inspiration than a guidebook. It is arranged in a series of short chapters with titles like "Don't Marry the Fly," "Use Loneliness," and "Trust Yourself." While they may strike some media writers as overly abstract, for others they will teem with applicable insights into how writers think, act, and work. She does offer some definite advice, for example, about freewriting, "composting" (or sifting through thoughts and experiences), soaking up specifics, and pepping up language.

But she is most reassuring and soothing in simply encouraging writers to press ahead: be flexible, stick to it, don't fret, move forward, take breaks, refresh yourself, use everything. She authors what may be the ultimate and inescapable message a writer must hear: "Keep your hand moving" (15). She also offers this solid advice:

> There is no perfection. If you want to write, you have to cut through and write. There is no perfect atmosphere, notebook, pen, or desk, so train yourself to be flexible. Try writing under different circumstances and in different places. . . . If you want to write, finally you'll find a way no matter what. (173–174)

Intimate Journalism: The Art and Craft of Reporting Everyday Life

Walt Harrington
(Sage, 1997)

As the subtitle suggests, Walt Harrington bows to both craft and magic in describing and producing what he calls "intimate journalism," or stories about "how people live and what they value" (xx). *Intimate Journalism* is an anthology, featuring 15 longer articles from 10 writers, with comments from the authors following each piece.

In a dazzling introductory essay, Harrington (a newspaper and magazine writer and teacher) constructs a bravely philosophical and sociological foundation for his work, then fortifies it with applied detail about conceiving, reporting, and writing. He provides helpful tips about scenes, voice, dialogue, interior monologues, time lines, physical detail, pacing, and creating "an interpretive and poetic tone" (xliv).

Harrington insists on compulsory shoe-leather reporting, but he also understands the essential gear shift required to lift writers into the creative mood:

> I suggest you stay at home one morning, pour a cup of coffee, put on classical music or gentle jazz, whatever your preference, sit down in a comfortable chair, stack all your notes to one side. On top of one legal pad, jot the word "themes" and atop another write "facts, quotes and details to use." Then start reading your notes, your transcripts of interviews, anything else you've collected. . . . Try to let the material wash over you . . . in the way that rocking your child to sleep late at night in a dark and quiet house might wash over you. . . . Make a sensory and emotional connection with your story. (xxxvii–xxxviii)

The Psychology of Writing

Ronald T. Kellogg
(Oxford, 1999)

Ronald Kellogg, a cognitive psychologist, presents a scholarly, multidisciplinary synthesis of research into how writers think and act. He is concerned less with offering how-to instruction than with understanding how writers try to make sense of what they know. To that end, he has compiled an eclectic and comprehensive body of anecdotes, surveys, and experimental research about writers' processes, personalities, and work habits.

His findings are reliably interesting and insightful. They do require a long-range outlook: Kellogg cites evidence that artists, even prodigies, usually need 10 to 20 years to produce outstanding work, a period of "deliberate practice" involving "highly effortful and sustained activities designed to attain excellence" (83).

Other findings are more immediately applicable. *The Psychology of Writing* has an excellent section, for instance, on using computers as "idea processors" as well as word processors.

Discussing prewriting strategies, Kellogg defines the goal for writers as "better retrieval and application of knowledge." The problem, he says, is "attentional overload," or overwhelming the brain and memory by trying to write too much too perfectly too soon. Writers are better off brainstorming; listing and then clustering ideas; using flow charts, boxes, and trees to quickly generate raw material; and, when stuck, simply using "an imperfect idea or expression in order to get on with the writing" (120–122). His message: maximize ideas, get started, keep moving, polish later.

Writing on Both Sides of the Brain: Breakthrough Techniques for People Who Write

Henriette Anne Klauser
(HarperSanFrancisco, 1987)

This small volume delivers exactly what its title intimates: a wealth of good counsel about stroking both the logical and creative hemispheres.

Henriette Anne Klauser ably distinguishes between craft and magic by applying the left-brain, right-brain model. To stimulate the right brain, she recommends techniques such as freewriting, branching, "spiral thinking," visualizing, and staging creative moments. Although she concentrates on the magical side, she also includes some forthright advice on specific matters like spelling, word usage, and squelching procrastination.

Throughout the book, Klauser proposes all sorts of exercises, some practical, some fanciful, for stirring the nonlinear chambers. For example, she recommends that your work space contain two different chairs, the "Writing Chair," where you write, and the "Ruminating Chair," a separate and safe space where you allow yourself to reflect, stare off, look out the window, and otherwise muse (40).

Klauser tends to see the right brain as the "writer" and the left brain as the "editor." Much of her philosophy concerns not just invoking inspiration but deflecting what she calls the "premature edit mode." This is the "dark monster" that "makes you bite your pencil, crumple your paper into a ball in frustration, cross out words as you write them, and beat on yourself for waiting this long to get started" (5). It does important work, she believes, but can stifle creativity if activated too early.

"Our motto is this," Klauser avows. "We do no editing before its time" (18).

Writing for Your Readers

Donald M. Murray
(Globe Pequot, 1992)

Enshrined as elder statesperson of the writing coach movement, Donald Murray has devoted a lifetime to writing, teaching, and mentoring, and almost everything he writes is wise and witty.

Writing for Your Readers, another hard-to-find volume, culls from his work as columnist and coach at the *Boston Globe.* Because Murray writes with such grace himself and has such elemental insight into writers and their work, the book succeeds on three reinforcing levels: as a model, as an inspiration, and as a compendium of smart advice.

Murray loves lists and aphorisms, and he fills the book with tips, examples, and zingers. One chapter, for example, begins this way: "One day I made a list of what I wish I'd known before I showed up for my first job on a newspaper. Here it is." He then reels off 20 pithy observations, from "Ask the Reader's Questions" to "Listen for the Initiating Line" to "Write Many Leads to Find the Lead" to "Be Accurate in Detail and Context" (105–109).

Other chapters cover finding the tension, reporting for surprise, tuning your voice, and revising and editing your own copy.

Murray also likes to quote others, and this book contains an immortal quote about writer's block, from Roger Simon:

> There is no such thing as writer's block. My father drove a truck for 40 years. And never once did he wake up in the morning and say: "I have truck-driver's block today. I am not going to work." (224)

On Writing Well: The Classic Guide to Writing Nonfiction

William Zinsser

(HarperPerennial, 1994)

William Zinsser is the guru of clarity. Through nearly a quarter century of multiple editions, *On Writing Well* has prodded and cheered generations of writers. Playing off what he calls "my four articles of faith: clarity, simplicity, brevity and humanity" (172), Zinsser cordially escorts us on a tour of writing's principles, forms, and methods.

"Clutter is the disease of American writing," he declares, in a chapter entitled "Simplicity." Three pages later he boldly reveals two pages from the first edition of *On Writing Well,* with dozens of changes he subsequently penciled in "eliminating every element that is not doing useful work" (11). It is an inspiring and instructive example, showing the profits of revision.

Other nuggets from Zinsser:

> "Most first drafts can be cut by 50 percent. They are swollen with words and phrases that do no new work." (17)
>
> "Little qualifiers," words such as *rather* or *quite* or *a little,* should be pruned because they "dilute your style and your persuasiveness." (71)
>
> "There's not much to be said about the period except that most writers don't reach it soon enough." (72)

SUMMARY

Why stop here? As I write this, I can see straight in front of me a bookcase loaded with volumes about writing. Each wooden shelf bows under the tonnage. There are guidebooks and anthologies, biographies and memoirs, textbooks and readers. Books fill my writer's lair. Pluck one from the shelf—say, *Reporting* by Lillian Ross or the collected columns of my childhood idol, Kays Gary of the *Charlotte Observer*—and writing comes alive. These books are old friends, marked with underlining and highlighter ink and scribbling in the margins. I have underscored great passages of sportswriter Jim Murray's excruciating description of his blindness, example after example in Richard Wydick's estimable *Plain English for Lawyers,* notes to myself about 18 different pages in Steve Weinberg's *The Reporter's Handbook.*

No writing bibliography should omit Strunk and White's *The Elements of Style,* a book so popular the word *classic* does not do it justice. Among reporting textbooks, I regularly refer to those by Carole Rich *(Writing and Reporting News)* and Melvin Mencher *(News Reporting and Writing).* Jane Harrigan *(The Editorial Eye)* and Thom Lieb *(Editing for Clear Communication)* have produced the two best editing texts I have seen. I recently cleared space for books on online writing, and the shelf already is half filled.

Each book represents in its way a writer writing to help other writers. Each is illuminating and inspiring. And each is incomplete. The conversation about writing is timeless and eternal. No one ever comes to its end. I have never met a single writer who felt in total mastery of the art. From neophytes to Nobel Prize winners, we all have more to learn.

I remember an early electronic game that I played with my son and daughters. We worked and worked and worked to conquer 10 seemingly interminable levels of the quest. When we finally and triumphantly subdued the last nemesis and claimed the promised treasure, the image on the screen dissolved, and a brand new, unadvertised digitized universe materialized, an entirely new game, and we were, again, back at screen one.

Every writing assignment takes us to screen one. The screen is always blank, ours alone to fill. We learn from others, we ply our craft, we tweak our magic, and we script our words into the everlasting conversation. It is a privilege and luxury to lead the writer's life. Make the most of it.

Index

253